The Spiritual Life and Prayer

According to Holy Scripture
and Monastic Tradition

THE SPIRITUAL LIFE AND PRAYER

ACCORDING TO HOLY SCRIPTURE AND MONASTIC TRADITION

by

CÉCILE BRUYERÈ, O.S.B.

TRANSLATED FROM THE FRENCH
BY THE NUNS OF STANBROOK ABBEY

Reprinted by

MEDIATRIX PRESS

MMXVI

The Spiritual Life and Prayer:
According to Holy Scripture and Monastic Tradition

ISBN: 0692722742

©Mediatrix Press, 2016

Published by Mediatrix Press
Post Falls, Idaho
www.mediatrixpress.com
Originally published by London and Leamington, 1900.

TABLE OF CONTENTS

HE FOLLOWING pages were written some years ago, and were not originally intended for public circulation. They were drawn up by the author with a view to one single religious family, to serve them both as a guide in the study of the numerous works on the subject of prayer bequeathed to us by Christian tradition, and as a clue in the maze of religious literature, which issues daily from the press, but in which truths and principles old as the world are not always sufficiently explained. As misapprehensions on such subjects are the source of serious mistakes, it was thought well to help souls by stating clearly the main points of doctrine which throw light on the spiritual life.

For this purpose a few copies of the work were printed in 1886, under the title, "Prayer, according to the Holy Scriptures and Monastic Tradition." Each copy was marked "Strictly private."

Persons of weight and authority having expressed a wish for a wider circulation of the book the author hesitated to comply, when a still more pressing invitation came from Germany. The book was translated into German by a religious, carefully revised by Dr Raich, of Mayence, and honoured by Mgr. Paul Leopold Haffner, Bishop of Mayence, with the following introductory notice printed at the beginning:

"The present treatise on prayer was first of all printed privately in the French language, and was intended exclusively for the instruction of the daughters of St Benedict. All souls, however, who are aiming at perfection may derive profit and edification from its pages. The spirit of the venerable Abbot Gueranger breathes through the whole work. What this distinguished man thought on the all-important subject of prayer, what he expressed in his conferences, and what he wrote in many parts of his classical work, "The Liturgical Year," is found here systematically arranged. Some of the chapters are real masterpieces; therefore we joyfully welcome the translation of this book into German, and we most earnestly encourage its circulation.

Mayence, September 10, 1896."

With such a recommendation the book was well received, and most favourably noticed by The Literary Review of Catholic Germany, published at Fribourg, in Brisgau, under the patronage of Dr. G. Heberg. The article was written by Dr. Paul Keppler, a Professor of Theology, one of the most eminent scholars of Germany, and now Bishop of Rottenbourg. The learned doctor criticizes only one point, in the following words: "The author is well read in the Fathers, and consults them with intelligence and discretion, but his confidence in Denis, 'the incomparable Areopagite,' who, he maintains, received the immediate tradition of the apostles, is not justified."

To this we briefly reply that the author, though not ignorant of what has been written on the subject, did not consider that it came within the scope of a spiritual treatise to enter upon a question of pure erudition. It sufficed that, thanks to St Thomas, the doctrine of St. Denis now forms part of the ordinary teaching of the Church, and in all simplicity the opinion of the Church in her liturgy was adopted. It is for this reason also that in quoting from the Scriptures the author abstains from using any other text than the Vulgate, in spite of the light that other versions, by their more powerful language, might throw upon certain passages.

Before the German translation appeared, a French copy of "L'Oraison" having come, in 1890, under the notice of Cardinal Manning, he warmly encouraged an English translation of the work, and this eminent prince of the Church condescended to peruse the pages, and annotate them himself. Moreover, it was his wish that the translation should come before the public with a preface by himself; the first lines of it were already written when death hindered the completion of his work.

In France several bishops and many eminent religious, after reading the work, expressed a desire that it should be published; but these requests, as well as the names of their authors and the support given by them are private property. Nevertheless as the work had unwittingly been brought forward, it would have seemed affected to persist obstinately in keeping it secret; and the general circulation of the book was resolved upon.

But some changes were needed before giving it to the public. A more logical order was adopted, and four new chapters were added to complete certain subjects; it was requisite also to throw greater light on some points, and it seemed expedient to change even the title of the book; "Prayer" being only one part of the spiritual life, the word seemed too exclusive for a treatise intended to view it in all its aspects.

This book does not aim at science or at learning. It contains nothing new; on the contrary, the author's ambition is to be wholly traditional and ancient. The end proposed will be fully gained if God should deign to make use of these pages to kindle some sparks of divine love in souls who, in the midst of our dark times, are truly seeking Him.

It is not to superficial souls nor to light minds taken up with worldly solicitudes that this book is addressed. Such as these would no doubt be tempted to smile if in their presence we touched upon the matters to be treated of here. To them prayer and contemplation seem, at best, nothing but pious dreaming, useless things, which the better sort style innocent, and the rest too gladly compare with wanderings of the brain and the phenomena produced by the follies of fanaticism and illusion. The true children of the Catholic Church think differently; they know that man is made for union with God, that God is man's end, and that his immortal soul has supernatural aspirations and aptitudes which are the fruit of the grace of Baptism and which cannot be violently restrained. They are well aware that, apart from a knowledge of extraordinary ways, man, by the very fact of his being a Christian and a child of God, cannot, without peril and fault, be indifferent to divine things or close his eyes to them. "We are not born to fix our gaze on created things, but to contemplate the Creator of these things—that is, to behold Him by the spirit. . . . We must contemplate God with the eyes of the soul, and not this world with the eyes of the body; for the eye is material as is the world which it contemplates; but God, Himself immortal, has willed that our soul should be immortal. To contemplate God is to honour Him, and with profound veneration to love Him as the common Father of mankind."[1]

Thus have the true philosophers of all ages thought; thus have they assigned to man's existence, even during his earthly pilgrimage, a destiny very different from the life of the senses.

But why speak of Christian philosophers? It is the Incarnate Word Himself that takes up the words spoken to Israel of old. He reiterates and sanctions them for ever by saying: "Not in bread alone doth man live, but in every word that proceedeth

---

[1] Non ergo nascimur, ut ea, quæ sunt facta, videamus, sed ut ipsum factorem rerum omnium contemplemur, id est, mente cernamus. . . . Non ergo mundus oculis, quia utrumque est corpus, sed Deus animo contemplandus est: quia Deus, ut est ipse immortalis, sic animum voluit esse sempiternum. Dei autem contemplatio est, venerari et colere communem parentem generis humani (Lactantius, De Falsa Sap,, iii, 9).

from the mouth of God."[2]

Now this spiritual food, more necessary to man than material bread, is no other than the Divine Word, the essential Truth, the Living Bread coming down from heaven, who also is the Bread of Angels and the object of their eternal contemplation. The great interest of our present life is the communion of our souls with that mysterious food, a communion which consists in knowing the "only true God, and Jesus Christ whom He has sent."[3] It matters little that few people heed these supernatural aspirations of the baptized soul. Neither does it matter that these subjects remain generally unknown to the man of worldly wisdom, "the disputer of this world."[4]

The author's design in writing this book is sufficiently justified by the great advantage accruing to souls eager for perfection, from the possession of exact, simple and clear principles, which will enable them to glean with discernment and reproduce in their conduct that which they should imitate in the examples and teaching of the spiritual life. For want of this discrimination false and inexact notions gain free circulation, and the very books that are intended for edification serve to foster delusion.

Assuredly the Spirit of God keeps what is His own, and a secret repugnance will often, without any difficulty, teach an upright soul the kind of doctrine suitable for it. If you put a sheep in the midst of rich pasture, it will not take indifferently all the herbs that are there; its very instinct will guide it surely to choose some and to reject others, and the choice will nearly always be judicious. Thus will it frequently happen with a

---

[2] Non in solo pane vivit homo, sed in omni verbo quod pro cedit de ore Dei (Deut. viii, 3; Matth. iv, 4).

[3] Solum Deum verum, et quem misisti Jesum Christum (Joann, xvii, 3).

[4] Conquisitores hujus sseculi (1 Cor. i, 20).

discreet soul in what concerns its spiritual food. A wisdom superior to human wisdom will help it to discern what is for its good, according to the state, the times and the phases of the spiritual life through which it is passing.

But the safest way is to consult an experienced guide in order to avoid groping in the dark and wasting time, as holy Scripture says:

"But be continually with a holy man, whomsoever thou shalt know to observe the fear of God, whose soul is according to thine own soul, and who, when thou shalt stumble in the dark, will be sorry for thee."[5] This also is what all masters of the spiritual life recommend.

It seems to us that in these matters it is wise to mortify curiosity and indefinite reading, in order not to overburden the mind with a great quantity of different notions; for just as too much food causes the stomach to be overworked, so the soul can be stifled under the exuberant surcharge caused by an immoderate and unbridled thirst after knowledge. It is expedient to be sober in the use of even good things, according to that sentence of the wise man: "Be not over just; and be not more wise than is necessary, lest thou become stupid."[6]

The Apostle gives the same advice with reference to the use of spiritual gifts: "For I say, by the grace that is given me, to all that are among you, not to be more wise than it behoveth to be wise, but to be wise unto sobriety, and according as God hath

[5] Cum viro sancto assiduus esto, quemcumque cognoveris observantem timorem Dei; cujus anima est secundum animam tuam, et qui, cum titubaveris in tenebris, condolebit tibi (Eccli xxxvii, 15, 16).

[6] Noli esse justus multum, neque plus sapias quam necesse est, ne obstupescas (Eccli vii, 17).

divided to every one the measure of faith."[7]

Furthermore it is certain that the soul's advancement in perfection does not depend upon the number of reflections which the mind accumulates, but upon her really digesting some of them. One single sentence of the Gospel can lead us to sanctity as our divine Master teaches: "Thou shalt love the Lord thy God with thy whole heart, and with thy whole soul, and with thy whole mind. This is the greatest and the first commandment. And the second is like to this: Thou shalt love thy neighbour as thyself. On these two commandments depend the whole law and the prophets."[8]

One of the most eminent doctors of the spiritual life, Saint John of the Cross, used to delight in inculcating these principles: "What is needed further, if anything is wanting, is, not writing more or speaking more, whereof ordinarily there is an abundance, but it is to be silent and to act. When, therefore, a soul has got the knowledge of all that is necessary for her advancement, she has no further need to give ear to others, or to speak herself; she only needs to put in practice what she knows, with generosity, silence and attention, in humility, charity and contempt of self; not turning aside incessantly to seek after novelties which serve only to appease the hunger for external consolations. They cannot really satisfy it, and they leave the soul feeble, empty and devoid of all the interior spirit of true virtue. The result is unprofitable in every way; for a man who before he has digested his last meal takes another, the

---

[7] Dico enim per gratiam quæ data est mihi, omnibus qui sunt inter vos: non plus sapere quam oportet sapere, sed sapere ad sobrietatem: et unicuique sicut Deus divisit mensuram fidei (Rom. Xii, 3).

[8] Diliges Dominum Deum ex toto corde tuo, et in tota anima tua, et in tota mente tua. Hoc est maximum, et primum mandatum. Secundum autem simile est huic: mandatis universa lex pendet, et Prophetæ (Matth. Xxii, 37).

natural heat not sufficing for so much food, sickness follows."[9]

In point of fact, nothing is of any worth in the spiritual life, except what ends in practice. High thoughts and sentiments which do not produce solid virtue are of no value; and doctrine is proved by acts. To love to be instructed in supernatural science is certainly the sign of a well-balanced mind, but to limit oneself to searching into truth without ever allowing the riches of the mind to bear upon the will for strenuous action is to show oneself illogical and to betray weak convictions.

The characteristic of our faith is that it ever tends to apply to ourselves all the truths that it teaches us. It has no theories which are not meant to be reduced to practice; dreamers, system-makers will have no success; faith moulds those only who act according to their belief. Men of upright heart, who draw all the logical consequences from their faith, who live by faith alone; in other words, the valiant are those whom St. Paul calls the saints.

It will not therefore be a matter of surprise to find in the following pages more principles than sentiments; truths destined to encourage action rather than to satisfy the mind. The author had no thought of feeding even the most legitimate curiosity, but of increasing in souls, even in this world, the desire of union with God, for the glory of the Father, of the Son and of the Holy Ghost, who will be the object of their contemplation for all eternity.

ST. CECILIA'S ABBEY,
Solesmes, 1899.

---

[9] Works of St. John of the Cross, letter iii.

CHAPTER I
Some General Principles

EVERY man's one great object in life is to reach the end God had in view in calling him out of nothingness. To learn the pathway thither, to discern the obstacles which can either arrest or turn aside, to obtain light as to the repugnances and opposing forces within our very selves, is a study the most reasonable, the most wise and the most necessary that can be undertaken.

The secrets of the spiritual life are not reserved exclusively for a few chosen souls, as people too often believe, nor for those only who make religion their speciality. All men are created by God; all are called to save their souls; all are regenerated by the same means, as St. Paul says: "One body and one Spirit, as you are called in one hope of your calling. One Lord, one faith, one baptism. One God and Father of all; who is above all, and through all, and in us all."[1] Finally, all will be made blessed for eternity by the same immediate vision of God.

Therefore all must go through a certain preparation. There are indeed differences of degree, according to God's measure of grace to each soul, but the end is the same for all: "Until we all meet into the unity of faith, and of the knowledge of the Son of God, unto a perfect man, unto the measure of the age of the

---

[1] Unum corpus et unus Spiritus, sicut vocati estis in una spe vocationis vestræ. Unus Dominus, una fides, unum baptisma. Unus Deus et Pater omnium, qui est super omnes et per omnia et in omnibus nobis. (Eph., iv, 4-6).

fulness of Christ."[2]

Now it is a fact that already, in our mere apprenticeship and preparation for our future life, the very same law fully holds, which is the law of eternity. The only concern of this life is to press on, through the shadows of faith, towards some experience of—some initiation into—that which will be eternal life in its full bloom.

All God's designs over us in this world are intended to bring about our supernatural perfection. Our faith is to become so clear-sighted and developed as to bring us to the very portals of the face to face vision of God; our hope is to give us sure certainty of gaining it; and our charity, in its strength and ardour, is to be here below the very same that we shall have in eternity.

All men, whether Christians or not, seek for happiness; but it is in their notion of what happiness is that they differ, as is shown by the means they adopt and by their manner of acting.

This is not surprising; but that many Christians should unwittingly drink in pagan ideas, and should mistake the conditions of happiness, going in search of it outside God and obedience to God, and wearying themselves on this fool's errand, is indeed amazing.

Happiness cannot be found without goodness; it would be deeply immoral were it possible for the full grown man to be happy with any true happiness, either here or in the next world, without being virtuous. Happiness comes from the possession of a good; such as the good is, such will the happiness be that flows from it. There is perfect equation between the cause and the effect. All gross enjoyment, all false and empty pleasure implies both a clinging to some created thing and a real forsaking of true good and of real happiness.

---

[2] Donec occurramus omnes in unitatem fidei et agnitionis Filii Dei, in virum perfectum, in mensuram ætatis plenitudinis Christi (Eph. iv, 13).

To seek happiness without seeking it in the true good is an illusion. These principles, so simple because so evident, are brought before us in the events of daily life. In vain will a nation multiply means of enjoyment, bring comfort and ease within the reach of all; if its moral standard is low, the sources of true happiness will ever remain closed to it; men will give themselves up to despair, to a state of melancholy pessimism, and even to disgust of life itself. Such is the terrible logic of facts, such is God's revenge, when men despise His law, which is the rule of true good and the way to happiness. "Thy word," says the psalmist, "is a lamp unto my feet, and a light unto my paths."[3]

Reason and experience suffice to prove the truth of what we have said; but our Christian teaching above all bears witness to it. In the Old Law God encouraged the observance of the commandments by promising rewards; in the New Law of perfection, our Lord points to the beatitudes as the recompense of heroic virtue, the delicious fruit of goodness; He makes use of a divine paradox to rectify our mistaken notions, showing that the very trials of our earthly pilgrimage are the condition and pledge of new happiness: "Blessed are they that mourn; blessed are they that suffer persecution";[4] and this blessedness is promised to the poor and persecuted even now without delay. These souls aimed at a more excellent good, hence the happiness resulting from it defies in some sort the sorrows of our exile and triumphs over poor nature; hence our Lord concludes: "Rejoice and be glad.";[5] For there is a happiness beyond that which comes from the enjoyment of visible things; no good less than God will satisfy us, neither will any

---

[3] Lucerna pedibus meis verbum tuum, et lumen semitis meis (Ps. cxviii, 105).

[4] Beati qui lugent .... beati qui persecutionem patiuntur propter justitiam (Matth. v, 5-10).

[5] Gaudete et exsultate (Matth. v, 12).

happiness less than the fulfilment of God's promise to pour His own eternal joy into our souls, "Enter into the joy of thy Lord."[6] As this happiness is the effect of no created cause, it does not depend upon the events of this world; it stands high above them all, and remains unchanged amidst the ever varying accidents of life. Although it can be only imperfect, since we are not yet in full possession of our sovereign Good, and we must still walk by faith, yet nothing external can diminish it; the weakness of our own will alone can risk its continuance.

While bringing forward these Christian truths, which seem more than ever necessary and opportune in the present day, God forbid that we should seem to lose sight of another great law—the law of reparation and expiation. Sorrow and suffering must ever be the authentic process of the rehabilitation of our sinful nature. The saints will ever be irresistibly drawn to fill up what is wanting in the Passion of our Redeemer; but like their divine Master, and Mary the Queen of martyrs, they will experience ineffable happiness in "suffering in their flesh for the body of Christ, which is the Church."[7] And just as our Lord, when forsaken by His Father, was straitened with anguish even unto death, yet all the while there was in His soul a fountain of joy flowing from His sacrifice itself and the perfection of His holocaust, so God's true servants, in partaking of our Lord's chalice, become inebriated at once with joy and with grief.

But it is useless and even dangerous, as all illusions are, to seek suffering for suffering's sake. This is a tendency much to be regretted in our sickly age, among people otherwise very good. Never has suffering been more extolled and sought after, yet valour is by no means a characteristic of our times. It is a sign of weakness, and a covering for all sorts of imperfections. Under this fair exterior, much cowardice and hysteria lie

---

[6] Intra in gaudium Domini tui (Matth. xxv, 21).

[7] Col., I, 24.

hidden. Duty-doing is made to give way to suffering, whereas every kind of suffering is not either necessarily holy or conducive to holiness. Instead of glorying in such suffering better far would it be to get rid of it as quickly as possible, for it breeds sadness, while at the same time it puffs the soul up by fostering presumption, vain boasting of virtue and of special designs in its regard on the part of God.

Nothing is absolutely good but God and His will. Suffering has but a relative and borrowed goodness; it is a means, not an end. There will be no suffering in heaven; here in this world it serves to enkindle our love, but it is by no means indispensable. Merit does not lie in suffering, though suffering is often an occasion of merit. Suffering must be united with love, otherwise its place is in those dark regions where the spirit of evil dwells.

Our principal aim, therefore, in this world must be to seek the sovereign Good; our principal occupation to tend towards it, if we would cooperate with God's designs in our regard. He created us to know Him, to love Him, to serve Him, to do His blessed will, and thus to enter into eternal life—that is into eternal beatitude. When we fulfil this programme, we give God that accidental glory which He intended to draw from the creation of man.

One thing, however, is required both as the condition and the means for bringing about our restoration; without it, man can attain only a philosophical and human perfection, quite inadequate to the supernatural being whereunto he has been raised. This essential is prayer. As in eternity man is fixed in the possession of the sovereign Good and established in perfection by the face to face vision of God, so, in the course of his life on earth, he will habitually tend towards that sovereign Good; he will be super naturally impelled to reach it by prayer. The intensity of his prayer, the attitude of his soul towards God, will be the measure of its advance towards the sovereign Good. We may not choose our own ways of reaching supernatural perfection. To pray or not to pray is no matter of choice; on the contrary, there is nothing more important than prayer, as we learn from many expressions in the writings of the saints—expressions which, at first sight, might seem to be mere pious exaggerations, whereas they are strictly true.

There can be no doubt that the choice of such or such a method of prayer is of secondary importance; but man cannot neglect to exercise his faith and to strive with perseverance after union with God, without real detriment to his soul. Neither can he seriously aim at perfection without taking some means of knowing the divine Type according to which he is to be reformed. "Look, and make according to the pattern that was shown thee in the mount."[8] Likewise, in the 44th Psalm, it is written: "Hearken, O daughter, and see."[9] Faith does indeed come first of all by hearing; but afterwards it enables us to see truth by a special light of its own which penetrates the intellect and the will. In this world our intercourse with God cannot be a matter of form; our hearts must really turn to Him, urged on by our understanding; we must find once more the secret of that familiar converse with God which Adam enjoyed in Paradise.

In view of this it is important to observe how much more effectually the study of dogmatic theology transforms the soul than does the study of moral theology. Eminent missioners have observed this in the case of their pagan converts. The study of dogma raises the soul to higher regions, and shows it the divine Exemplar of the true, the good and the beautiful. Hence souls cannot be too strongly urged to learn to know God in order to reform themselves, and not to rest satisfied with what is commonly known as "the faith of the rustic." In an age like ours, when men are striving to learn everything, to know

---

[8] Inspice, et fac secundum exemplar quod tibi in monte monstratum est (Exod. xxv, 40).

[9] Audi filia, et vide (Ps. xliv, 11).

everything, to search into everything that can possibly be known, shall the queen and mistress of all sciences, the science which throws light upon all others, be alone neglected? How shall Christians put aside the only study that is useful for the real advancement of their souls, and cultivate exclusively the knowledge of the things which lie round about them? The knowledge of God is necessary both for our intellectual and for our moral progress. There are certain weaknesses and falls which this knowledge does away with altogether; the soul rights itself, when once it knows the God from whom the moral law emanates, and who teaches it by the voice of conscience and by the Church.

The knowledge of doctrinal truth is the root of prayer, hence its great importance; it is likewise the safeguard against many illusions of the imagination, the corrective of pious dreaming and of false mysticism. It is absolute presumption to expect to obtain, by immediate light from God, that knowledge which we can and ought to acquire for ourselves as part of our work in this world. We must not voluntarily rest satisfied with vague notions about the truths into which our baptism has initiated us, otherwise we should be guilty of culpable idleness. God may perhaps be waiting for this labour in the sweat of our brow, before filling up by His grace the measure of knowledge needful for the complete development of the spiritual life within us. For there are two forms of infused knowledge; the one teaches that of which we are altogether ignorant, and the other widens and makes fruitful the knowledge which the mind has already acquired by study. To conclude, God so truly takes pleasure in beholding our efforts to arrive at the knowledge of Himself, that we find Him raising all the canonized saints to a high degree of it by the one or by the other of these ways.

If it sometimes happen that extensive knowledge of theology does not bring with it, as a consequence, sanctifying union with God, we must beware of looking upon this knowledge as a snare and an obstacle, which God forbid. The cause of this strange anomaly can be easily assigned; for this happy result can never be brought about by mere keenness of wit, nor by curiosity, nor by that scholastic eagerness which in theology seeks for nothing but subtleties, strict definitions and superficial flashes of truth.

Too often we find souls clinging to set forms, and unwilling to enter the regions of true supernatural prayer. There, God will have the soul empty itself of all images and created forms, that He may unite it to Himself by a mystic knowledge higher than the soul—that is higher than its own natural way of acting. But this is God's work; no efforts of human industry can bring it about. We must not, however, argue from this against the importance of a solid study of the revealed truths which are the objects of our faith.

The "sublime ignorance" spoken of by theologians has nothing in common with ordinary ignorance; the former disdains one kind of knowledge for a higher, whereas the latter cannot disdain what it does not possess. The truth will always remain that, as long as God Himself does not directly intervene to instruct us, one of our principal duties will be to study those truths which He has deigned to reveal to us, and without knowledge of which we cannot enjoy intimacy with Him. "If you continue in My word, you shall be My disciples indeed; and you shall know the truth, and the truth shall make you free."[10]

Our freedom then will come from truth, truth known and lived, which will set to rights all our imperfections, retrieve all our losses and correct all our vices, as the Church teaches in her prayer: "O God, who by the means of this venerable Sacrament hast made us partakers of the one supreme Divinity, grant, we beseech Thee, that as we know Thy truth so we may

---

[10] Si vos manseritis in sermone meo, vere discipuli mei eritis, et cognoscetis veritatem, et veritas liberabit vos (Joann. viii, 31, 32).

accompany it by a worthy life."[11] Mental prayer, which brings the soul into direct contact with God, is the means whereby we shall become perfectly assimilated to that divine principle which is to restore us and qualify us to enter into the eternal mansions.

---

[11] Deus, qui nos per hujus sacrificii veneranda commercia, unius summæ divinitatis participes efficis: præsta quæsumus; ut sicut tuam cognoscimus veritatem, sic eam dignis moribus assequamur (Secreta Dom. XVIII post Pent.).

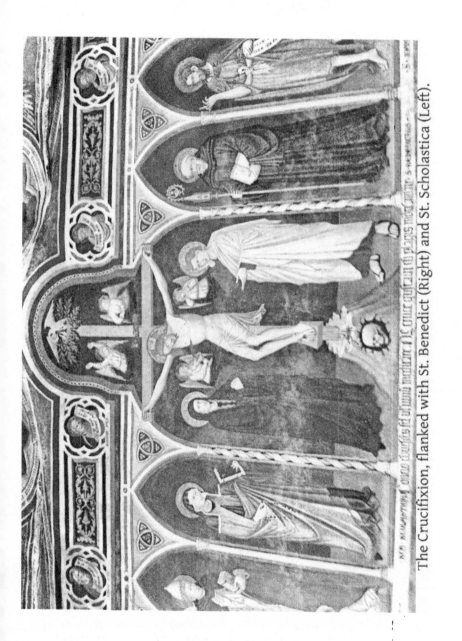

The Crucifixion, flanked with St. Benedict (Right) and St. Scholastica (Left).

CHAPTER II
What is the Spiritual Life?

HEN in so many places the holy Scripture declares that there is antagonism between what it calls the "carnal or animal man" and the interior "heavenly or spiritual man," it evidently does not intend to define states, nor to create real categories or, as it were, castes. The clearly marked distinction between the "carnal man" and the "spiritual man" arose from the fact that in the early Christian Church holiness shone forth with so much lustre in the midst of the pagan world that it brought into full daylight the superiority of the Christian over the pagan. It came about that even error took hold of these contrasts, exaggerated them, and then falsified doctrine by pushing to extremes contrasts only too real.

The "animal man," in Scripture language, sometimes means the man who buries himself in abject materialism or simply in practical sensuality, persuading himself that nothing is real but that which he can touch and handle. Sometimes even the apostle will give the name of "animal man" to that body of disorderly or of even purely human tendencies existing in the Christian whose higher life is imperfectly developed, and by their base allurings so often making him lose sight of the supernatural spirit. The "spiritual man" and child of God is he who lives in obedience to the leadings of the Spirit of God: "For whosoever are led by the Spirit of God, they are the sons of God."[1] Of the others Scripture says: "These are sensual men,

---

[1] Quicumque Spiritu Dei aguntur, hi sunt filii Dei (Rom. viii, 14).

having not the Spirit."[2]

Such, in fact, is the line of demarcation between the "animal man" and the "spiritual man." Elsewhere St. Paul expresses it still more clearly. "But the sensual man," he says, "perceiveth not these things that are of the Spirit of God; for it is foolishness to him, and he cannot understand, because it is spiritually examined."[3] He who has not the Spirit of God within him is a "carnal man," and does not live by the spiritual life—that is by that higher life which is given to us in baptism.

Hence the "spiritual man" is regenerated man; the man who has received the spirit of adoption, who has fellowship with the Father and with His Son Jesus Christ. He lives spiritually, and he has the fulness of spiritual life when he lives up to the duties of his high state; on the other hand, the apostle does not hesitate to number among "carnal men" those who by their conduct belie the promises they made at their baptism: "For whereas there is among you envying and contention, are you not carnal, and walk according to man?"[4] Thus then, in the apostle's sense, the movements or actions of the soul reveal the nature of her life.

The spiritual or interior life begins in us at our baptism, which is a real second birth, and, according to St. Denis, "the principle of the sacred action of the most holy sacraments, a principle which transforms our carnal dispositions, that we may be apt to receive the other sacraments."[5] This spiritual life is capable of increase and development like our natural life. A

---

[2] Hi sunt ... animales, Spiritum non habentes (Judæ 19).

[3] Animalis autem homo non percipit ea, quæ sunt Spiritus Dei: stultitia enim est illi, et non potest intelligere, quia spiritualiter examinatur (1 Cor. ii, 14).

[4] Cum enim sit inter vos zelus et contentio, nonne carnales estis, et secundum hominem ambulatis? (1 Cor., iii, 3).

[5] Hier. Eccl., ii.

long and laborious career, marked by diverse phases, opens out before the soul from the day she receives the principle of her new life in baptism till she attains the perfect age of Christ. Among the numberless passages of St. Paul's Epistles describing this onward march of the soul there is one, taken from the Epistle to the Ephesians, which, we think, contains a very complete programme of the spiritual life. Moreover it is set forth in a solemn and majestic form, showing the importance which St. Paul attached to it: "For this cause I bow my knees to the Father of our Lord Jesus Christ, of whom all paternity in heaven and earth is named, that He would grant you, according to the riches of His glory, to be strengthened by His Spirit with might unto the inward man. That Christ may dwell by faith in your hearts; that being rooted and founded in charity, you may be able to comprehend, with all the saints, what is the breadth and length and height and depth. To know also the charity of Christ, which surpasseth all knowledge, that you may be filled unto all the fulness of God."[6] It was necessary to read this magnificent exposition to the end, but we must return to it, and consider in detail each word of the incomparable master.

In his zeal for those to whom he has preached the Gospel, St. Paul ardently desires for them all that is highest and best; and it is from God the Father, whose Spirit they have received, that he asks the inestimable grace of seeing them complete a perfect career. God having various measures in the distribution of His grace—the *lenticula* or "little vial" of Saul: "And Samuel

---

[6] Hujus rei gratia flecto genua mea ad Patrem Domini nostri Jesu Christi, ex quo omnis paternitas in coelis et in terra nominatur, ut det vobis secundum divitias gloriæ suæ virtute corroborari per Spiritum ejus in interiorem hominem, Christum habitare per fidem in cordibus vestris, in caritate radicati et fundati, ut possitis comprehendere cum omnibus sanctis, quæ sit latitudo, et longitudo, et sublimitas, et profundum: scire etiam supereminentem scientiæ caritatem Christi, ut impleamini in omnem plenitudinem Dei (Eph. iii, 14-19).

took a little vial of oil, and poured it upon his head, and kissed him";[7] or the large measure of David: "Then Samuel took a horn of oil, and anointed him in the midst of his brethren,"[8]—what the apostle asks is that God would pour out His supernatural gifts "according to the riches of His glory." Most certainly, if we consider the fruits of holiness in the early Church, the apostle's prayer was heard. Now the first working of grace which the apostle solicits is this: "That God would grant you to be strengthened by His Spirit with might unto the inward man."[9] The inward man can then be diversely developed within us; and our all important interest during the time of our probation consists in bringing about this growth under the combined effort of divine grace and our own cooperation.

The first phase of the spiritual life here described by St. Paul is the PURGATIVE LIFE, in the course of which the soul strives to combat both her internal and her external enemies, to free herself from the tyranny of the senses and to prepare the way of the Lord. It is to this phase that exhortations such as these belong: "Purge out the old leaven, that you may be a new paste, as you are unleavened."[10]

The apostle repeats the same teaching in his Epistle to the Ephesians: "But you have not so learned Christ; if so be that you have heard Him, and have been taught in Him, as the truth is in Jesus. To put off, according to former conversation, the old man, who is corrupted according to the desire of error. And be renewed in the spirit of your mind, and put on the new man,

---

[7] Tulit autem Samuel lenticulam olei, et effudit super caput ejus, et deosculatus est eum (1 Reg., x, 1).

[8] Tulit ergo Samuel cornu olei, et unxit eum in medio fratrum ejus (1 Reg., xvi, 13).

[9] Virtute corroborari per Spiritum ejus in interiorem hominem (Eph. iii, 16).

[10] Expurgate vetus ferinentum, ut sitis nova conspersio, sicut estis azymi (I Cor. v, 7).

who according to God is created in justice and holiness of truth."[11]

Elsewhere St. Paul further insists upon the labours of this first period, and everywhere he points to the same end. This time he is addressing himself to the Colossians: "Mortify therefore your members, which are upon the earth. .... Lie not one to another, stripping yourselves of the old man with his deeds, and putting on the new, him who is renewed unto all knowledge, according to the image of Him that created him."[12]

But the apostle's ambition is not limited to the powerful strengthening of the inward man by the Holy Spirit; he points to a further advance, saying: "That Christ may dwell by faith in your hearts."[13] This is exactly what our Saviour Himself expressed when, speaking to the multitude that surrounded Him, He said: "Walk whilst you have the light, that the darkness overtake you not; and he that walketh in darkness knoweth not whither he goeth. Whilst you have the light, believe in the light."[14] And again: "I am the light of the world; he that followeth Me walketh not in darkness, but shall have

---

[11] Vos autem non ita didicistis Christum, si tamen illum audistis, et in ipso edocti estis, sicut est veritas in Jesu; de ponere vos secundum pristinam conversationem veterem hominem, qui corrumpitur secundum desideria erroris. Renovamini autem spiritu mentis vestræ, et induite novum hominem, qui secundum Deum creatus est in justitia et sanctitate veritatis (Eph. iv, 20-24).

[12] Mortificate ergo membra vestra, quare sunt super terram. . . . Nolite mentiri invicem, exspoliantes vos veterem hominem cum actibus suis, et induentes novum, eum qui renovatur in agnitionem, secundum imaginem ejus qui creavit illum (Coloss., iii, 5, 9, 10).

[13] Christum habitare per fidem in cordibus vestris (Eph., iii, 17).

[14] Ambulate dum lucem habetis, ut non vos tenebræ comprehendant; et qui ambulat in tenebris, nescit quo vadat. Dum lucem habetis, credite in lucem ut filii lucis sitis (Joann xii, 35, 36).

the light of life."[15]

By following Him who has deigned to make us His brethren by adoption, man will therefore possess the true light of the spiritual life; he will enter into the Illuminative Life, which heretofore was not his: "For you were heretofore darkness, but now light in the Lord. Walk then as children of the light. For the fruit of the light is in all goodness and justice and truth."[16] And: "For all you are the children of light, and children of the day; we are not of the night nor of darkness."[17]

The same signs of the development of the inward man are brought forward by St. John. "God is light," he says, "and in Him there is no darkness. If we say that we have fellowship with Him and walk in darkness, we lie, and do not the truth. But if we walk in the light, as He also is in the light, we have fellowship one with another, and the Blood of Jesus Christ, His Son, cleanseth us from all sin."[18]

From the Old Testament times, the Holy Spirit has ever urged souls on to the Illuminative Life: "Come ye to Him, and be enlightened, and your faces shall not be confounded."[19] Other similar passages are so numerous that they could not be

---

[15] Ego sum lux mundi; qui sequitur me, non ambulat in tenebris sed habebit lumen vitæ (*Ibid.*, viii, 12).

[16] Eratis enim aliquando tenebræ, nunc autem lux in Domino. Ut filii lucis ambulate; fructus enim lucis est in omni bonitate, et justitia, et veritate (Eph. v, 8, 9).

[17] Omnes enim vos filii lucis estis et filii diei; non sumus noctis, neque tenebrarum (Thess. v, 5).

[18] Quoniain Deus lux est, et tenebræ in eo non sunt ullæ. Si dixerimus quoniam societatem habemus cum eo et in tenebris ambulamus, mentimur, et veritatem non facimus. Si autem in luce ambulamus, sicut et ipse est in luce, socictatem habemus ab invicem, et sanguis Jesu Christi, Filii ejus, emundat nos ab omni peccato (1 Joann, i, 5, 6, 7).

[19] Accedite ad eum, et illuminamini, et facies vestræ non confundentur (Ps. xxxiii).

pointed out. The New Testament shows above all that our Lord came to increase the brightness of the light, and to make access to it more easy and more general. The prince of the apostles bears witness to this when he says, in the enthusiasm of his pastoral love: "That you may declare his virtues, who hath called you out of darkness into His marvellous light."[20]

However splendid the spiritual life in its "illuminative" stage may appear to us, this is not the utmost advance to which the inward man may aspire, the man that is, who has received that precious germ which, when fully developed, is to bring him to the perfect age of Christ. It is here that St. Paul, writing to the Ephesians, surpasses himself in his description of the spiritual life. In the passage alluded to he gives the secret of its last phase, which comprises heavenly beatitude itself. The Unitive Life, for it is of this that we are now speaking, is thus described by the apostle; "To be rooted and founded in charity." All the rest is but a development of this admirable state, wherein the inward man, now truly an adult, truly united to the Incarnate Word, whose perfect age he has attained, is led, by a marvellous assimilation, to the mysteries wherein Christ manifested His incomprehensible charity, that by Him and in Him he may be brought to enjoy even the fulness of God:

"That, being rooted and founded in charity, you may be able to comprehend, with all the saints, what is the breadth and length and height and depth. To know also the charity of Christ, which surpasseth all knowledge, that you may be filled unto all the fulness of God."[21] Farther on we will develop the splendours of the "unitive life"; for the present it is sufficient

[20] Ut virtutes annuntietis ejus qui de tenebris vos vocavit in admirabile lumen suum (1 Pet. ii, 9).

[21] In caritate radicati et fundati, ut possitis comprehendere cum omnibus sanctis, quæ sit latitudo, et longitudo, et sublimitas, et profundum: scire etiam supereminentem scientiæ caritatem Christi, ut impleamini in omnem plenitudinem Dei (Eph., iii, 17-19).

for our purpose to have pointed out with the apostle this true end of the spiritual life, as an object greatly to be desired, and worthy of our most generous efforts.

The three stages of the spiritual life here mentioned, which stages we have purposely drawn from the teaching of the apostle St. Paul, were acknowledged very early in the Church. St. Denis, in his two "Hierarchies," founds all his teaching upon this triple form of the spiritual life, PURGATIVE, ILLUMINATIVE and UNITIVE. He seems to have gathered the tradition from the lips of the apostles themselves; but among the fathers he is not the only one that has pointed out these three definite stages. St. Gregory of Nyssa, a father who treats with the greatest profundity of the divine workings, also divides the spiritual life into three distinct parts, linking each with the Sapiential Books of Scripture. He assigns Proverbs to the "Purgative Life," Ecclesiastes to the "Illuminative Life," and the Canticle of Canticles to the "Unitive Life."[22]

St. Gregory the Great in his exhaustless "Morals" keeps the same divisions. "There are three states," he says, "for those who are converted—the beginning, the middle, and the perfection."[23] He repeats the same in one of his Homilies on Ezechiel: "For the beginnings of virtue are one thing, the progress another, and the perfection another."[24] St. Maximus of Constantinople, an abbot and martyr of the eighth century, calls the first state "Exercise of Practice"; the second, "Theory," which forms to the knowledge of things material and spiritual; the third, "Theology," which the soul reaches when, united to God by the grace of the Holy Ghost, it contemplates eternal truth and

---

[22] S. Greg. Nyss. In Cant. Homil. 1.

[23] Tres sunt modi conversorum: inchoatio, medietas atque perfectio (*Mor.* XXIV, viii).

[24] Aliud namque sunt virtutis exordia, aliud provectus, aliud perfectio (in Ezech. Lib. II, Homil. 3).

delights therein.

In the course of time the science of the spiritual life followed the impulse given to theology. When this latter was organized and classified by the schoolmen, and teaching became more condensed, more precise, more concrete, though not more extensive, the notions of the spiritual life were at the same time established. The doctrine of the angelic St. Thomas Aquinas has fixed and defined for ever the three stages of which we have been speaking. Moreover, from the very beginning, the Church adapted her children to them in a practical way by means of the sacred liturgy; this it is that Dorn Gueranger has so well explained in the simple and vigorous language of his "Liturgical Year."

Hence man, having received in baptism the first fruits of the Spirit, ought unceasingly to aspire after his full growth. He must not limit his desires in the supernatural order, as he does not certainly wish to do so in the natural order. No one makes it the object of his ambition to attain merely the age of childhood or of youth; every man desires to reach his full development. Thus ought we ever to desire to attain the fulness of that divine life of which we have the principle within us: "If we live in the Spirit, let us also walk in the Spirit."[25]

---

[25] Si Spiritu vivimus, Spiritu et ambulemus (Gal. v, 25).

CHAPTER III
Who are apt for the Spiritual Life?

AS A RULE, books treating of the spiritual life seem to be addressed exclusively to a certain class of men, to persons gifted with a special vocation. Such we think is not the Church's intention, nor that of our Lord Jesus Christ. This way of distinguishing and separating seems to divide the mystic body of the Lord, which is founded on the unity of one same life, whose sole principle is the Spirit of God. "One body and one Spirit, as you are called in one hope of your calling. One Lord, one faith, one baptism, one God and Father of all, who is above all, and through us all, and in us all. But to every one of us is given grace according to the measure of the giving of Christ."[1] So then the Holy Spirit, who forms the spiritual life within us, is the bond that unites all who are baptized. It is quite true that all do not receive the same measure of grace, and that, in some souls grace itself is crowned with those spiritual gifts which God distributes according to His good pleasure:

"Now there are diversities of grace, but the same Spirit; and there are diversities of ministries, but the same Lord; and there are diversities of operations, but the same God, who worketh all

---

[1] Unum corpus, et unus Spiritus, sicut vocati estis in una spe vocationis vestræ. Unus Dominus, una fides, unum baptisma. Unus Deus et Pater omnium qui est super omnes et per omnia, et in omnibus nobis. Unicuique autem nostrum data est gratia secundum mensuram donationis Christi (Eph. iv, 4-7).

in all."[2] Thus, according to the teaching of the apostle, grace is not distributed to all in equal measure. Moreover, the diverse gifts of the Holy Spirit, which determine the ministry and action of each one in the Church, or what St. Paul calls "the manifestation of the Spirit unto profit,"[3] depend more still than the rest upon God's good pleasure, and are the privileged matter of His free liberality; "For in one Spirit were we all baptized into one body. . . . For the body also is not one member, but many."[4]

This unequal distribution of grace sometimes gives rise to a pernicious error, which would aim at nothing less than discouraging the Christian in his aspirations after God. "I cannot help it," some will say, "God does not call me by His grace to the heights of the spiritual life." Let us have a right understanding of the matter. In admitting that God is essentially free in the distribution of His grace, we do not mean to say that He ever measures it out so sparingly as to make it impossible for certain souls to attain the fulness of the spiritual life. No doubt the greater number of those who are saved do not before their death come to this union with God, but we must not conclude that they might not have done so, or that God denied them the necessary grace.

Our faith obliges us to believe that all men have been redeemed by Jesus Christ; and yet how many are lost without being able to impute this misfortune to any one but to themselves! We cannot then gather the law from the fact, nor

---

[2] Divisiones vero gratiarum sunt, idem autem Spiritus: divisiones ministrationum sunt, idem autem Dominus: et divisiones operationum sunt, idem vero Deus, qui operatur omnia in omnibus (i Cor. xii, 46).

[3] Manifestatio Spiritus ad utilitatem (Ibid).

[4] Etenim in uno Spiritu omnes nos in unum corpus baptizati sumus .... nam et corpus non est unum membrum, sed multa (Ibid, xii, 13, 14).

can we argue from the condition to which man reduces himself, what God's intentions are in his regard. But if we open the holy Scriptures, we there find the most generous, vehement and repeated invitation to the Unitive Life, whilst nowhere do we see a systematic exclusiveness, which would repel far from God and from union with Him a certain number of souls purposely overlooked by divine Providence. "Behold, I stand at the gate and knock. If any man shall hear My voice and open to Me the door, I will come to him, and will sup with him, and he with Me." If this text shows us clearly how intimate is the bond of union which our Lord wishes to contract with us even in this world, and how He is first to make the advance, since He stands at the door and knocks, it also shows that man, on his side, must correspond to these merciful advances; he must open the door, under pain of preventing our Lord from abiding with him. Let us then assert boldly that the fact of the unequal distribution of grace does not close the way to divine union, any more than the "diversities of ministries" prevent us from belonging to the mystical body of Christ.

The doctrine of the Church on purgatory alone seems to prove that our Lord has given all men the power of attaining to divine union. For if it were not strictly possible for all Christians, before their death, to reach the Unitive Life, how could God reproach them afterwards, and give them over to the rigorous requirements of His justice, for having neglected the means whereby they might have come before Him free from all their debts. Nothing then could be more strange than the conduct of a Christian who should limit his efforts in the supernatural life merely to reaching the place of expiation, when, at the very outset, all baptized souls are established in a holy state which gives them the right of immediate entrance into the eternal sanctuary, there to enjoy the face to face vision of God.

So then all Christians may attain union with God, without any other call to it than that given in their baptism; they can do so in virtue of their simple title of children of God, and without entering upon any other way but that of the precepts: "He that hath My commandments and keepeth them, he it is that loveth Me. And he that loveth Me shall be loved of My Father; and I will love him, and will manifest Myself to him."[5] But what shall we say of the new facility offered to those who make the evangelical counsels their law, and who have heard the word, "He shall receive a hundredfold, and shall possess life everlasting"?[6]

Supported by Scripture and tradition, St. Benedict, in his Rule, simultaneously opens to his children the gates of the spiritual life and points to its highest reach. "To thee therefore now my speech is directed," he says, "who, renouncing thy own will, being to fight under our Lord Jesus Christ, the true king, takest unto thee the most strong and bright armour of obedience."[7] A little farther on he adds: "But in process of practice and faith, the heart being once dilated, the way of God's commandments is run with unspeakable sweetness of love."[8]

By this advance in holiness of life and faith, an advance which goes so far as to make the soul run with joy and gladness in the way of the divine commandments, it is easy to recognize the perfection of the spiritual life in which love makes all things light. The holy patriarch has no distinctions among his

---

[5] Qui habet mandata mea et servat ea: ille est qui diligit me. Qui autem diligit me, diligetur a Patre meo, et ego diligam eum et manifestabo ei meipsum (Joann., xiv, 21).

[6] Centuplam accipiet, et vitam æternam possidebit (Matth., xix, 29).

[7] Ad te ergo nunc mens servo dirigatur, quisquis abrenuntians propriis voluntatibus, Domino Christo vero Regi militaturus, obedientiæ fortissima atque præclara arma assumis (S. Reg. Prol.).

[8] Processu vero conversationis et fidei, dilatato corde, inenarrabili dilectionis dulcedine curritur via mandatorum Dei (S. Reg. Prol., sub fine).

children; in his view the career is open to all, and nothing remains but to run for the prize. To aspire after the highest reach of the spiritual life, which is union, is the normal state for the Christian, and especially for the religious. The soul which has entered the state which aims at perfection must, however, take heed lest a want of generosity and energy in overcoming herself should hinder the carrying out of this divine programme.

Thus thought Dom Gueranger, when he drew up his "Rudiments of the Monastic Life." "God," it is there said, "has revealed Himself to man by faith. He has excited his hope of eternal union with the sovereign Good; He has commanded him to love his Creator and Redeemer; but He has done all this for an end, which is to be realized by man even in this present life. This end is that man should aspire, even in this world, to perfection.

"Perfection is the entire agreement of the creature with his God, as far as the creature is capable of it. It results from the conformity of the creature with the sanctity of God, by the exemption from sin and the realization of all virtues, of which charity is the most exalted, spreading its influence over every other.

"Hence it follows that there is a real obligation incumbent on every Christian, of desiring perfection and of endeavouring, according to the graces granted to him, to attain it. Were it not so, we should have to say that God cares not for His creature's fulfilling the plan He has marked out, or that His creature may, if he please, refuse to fulfil that end for which God drew him out of nothing, and redeemed him from hell. To assert either of these is worse than folly. Hence, in order to preclude all illusion with regard to this precept of perfection which includes all other precepts, our Lord says to us: 'Be perfect, as your heavenly Father is perfect.'[9] In these few words He shows us the divine Type according to which we should regulate, not only our actions, but also our thoughts and desires."[10]

There are not then two forms of Christianity, as the Gnostics taught, nor two supernatural states to which man may be successively called, in virtue of two distinct predestinations. Only let man be faithful, and God will not be wanting; the holy Scriptures give us the infallible assurance of this. "Think of the Lord in goodness, and seek Him in simplicity of heart. For He is found by them that tempt Him not, and He showeth Himself to them that have faith in Him."[11] Thus the way is thrown open broadly before all whom baptism has made children of God. Even during their earthly pilgrimage, if they are faithful to their supernatural engagements, they may already attain to intimacy with God their Father.

---

[9] Estote ergo vos perfecti, sicut et Pater vester coelestis perfectus est (Matth. v, 48).

[10] Rudiments viii.

[11] Sentite de Domino in bonitate, et in simplicitate cordis quærite illum: quoniam invenitur ab his qui non tentat illum, apparet autem eis qui fidem habent in illum (Sap., i, 1, 2).

CHAPTER IV
That Union with God is a Grace, although it is the End set before all Christians

NION with God, even in this world, is the end whereunto all spiritual life tends. But this union is, at the same time, a grace which all man's efforts and works can never naturally attain. Hence many argue thus within themselves: "If union with God is a grace, it is above my reach; I can only remain in peace and expect it from the gratuitous liberality of God. How can we reconcile these two things, namely, that union is a grace and, at the same time, that it is the end set before all Christians?" As if everything that comes to us from God were not a gift, down to our very being, to which we certainly had no claim. But while leaving to the word "grace" its proper signification, namely, a gratuitous help in the supernatural order, it is easy to see that we cannot shelter our cowardice under the plea of incapacity to accomplish the work as though, from the fact that union is a grace, we had nothing more to do but to await it from God's hands, without making any effort to obtain it. We wish to show that these two views may be easily reconciled. Final perseverance is also a grace; but though it is a grace, and for the very reason that it is a grace, we are bound in conscience, while doing everything necessary to obtain it, to hope constantly and firmly that it will be granted us.

Therefore when we use the word "grace," we understand simply a good which God does not owe us in virtue of His justice, a good which is above our efforts and our natural wants. Having said this, let us beware of believing that the soul

27

cannot prepare the way of the Lord, and make straight the paths by which He will come.

Exact fidelity in conquering self, constant seeking after virtue, persevering imitation of our Lord Jesus Christ, loyal obedience to all God's commandments, these are the efficacious means for obtaining the grace of divine union; but even then it is from God only that it can be obtained. Moreover, our Lord often shows that this is the domain of His free generosity. At one time He unites Himself almost suddenly to a soul that has done nothing to prepare herself for this high favour; at another time He refuses it for years to one who seems most exact and fervent in God's service.

Far from lessening our desire after divine union, or causing us to relax in our efforts, this fact ought, on the contrary, to animate us to multiply those acts which may draw upon us the look of our divine Lord. Can we be astonished that the most excellent gifts that divine liberality can bestow upon us should often call for many desires, efforts and prayers? If so few souls reach this end, the fault is not on God's side; He has not become sparing in His dealings with souls. The grace of the Unitive Life would be much more common among Christians if it were better understood, more highly esteemed and more ardently longed for.

When we consider what fasts, watchings, and humiliations the fathers of the desert undertook; when we see the long hours they devoted to prayer, both mental and vocal, their admirable detachment from all things, their incomparable submission to the spiritual guides under whom they had placed themselves, we cannot be surprised that God rewarded so many labours by an eminent gift of contemplation and union with Himself. It was always a gift, a gift bearing no proportion to their labours; but it astonishes us less in them than when it comes, as it were, on a sudden to reward our dispositions as yet so far from generous.

We ought at least to persevere in the little that we are
doing, striving daily to do more, and then to keep full of
confidence in God's infinite goodness. "I believe to see the good
things of the Lord in the land of the living. Expect the Lord, do
manfully, and let thy heart take courage, and wait thou for the
Lord."[1] The Gospel gives us the precious assurance that this
waiting will not be in vain: "Blessed are those servants whom
the Lord, when He cometh, shall find watching. . . . And if He
shall come in the second watch, or come in the third watch, and
find them so, blessed are those servants."[2] Why "blessed," if not
that great and choice favours are reserved for this vigilance?
God will sometimes leave us waiting and longing till the third
watch, and then He will come. How great would be the soul's
loss and misfortune, had she grown weary of waiting on the
eve or fore-eve of her Lord's visit.

Moreover, in the Old Testament, God was not slow in
making known His full will on this subject: "Wisdom is
glorious, and never fadeth away, and is easily seen by them that
love her, and is found by them that seek her. She preventeth
them that covet her, so that she first showeth herself unto
them. He that awaketh early to seek her shall not labour, for he
shall find her sitting at his door."[3]

The same thought inspires the Church to sing as follows, on
the feast days of saints: "Thou hast given him his heart's desire,

---

[1] Credo videre bona Domini in terra viventium. Exspecta Dominum,
viriliter age, et confortetur cor tuum, et sustine Dominum (Ps. xxvi,
13-14).

[2] Beati servi illi, quos, quum venerit Dominus, invenerit vigilantes
. . . Et si venerit in secunda vigilia, et si in tertia vigilia venerit, et ita
invenerit, beati sunt servi illi (Luc., xii, 37-38).

[3] Clara est, et quæ numquam marcescit sapientia, et facile videtur ab
his qui quærunt illam. Præoccupat qui se concupiscunt, ut illis se
prior ostendat. Qui de luce vigilaverit ad illam, non laborabit;
assidentem enim illam foribus suis inveniet (Sap., vi, 13-15).

and hast not withholden from him the will of his lips. For Thou hast prevented him with blessings of sweetness. . . . He asked life of Thee, and Thou hast given him length of days for ever and ever."[4] This saint asked for the true life, and God gave it to him with an abundance and development beyond all his expectations.

Our Lord is so desirous of giving Himself to souls, the expansive force of His love is so great that, far from always waiting till the grace is asked of Him, He sometimes with ineffable sweetness anticipates the soul's action, even when that soul is far off from Him: "The Lord hath appeared from afar to me. Yea, I have loved thee with an everlasting love, therefore have I drawn thee, taking pity on thee. And I will build thee again, and thou shalt be built, O virgin of Israel."[5] Admirable indeed is the work of divine mercy and compassion which we have daily before our eyes, and which gives joy to the angels of God! Yet, it is not the supreme effort of God's essential goodness. St. Paul reveals this fact, when quoting another prophet he says: "But Isaias is bold, and saith: I was found by them that did not seek Me; I appeared openly to them that asked not after me. But to Israel he saith: All the day long have I spread My hands to a people that believeth not, and contradicteth Me."[6]

---

[4] Desiderium cordis ejus tribuisti ei, et voluntate labiorum ejus non fraudasti eum; quoniam prævenisti eum in benedictionibus dulcedinis. . . . Vitam petiit a te, et tribuisti ei longitudinem dierum in sæculum et in sæculum sæculi (Ps., xx, 35).

[5] Longe Dominus apparuit mihi. Et in caritate perpetua dilexi te; ideo attraxi te, miserans. Rursum ædificabo te, et ædificaberis, virgo Israël (Jer., xxxi, 3, 4).

[6] Isaias autem audet et dicit: Inventus sum a non quærentibus me: palam apparui iis qui me non interrogabant. Ad Israël autem dicit: Tota dic expandi manus meas ad populum non credentem, et contradicentem (Rom., x, 20, 21).

In His ardent desire of drawing souls fully to Himself, and to that closeness and intimacy which we call union, our Lord employs a further stratagem—He invariably inspires those who have reached divine union to solicit a like favour for others. The nearer souls are to God, the more are they a force of attraction for others, and the more earnestly do they offer violence to heaven in order to obtain for other souls the grace of which we are speaking. Thus it is that an invisible world already reveals itself—a world which, later on, will open out before our ravished gaze, a world in which we shall contemplate the mysterious fact of a supernatural filiation—not only in the sense usually understood, but in a deeper sense in which we may say that saints are born from saints, according to an ineffable generation "of God—*ex Deo.*"

The most striking example of this fruitfulness is found first of all in our Lord Jesus Christ. In the holy Gospel we see Him giving Himself to prayer in order to obtain from His Father the graces necessary for His apostles. It is after a night spent in prayer on the mountain, that our Saviour chooses them. They are truly the children of Christ's prayer: "I pray for them. I pray not for the world, but for them whom Thou hast given me, because they are Thine."[7] And when there is question of Peter's infallibility, our Lord permits us to see that it also rests upon His all-powerful prayer: "I have prayed for thee that thy faith fail not; and thou, being once converted, confirm thy brethren."[8] The Old Testament also brings before us the vocation of Eliseus as due in part to the prophet Elias.[9] And who has not been equally struck by the link existing between the prayer of the

---

[7] Ego pro eis rogo. Non pro mundo rogo, sed pro his, quos dedisi mihi, quia tui sunt (Joann., xvii, 9).

[8] Ego autem rogavi pro te ut non deficiat fides tua; et tu aliquando conversus confirma fratres tuos (Luc. xxii, 32.)

[9] 3 Reg., xix, 19.

glorious deacon St. Stephen and the conversion of Saul, who
had kept the garments of his murderers? And what accents of
prayer for those whom he has begotten in Jesus Christ do we
not hear from St. Paul in his Epistles! If we open the acts of the
martyrs, there again we meet this mysterious transmission of
holiness and this fruitfulness of prayer. The lives of the fathers,
too, offer many examples of it. Who has not read the story of
St. Paul, the first hermit, receiving St. Antony and saying to
him, "Long ago God promised me that you should spend your
life like me in His service"?[10]

Monastic chronicles are not less eloquent. That to which we
are now drawing attention is to be seen principally in the
beginnings of the Benedictine Order; St. Maurus and St. Placid
take pleasure in showing that they owe everything to the
prayers of their holy patriarch. Again, how can we fail to
recognize this law in the succession of holy abbots at Cluny,
and in the active vigilance with which each of them prepared
his successor? Furthermore, at Helfta we find traces of this
supernatural filiation when we learn that those holy nuns could
not rest until the gift—thus they spoke of the unitive life—was
granted to some one among them. Here we have the secret
cause of St. Mechtilde's zeal for St. Gertrude. And no doubt this
is why holy Scripture attaches so much importance to the
expression, "God of our fathers"; for to our mind it signifies, in
most places, a transmission of the divine blessing and of
holiness, rather than a carnal filiation. We doubt not that this
is also the reason why the ancient fathers, and in particular St.
Benedict, as may be seen in his Rule, attribute so great
importance to the Abbot's prayer.

Nor must we be astonished that God desires to be earnestly
entreated to admit His rational creatures to intimate union with
Himself; for that union is both the end that He proposed to

---

[10] E Vita S. Pauli Erem., x.

Himself in His works and the pledge of the supernatural prosperity of the Church. Let those who love the Church give a thought to this. If they would work for her, the most efficacious process for so doing is to possess the science of the saints, and to be able, by means of it, to have weight in that centre where human events are controlled. It was through this kind of powerful intervention that Moses won the battles for his people; "And when Moses lifted up his hands, Isræl overcame."[11] The same means enabled him to conquer the Lord Himself, when he said: "Either forgive them this trespass, or if Thou do not, strike me out of the book that Thou hast written."[12] In like manner through prayer Nehemias obtained the favour of witnessing the end of the captivity. In this way the prophets showed themselves to be as much men of prayer as they were inspired preachers; and in this way Esther gained favour with Assuerus, and saved her people.

Holiness of life and the spirit of prayer are all-powerful in this world; and when our Lord does not find these elements on our earth, He complains of their absence as if He could no longer show mercy. It is in these terms that He says to Ezechiel: "And I sought among them for a man that might set up a hedge, and stand in the gap before me in favour of the land, that I might not destroy it; and I found none. And I poured out my indignation upon them."[13] Such is undoubtedly the secret of many revolutions in the history of empires. Hence we understand that both private and social interests call for an increase in the number of souls truly united with God. Most

---

[11] Cumque levaret Moyses manus, vincebat Isræl (Exod., xvii, 11).

[12] Dimitte eis hanc noxam; aut si non facis, dele me de libro tuo quem scripsisti (Exod., xxxii, 31, 32).

[13] Quæsivi de eis virum qui interponeret sepem, et staret oppositus contra me pro terra, ne dissiparem eam: et non inveni. Et effudi super eos indignationem meam (Ezech., xxii, 30, 31).

certainly such an increase is a grace; but once again, it is none the less a grace promised to ardent and generous prayer.

The Holy Ghost, to encourage this ardour in souls, opens the sacred Canticle with the expression of a most vehement desire: "Let him kiss Me with the kiss of his mouth."[14] And when, later on, the Bride glances back, after many struggles and labours, she considers that she has not paid too dearly for the much desired union: "If a man should give all the substance of his house for love, he shall despise it as nothing."[15] Yet she had wholly given herself with all she possessed; but it is as nothing, so inestimable is the good with which she has been enriched.

Let us then be generous with our Lord; let us offer Him, without reckoning the very marrow of our being, as though everything depended upon our generosity and our effort. But when we have given all, let us follow that counsel of our beloved Master: "When you shall have done all these things that are commanded you, say, 'We are unprofitable servants; we have done that which we ought to do.'"[16] It is very remarkable that our Lord does not say: "You are unprofitable servants," but rather, "Say, 'We are unprofitable servants.'" God holds to the asserting of His divine freedom; He tells us so in a formal way: "Friend, I do thee no wrong; didst thou not agree with me for a penny? Take what is thine, and go thy way. I will also give to this last even as to thee."[17]

We cannot be too much on our guard against the desire to

---

[14] Osculetur me osculo oris sui (Cant., I, 1).

[15] Si dederit homo omnem substantiam domus suæ pro dilectione, quasi nihil despiciet eam (*Ibid.*, viii, 7).

[16] Cum feceritis omnia quæ præcepta sunt vobis, dicite: Servi inutiles sumus: quod debuimus facere, fecimus (Luc., xvii, 10).

[17] Amice, non facio tibi injuriam: nonne ex denario convenisti mecum? Tolle quod tuus est, et vade: volo autem et huic novissimo dare sicut et tibi (Matth. Xx, 13, 14).

bring God down to our level; many of our errors arise from it.
We are indeed made after God's image and likeness, and we
know that the human nature of the Incarnate Word has brought
the Divinity within touch of us, according to that sentence of
St. John: "For the life was manifested; and we have seen and do
bear witness, and declare unto you the life eternal, which was
with the Father, and hath appeared to us."[18] But we must
beware, we repeat, of limiting God to the proportions of our
nature. Therefore, when God makes a formal engagement with
us, we know by the very tenor of His promise what He strictly
engages Himself to do; but should it please His Divine Majesty
freely to go beyond His first generous engagements, we have
no right to say: "Thus far shalt Thou go and no further." God in
His munificence always surprises us, "Give, and it shall be
given to you; good measure and pressed down and shaken
together and running over shall they give into your bosom."[19]

Here it seems useful to settle a question in advance. There
exists an opinion too widely spread and accredited perhaps by
the mystic treatises of modern times, and the way in which
many lives of the saints are written; it is that sanctity consists
merely in those extraordinary manifestations which sometimes
signalize it, or else in those processes which our Lord makes
use of to prepare, to increase, or to make known holiness, when
it so pleases Him, processes which sometimes are a means for
attaining the fulness of charity, sometimes the indication of the
disproportion existing between our present state, and that to
which God, in His ambitious love, desires to bring us; but

---

[18] Vita manifestata est, et vidimus et testamur, et annuntiamus
vosbis vitam æternam quæ erat apud Patrem, et apparuit nobis
(Joann. I, 2).

[19] Date, et dabitur vobis; mensuram bonam, et confertam, et
coagitatam, et superefflueatem dabunt in sinum vestrum (Luc., vi,
38).

processes which are neither sanctity nor the essential revelation of sanctity.

The proof of this is, that these same phenomena can be brought about externally and physically by diabolical or by natural causes, and that they are of no value except inasmuch as they come from God. If their cause is divine, the effects are worthy; if these phenomena do not come from God, the effects are deplorable. Even when the cause is divine, there is no reason to attach great importance to them, since they cannot reveal the real depth and worth of God's working, which is generally the more intense the less it betrays itself outside: "God is a spirit";[20] and when He unites Himself to the substance of the soul, without sign or medium, He produces no phenomena, because in a union such as this the senses perceive nothing. Phenomena of this kind always fall short; they are but feeble, distant and inadequate indications of what really takes place in the soul; and it is not in such a poor outward expression that the real spiritual life consists.

In reading attentively the lives of the fathers and the great contemplatives of old, we are struck with the almost absolute silence which they kept with respect to the external effects of supernatural contemplation. One would think that these effects were accidents of which they made no account, because they are of no value either in themselves or as proofs. In the mind of these masters union with God, true holiness, consists in the heroic practice of the theological and cardinal virtues. All the rest seems undeserving of mention, and scarcely do we find any allusion to it in their writings. St. John of the Cross, though modern, belongs to this admirable school, which has the advantage of securing holiness from the irreverent inquiries of materialistic science.

In the lives of the saints, the exaggerated stress laid upon

---

[20] Spiritus est Deus (Joann., iv, 24).

the supernatural phenomena of ecstasy, rapture and the like constitutes a peril, and prepares the way for dangerous illusions. No doubt, while bringing forward these extraordinary facts, the danger of aspiring after graces of this kind is with reason insisted upon. And yet in that insistence there is an evident contradiction, for if these favours constitute holiness, and if, though not the cause, they are at least the essential indications of it, why forbid souls to esteem and desire them? Holiness should be more than merely desired by Christians; it should be the object of our highest and most salutary ambition, as our Lord Himself declares: "Be ye perfect, as your heavenly Father is perfect."[21] How is it possible to desire the end without desiring the means? There is a subtle temptation here, arising from inexact notions; there is also a danger of illusion and an opening given to the devil's fraud—danger of illusion, because to make much of extraordinary things calls for and provokes it; also physical temperament, weakness, want of energy and of self-control may predispose a person for certain phenomena, independently of the holy cause which ordinarily produces them. Moreover, it is a matter of positive experience that when these graces are brought about by God's working, their effects are very different in different subjects. Though the soul itself is the same in all, physical temperaments are very various and they react upon the soul in different ways. Some are too easily carried away by supernatural impressions, and thus they excite, entertain and, to a certain extent, bring back to themselves the state which they have experienced. If an imprudent director betrays admiration for these phenomena as if they were supernatural graces much to be desired, he does serious injury to souls. Again, if on their side, souls set too high a value on extraordinary graces, they not only prejudice themselves, but

---

[21] Estote perfecti, sicut et Pater vester ccelestis perfectus est (Matth. v, 48).

they ruin their health without gaining any spiritual profit. More than one failure in the spiritual life has had no other cause than this.

On his side the demon, bent upon ensnaring souls and mimicking God, hastens to make good interest out of all esteem, all love, all seeking for these phenomena which God's action may produce, but which belong to a world where the demon finds access. What a subject of joy for the "ape of God"—as Tertullian calls the devil—when he can find servants of God, either men or women, ready to be the innocent accomplices of his fraud, simply because they are not sufficiently on their guard against yielding to those external, sensible and physical accidents which sometimes accompany God's grace! What a satisfaction for the devil, when he succeeds in making a creature of God lose his time and his health, whereas, with more energy and sound spiritual life, he might be dealing him some hard blows!

Further, let us add that the word "extraordinary" is not synonymous with the word "supernatural"; the distinction to be made between the two is a very important one. The intuitive vision of God, which is the final term of the supernatural, cannot be called "extraordinary," since it becomes the portion of all who are saved. Thus there may be a very high grace of union, and yet it may not take any extraordinary form, while certain extraordinary graces do not necessarily result in divine union. St. John of the Cross has no mercy for those who seek visions, ecstasies and even the gift of miracles; but he nowhere says that we must not aspire to union with God. On the contrary, it is to make this union more perfect that he counsels souls not to stop at the processes by which it may please God to bring it about. It is as though he would recommend us not to waste our time admiring the magnificence of the halls in the royal palace, as long as we have not reached the apartment where the king himself resides.

It will always be lawful to aspire after union with God, which is our end, without on that account desiring the extraordinary ways and phenomena which sometimes lead to it, but which are not indispensable, which even disappear, little by little, when the soul attains the highest stage of the supernatural life.

We will rather seek the means which God has given for producing in our souls, with sovereign efficacy, His own proper perfection, by kindling in our hearts that fire which He came to cast upon the earth. Surely, He has willed to accomplish in favour of the true Israel what he promised to Israel of old: "As the eagle enticing her young to fly and hovering over them, He spreads his wings, and hath taken him and carried him on His shoulders."[22]

---

[22] Sicut aquila provocans ad volandum pullos suos, et super eos volitans, expandit alas suas, et assumpsit eum, atque portavit in humeris suis (Deut., xxxii, 11).

CHAPTER V
God, by means of the Sacraments, makes His Designs still more evident

BY coming into this world our Lord Jesus Christ wished to bring holiness within the reach of all men. For this end He provided certain means to fill up all their deficiencies, and supply all their needs in the supernatural order.

Those wonderful means of sanctification are the Sacraments. Their outward signs harmonize admirably with the grace which they contain, and with the effects which they produce. By their means, in a truly divine order of things, creatures, which have so often captivated man and drawn him away from God, become instruments for bringing him back. Themselves rehabilitated and ennobled by the use now made of them, these lower creatures will no longer appear hurtful, but rather good and wholesome, just as when they first came from the hand of the same Creator that made all things, both those that are visible and those that are invisible. The economy of the Sacraments is the power of God exerted in behalf of man's sanctification. The principal mission of the ecclesiastical hierarchy, which is itself constituted by the sacrament of Holy Orders, is, first of all, to render glory directly to God by the sacrifice, and then to confer the Sacraments upon all men. It is in these Sacraments that God has concentrated the certain and authentic help of His grace; it is there that, without fettering in any way the liberty of His divine munificence, He has guaranteed to us the complement indispensable to our nature, in order to perfect us and unite us to Himself.

The superiority of the Sacraments over all other forms by

which grace comes to us is evident, since, in the language of the schools, they give grace *ex opere operato*, and not simply ex *opere operantis*. Grace is produced in the soul of man in this latter way, when God gives it through the dispositions of the individual, in consequence of his personal acts; whereas when grace is produced *ex opere operato*, as in the Sacraments, it is bestowed by virtue of the divine ordinance, independently of the virtues or the merit of the agent. Certain dispositions are indeed needed, but only as conditions, as removing an obstacle, but not as intrinsically modifying the grace inherent in the sacramental form, nor as determining the bestowal of that grace.

We maintain, then, that the Sacraments, with the power proper to them, are the means instituted by God for enabling man to attain to holiness, without there being any need to look for extraordinary means. To desire these latter is not to desire perfect sanctification, but rather to aspire after a less sure mode of sanctification, one which is open to delusion. It is to enter that way by an act of self-will, whereas here, more than anywhere else, the law imperatively requires an absolute renouncing of what is one's own.

The Sacraments being the regular, normal, certain and authentic means of our sanctification, our principal concern should be, rightly to receive them, and to make good use of the forces which they have laid up within us. They contain God, whilst at the same time they veil His splendour; they communicate God to man, and hence they all tend to divine union; they are provided with the energy necessary to bring it about, and they enable us fully to attain our end.

God forbid that we should seek to confine His liberality within the limits of the Sacraments. If a right esteem of these powerful and ever-ready sources of grace is of the utmost importance for the attainment of that holiness to which all Christians should aspire, we know that God has left Himself perfectly free to bring about man's sanctification by special and different ways according to His good pleasure. God determines these things in His sovereign wisdom, which can have no law but itself; and we see by the results that His gifts surpass His promises. We cannot read the lives of the saints, or the records of God's graces to men, in this land of our exile, without experiencing much consolation, and being drawn to admire God's admirable condescension and the prodigious variety of the artifices of His love. This admiration will be all the more pure, as it is free from any secret and dangerous envy, regret, or falling back upon self, seeing that God has elsewhere guaranteed to all souls the means of reaching divine union; for we know by our faith and by experience that God has abundantly provided for all men's sanctification.

If visions, ecstasies and raptures, with their external phenomena, had been the necessary accompaniment of our sanctification, God would not have failed to make this known to us; but, on the contrary, He has passed over in silence the accidental things of the supernatural life, leaving them quite in the shade; whereas He has brought forward HIS SACRAMENTS, and imposed them upon all men as the law.

In Baptism spiritual life is given to us. Therefore this sacrament cannot be repeated; for as we are not born twice over into our natural life, so we are born once only to grace. The character of a child of God, once stamped upon us in Baptism, is ineffaceable, even were we to lose our grace, so deeply does it penetrate the very substance of our being. Together with this character God bestows upon us all the virtues and the energies necessary for our full spiritual life. As a son of our Father's family, we receive the patrimony which will enable us to live up to our rank without ever derogating from our dignity.

To live in the thought of our Baptism, of the nobility which it has conferred upon us, of the energies with which it has endowed us, of the obligations which it has imposed upon us, and to be ever striving more perfectly to fulfil these obligations—all this constitutes in itself a very extensive and important outline of perfection. The apostle St. Paul, who has said all that can be said on these matters, places no other before the Christians of his time. "Call to mind," he says, "the former days, wherein being illuminated,"[1] etc. He gives the same advice with reference to all the Sacraments which impress a character upon the soul, because by thus living in the thought of the grace which we have received, and desiring to be ever in the good dispositions which we had when we received it, the energy of the sacrament is kept up and increased within us. "Neglect not the grace that is in thee," wrote St. Paul to his beloved Timothy, reminding him of his ordination, "which was given thee by prophecy, with the imposition of the hands of the priesthood."[2]

Just as our dispositions prepare the way for the reception of sacramental grace, and give to it its field of action, so, when we remove all obstacles, we encourage the working and expansion of this grace, which should take possession of our being, and transform it into God. We may safely assert that any soul, relying on the grace of baptism, would speedily reach a high degree of sanctity if she made it her business to shun habitually all that she renounced at her baptism, to advance in this renunciation according to her light and, in spite of all obstacles, to identify herself daily more and more with her noble titles, child of God, coheir of Jesus Christ, and temple of the Holy Ghost.

A tree, however high its branches may grow, proceeds from its first germ, and not from any increase of energy from without; the power of that full development which delights all

---

[1] Rememoramini pristinos dies, in quibus illuminati (Heb., x, 32).

[2] Noli negligere gratiam quæ in te est, quæ data est tibi per prophetiam, cum impositione manuum presbyterii (1 Tim., iv, 14).

who sit under the shade of the noble tree is in the seed. It fell upon good ground, and it was carefully cultivated. Even if the ground were not of the best, this careful culture supplied what was wanting. By its side fell an equally good seed; but the ground was stony and covered with briars, so the tree grew up poor and ill shaped, suggesting only an idea of barrenness. Thus Baptism has always its own intrinsic power; but if generous cooperation is wanting on the part of the Christian, his growth is hindered and retarded, and his supernatural energies are weakened. If spiritual death does not follow, the hour of natural death will come, and the fire of purgatory will have to do the work which, through want of courage and energy, or perhaps through levity, indifference or slothful ignorance, he has left undone. To gain that fulness of life which is consummate perfection we must carefully cultivate the grace of Baptism without growing weary, or taking any rest until all that is natural in us is brought into perfect subjection to grace and to all God's leadings.

This radical transformation, this fulness of the life of Christ within us, this perfect development of the grace of Baptism manifests itself in the soul of man by a sure sign; that sign is when there is accomplished in her that mystery which St. Paul thus beautifully expresses: "For the Spirit Himself giveth testimony to our spirit that we are the sons of God."[3] When the Holy Spirit makes the soul see clearly that she is in very deed the child of God, that vision implies that, within her, order is well nigh restored, and that nothing now abides there detrimental to her character as a child of God. We will borrow from the Jesuit, Pere Surin, a passage which admirably describes how this precious and almost certain indication of the fulness of supernatural life existing in the soul is given. "Grace

[3] Ipse enim Spiritus testimonium reddit spiritui nostro sumus filii Dei (Rom., viii, 16).

works in the soul," he says, "in such a way that she experiences
a certain elevating confidence and peace proper to the good and
faithful friends of God; and the Holy Ghost, who, as our faith
tells us, dwells within us, by a further working of His grace
makes His presence manifest—'Because of His Spirit that
dwelleth in you.'[4] This is brought about in a way so high and
free that the faithful heart is persuaded, not in the ordinary way
by faith only, but by a sentiment so filial, so sweet that, without
any fear of delusion, she recognizes and knows that in all
probability she is God's own. I do not say that this is an express
revelation, such as God has sometimes given to saints, but a
probability, which gives rise to a surpassing peace and
confidence, causing the soul to rest in perfect tranquillity."[5]

St. John in his epistle teaches the same truth; "He that
believeth in the Son of God hath the testimony of God in
himself."[6] To experience this it is not sufficient to be merely in
a state of grace, we must moreover unreservedly serve God,
sincerely seek Him, and we must have entered resolutely on the
way of perfection. Then the spirit of adoption teaches the soul
to say: "Abba, Father."[7] This is the unceasing cry of the inmost
being, the filial persevering self-surrender of those who have
become the brethren and the coheirs of our Lord Jesus Christ.

All that we have said of the sacrament of regeneration holds
good of the sacrament of Confirmation, which, though distinct
from the first of the sacraments, is as it were its completion.
According to the principle laid down by our divine Master,

---

[4] Propter inhabitantem Spiritum ejus in nobis (Rom., viii, 11).

[5] Surin, Traité de l'Amour de Dieu (I, 1, cap., ii).

[6] Qui credit in Filium Dei habet testimonium Dei in se (1 Joann., v, 10).

[7] Abba, Pater (Rom., viii, 15).

"Without Me you can do nothing,"[8] our growth as well as our birth is the result of a divine work. But this growth must be fostered by our own care; that which is given to the soul in power must be brought into action. The soul is bound to make use of the grace which she has received in the Sacrament; for just as our physical organs lose their power for want of exercise, and our muscles refuse to work if we do not use them, so is it with the supernatural powers if they remain idle within us. Now the sacrament of Confirmation enables us to act manfully in the supernatural order and to manifest, while seeking after virtue and confessing the faith of our Baptism, that vigour, energy and calm confidence which are the signs of true strength. This supernatural vigour is moreover the stamp of a perfect Christian who finds himself at ease amidst strong works, and who is not withdrawn from contemplation by the labours and toils accompanying the acquisition of virtue.

But did God consider that man thus exalted could always maintain his high position and walk on without fainting, if no food were given to him to restore his strength? Our Lord, when on earth, was tenderly solicitous for those who followed Him. "I have compassion," He said, "on the multitude; for, behold, they have now been with me three days, and have nothing to eat. And if I shall send them away fasting to their homes, they will faint in the way, for some of them come from afar."[9] This was like a prelude to the fulfilment of that pressing invitation made by eternal wisdom in the Old Testament: "Whosoever is a little one, let him come to Me. And to the unwise she said: Come, eat my bread, and drink the wine which I have mingled

---

[8] Sine me nihil potestis facere (Joann., xv, 5).

[9] Misereor super turbam; quia ecce jam triduo sustinent me, nec habent quod manducent; et si dimisero eos jejunos in domum suam, deficient in via; quidam enim ex eis de longe venerunt (Mar., viii, 2, 3).

for you."[10] Such was the loving heart of our God; and such it is
now that the mysteries of our redemption are accomplished. He
has provided with divine liberality for all our supernatural
needs. As the end which He had in view was to unite us to
Himself, He would give us no other food to repair our strength
but Himself. For if in the natural order our bodily strength is
renewed by the food which we assimilate and which becomes
part of ourselves, our supernatural food, having superior energy
by reason of its dignity, communicates to us a life all divine: "I
am the living Bread which came down from heaven. If any man
eat of this Bread he shall live for ever."[11] And not only shall we
live "in the strength of that food,"[12] but we shall have the same
life as this Bread: "As the living Father hath sent Me, and I live
by the Father, so he that eateth Me, the same also shall live by
Me."[13] And, lest any one should misunderstand the nature of
this divine food, our Lord showed the effects of receiving it
when He said: "He that eateth My flesh and drinketh My blood
abideth in Me, and I in him."[14] What union was ever so close as
this?

But as the Jews loudly protested against these words, our
Lord answered: "Amen, Amen, I say unto you; except you eat
the flesh of the Son of man and drink His blood, you shall not

---

[10] Si quis est parvulus veniat ad me; et insipientibus locuta est:
Venite, comedite panem meum, et bibite vinum quod miscui vobis
(Prov., ix, 4-5).

[11] Ego sum panis vivus, qui de cœlo descendi. Si quis manducaverit
ex hoc pane, vivet in æternum (Joann., vi, 51, 52).

[12] In foritudine cibi illius (3 Reg., xix, 8).

[13] Sicut misit me vivens Pater, et ego vivo propter Patrem: et qui
manducat me, et ipse vivet propter me (Joann., vi, 58).

[14] Qui manducat meam carnem et bibit meum sanguinem, in me
manet, et ego in illo (Joann., vi, 57).

have life in you."[15] In this passage our adorable Master is certainly not speaking of a condition necessary for salvation, as Catholic theologians freely admit that certain circumstances may lawfully hinder the Christian from receiving the Body of the Lord. However we should like to ask with reference to these words, whether this eternal life which they pledge to us in the Eucharist, while being the blessed life of eternity, is not also that life of union with God which is an anticipation of the life of eternity, the germ of which is deposited for us in the divine Eucharist.

But are we right in saying that we possess only the germ of heavenly life by holy Communion? Does not God initiate us fully into this life? Does He not, in His ineffable and divine impatience, anticipate our eternal state? Yes, union is complete in this mystery; our contact with God, through the sacred Body of the Incarnate Word, is immediate and substantial; no divine operation in the soul of man can give more than we receive by this Sacrament. The union is complete if he who receives the Eucharist already has within him the life of grace. The child of God, being made a perfect Christian by means of Confirmation, approaches, and in him the words of St. Paul are realized: "The charity of God is poured forth in our hearts by the Holy Ghost, who is given to us."[16] He is then already purified, already illuminated, and possessing divine charity he is made capable of consummating and perfecting his union with God.

The blessed in heaven possess God by the beatific vision, which establishes them for ever in the essential good, truth and beauty. They are irrevocably fixed in it; and without changing

---

[15] Amen, Amen dico vobis: nisi manducaveritis carnem Filii hominis, et biberitis ejus sanguinem, non habebitis vitam in vobis (Joann., vi, 54).

[16] Caritas Dei diffusa est in cordibus nostris per Spiritum sanctum, qui datus est nobis (Rom. v, 5).

their nature they acquire constancy, power and nobility from the divine Object of their contemplation. Feeding upon God, filled with God by the beatific vision, they are, in a sense, transformed into Him.

Here upon earth, under the veils of the "Mystery of faith," the Christian feeds upon God; God gives Himself to him, just as in heaven He gives Himself to the elect—not by vision, but by the Sacrament. He does this in order that we may not be deprived of union with Himself, even while we are still in the condition of mere wayfarers. The blessed in heaven love God, and possess Him in vision; Christians on earth love God and possess Him in faith, without medium or hindrance. If our faith were so living and so deep that its voluntary action gave God the place in us, by faith and the Eucharist, which the sight of Him in eternity gives, the effects produced would bear comparison. How could such food not have the power really to transform and unite us with God?

At the time when our fathers in the faith had to observe the "discipline of the secret," they had an admirable way of expressing this teaching. In their paintings and in their writings they represented the divine Eucharist under the symbol of milk. Milk is the child's food, given by God in a mysterious way to the mother. It is the mother's food, adapted to the child's tender age. Thus, as long as we are in this life, we are but children, and our mother the Church has received for us the milk of the Eucharist, that is, divine food suited to our weakness—the food of the angels themselves and of the elect, which is to last until we have attained the age of perfect men, "unto the measure of the age of the fulness of Christ."[17] It is in this sense that certain passages of the Canticle of Canticles are interpreted when applied to the Church. For instance: "We will be glad and

---

[17] In mensuram ætatis pelitudinis Christi (Eph., iv, 13).

rejoice in thee, remembering thy breasts more than wine."[18] The milk here spoken of is indeed richer than wine, but still it is milk, and the food of our childhood here below.

After this who will care to say that in this life union with God is a privilege reserved for the few only, when our Lord Jesus Christ, eager to give us the full possession of God, has in His incomparable love prepared for all the means of union with Himself—"With desire have I desired to eat this Pasch with you before I suffer"?[19] And lest the Christian should hesitate in presence of this ineffable mystery, our Lord says again: "Do this for a commemoration of Me."[20]

The state to which our divine Lord reduces Himself in the Eucharist in order to satisfy the requirements of His tender love, brings Him before us exactly in that form of holiness which our own spiritual life should assume. According to His own teaching, abnegation and perfect mortification are indispensable if we would learn to live by the Spirit. Poverty and total riddance of self are essential if we would become disciples of Jesus Christ and attain perfection. The obedience, dependence and detachment from creatures in which we ought to be rooted, whatever our vocation may be, makes us use the world as though we used it not, as the law of Christ requires. Now our Lord's Eucharistic life is one of total abnegation, silence, poverty, obedience, absolute isolation and tranquil self-surrender which seems the ideal of what the soul's life will be when it has become perfectly united with God. Provided we surrender ourselves wholly and entirely to Him, He will fashion us according to His sacramental life; He will form us to the

---

[18] Exsultabimus et lætabimur in te, memores uberum tuorum super vinum (Cant. I, 3).

[19] Desiderio desideravi hoc pascha manducare vobiscum, antequam patiar (Luc., xxii, 15).

[20] Hoc facite in meam commemorationem (Luc., xxii, 19).

highest holiness that we can attain while yet we live in the land of faith. By modelling our souls to the likeness of His sacramental life, He leads them to adoration in its most perfect form, the property of adoration being to annihilate him who adores before Him who is adored.

This is not yet all. By reason of the higher life that our divine Lord brings to us, it is not He that is changed into us, but we that are changed into Him. His divine life assimilates to itself our life, and in assimilating elevates it. As in the Consecration our divine Lord transforms the bread and wine, so by the Sacrament He takes possession of us in order to transform and make us godlike.

In presence of these wonders and of the prodigality of God's love, we involuntarily ask ourselves how it comes to pass that holiness is so rare upon earth? Is it that we forget how rich we are? Or is it perhaps that we do not know how to use our riches as we ought? Most certainly preparation is needed for fruitfully receiving the Sacrament, but in what precisely does this preparation consist? To receive worthily the divine Food prepared for him, the baptized Christian need abstain from only those things which he renounced in Baptism, and behave himself as a loyal child of God, full of health and strength.

To assimilate our natural food nothing more is needed than to be in good health and to have an appetite. Then food supports, strengthens, gladdens and restores us. And so the Living Bread when it finds the soul healthy and vigorous gives an increase of health and of life. Health of soul, not holiness, is required for fruitfully receiving the divine Food. However health-giving a repast may be, it is never prepared for a dead man; it might even aggravate the malady of a sick man, and cause his death; but there exist many infirmities, especially those resulting from weakness, which can be cured by good food. Hence the Eucharist is not prepared for those who are not in the state of grace, and souls that are still weak must use it according to the discreet laws of the Church; but this divine food heals certain accidental infirmities, weaknesses of soul to which we do not cling; by its own divine energy, it gives and preserves health, increasing it even to the perfection of holiness.

St. Paul witnessed all this in the Church of Corinth, where spiritual gifts were seen in marvellous profusion; and yet because some of its children did not discern, as they should have done, the Body of the Lord, the Sacrament exercised not in them its supernatural efficacy, but inflicted even death: "Therefore are there many infirm and weak among you, and many sleep. But if we would judge ourselves, we should not be judged."[21]

But the apostle at the same time indicates the means of securing the life-giving effect of the Sacrament: "Let a man prove himself; and so let him eat of that bread, and drink of the chalice."[22] We shall not speak of those who have no life in them and who therefore cannot obtain an increase of supernatural life by receiving the Holy Eucharist, because they have within them a positive obstacle to the grace proper to the Sacrament. The words of the apostle, "Not discerning the Body of the Lord," imply most clearly the necessity for such a discernment and for such an appreciation in order that the soul may not liken the Body of the Lord to common food, nor loving its death and wilfully abiding in it, may not advance to receive this sacred Body like a galvanized corpse. Whereas the Sacrament was instituted not to give supernatural life, but to unite to God souls already possessing this life.

---

[21] Ideo inter vos multi infirmi et imbecilles, et dormiunt multi. Quod si nosmetipsos dijudicaremus, non utique judicaremur (1 Cor., xi, 30, 31).

[22] Probet autem seipsum homo: et sic de pane illo edat et de calice bibat (1 Cor, xi, 28).

Who then are the spiritually "infirm and weak," of whom the apostle here speaks? It was not his intention to include under these two heads all who fall into venial sins. Without a special grace venial sins cannot for any length of time be avoided; moreover, one of the effects proper to the Sacrament, is to efface these light faults and to prevent a relapse into them.

The "infirm" then, are those who, while receiving holy Communion, still retain an attachment to self, a certain clinging to their faults and imperfections, though they weep over the sinful acts themselves. This error or contradiction is frequent in persons professing a spiritual life; they disown the fruits, but they do not destroy the tree that produces them. They are like the Hebrew people who, on entering the Promised Land, did not destroy its inhabitants as God had commanded; and so, through the neglect of this first precaution they could never enjoy perfect peace in that chosen land flowing with milk and honey. The Holy Eucharist, finding in these infirm souls a sluggish remissness to which the will clings, does not obtain its full effect, which is to strengthen the spiritual life and elevate it to the perfection of union with God in faith, according to that promise made by Him to the prophet: "And I will espouse thee to me in faith; and thou shalt know that I am the Lord."[23]

It is not the number of our Communions that sanctifies us; it is the fervour with which we approach that gives the Sacrament its full power of action. It is in the highest degree profitable to the soul to communicate with suitable attention and fervour. This holy Sacrament is a powerful lever of progress in the spiritual life. God stretches out His hand to us, He makes Himself our way, our life, our strength, the milk of the weak, the bread of the strong.

Let us then strenuously reject all systems that would reduce Holy Communion to a mere means useful only to the imperfect;

---

[23] Sponsabo te mihi in fide: et scies quia ego Dominus (Osee ii, 20).

but at the same time let us beware of that odious parsimony which would grant this Bread of Life to souls of only consummate holiness. As is often the case, truth lies between these two extremes. For the Sacrament to have its full efficacy, our Lord does indeed require actual fervour of soul and habitual generosity in the labour of the spiritual life; but it is no less certain that the only indispensable disposition for holy Communion and for gaining by it an increase of charity is renunciation of mortal sin and a firm purpose of perseverance in this renunciation. With these dispositions the Christian may approach that God who, even in this world, deigns to offer him the fullest possession of Himself in the "Mystery of Faith," who thus bends down to His creature to raise him to Himself.

In the post communions of the Mass, which form quite a treatise on the Holy Eucharist, the Church teaches us all these truths. St. Denis also expresses them in the following words: "The Lord coming forth from the hiddenness of His divinity, lovingly became like unto us, assuming yet not absorbing our entire human nature. He clothes Himself in our compound nature, without altering His essential unity; and by an effect of this same charity He invites the human race to a participation of His essence and of His own riches, provided that we actively unite ourselves to Him by the imitation of His divine life; for thus we shall be truly associated to the Divinity, and shall share its riches."[24]

If we desire to know whether we are with fitting dispositions receiving this supernatural Food, we must judge by its effects. We cannot of course have any sensible perception of the divine life infused by it into us, but we are made aware of the presence of that life by the evident change wrought by it in the habits of the soul. We do not receive the Holy Eucharist for the purpose of being sensibly moved, of experiencing great

---

[24] Hier., Eccl., iii, n. 13.

consolation in sweet colloquies with our Lord, or of being made aware of the presence of our divine Guest by a kind of physical emotion; but we approach the Holy Table because the Sacraments work what they signify, and signify what they work, and since the Living Bread is the Mystery of faith, it enables us to live by God, with a life which is not directly perceived nor grasped in itself, but which manifests its presence by the growth of holiness and of the theological and moral virtues, by the gradual removal of all obstacles, and the cessation of all search after anything but God.

From all this we must conclude that Holy Communion cannot, without irreverence, be likened to other practices of piety. The Holy Eucharist is not given even as a means of intercessory prayer, although our intercession may be more efficacious when we are more united with our Lord; for it is in His name that we obtain every perfect gift from our heavenly Father. But as, in order to benefit fully by a divine ordinance, it is especially requisite to enter into the views of Him who institutes it, we must understand that the Eucharist was created to feed our souls. Before pouring ourselves out in intercession and the prayer of petition, charity will inspire us to think first of God and of ourselves—of God more than of ourselves. We shall place ourselves before God in the attitude and the dispositions which are befitting, and which will then secure the efficacy of our intercession and of our petitions.

Certain utilitarian tendencies of our times are a serious danger for the sanctification of souls, even in the religious state. All the energy of their mind is turned to the interests of their neighbour; and this ill-regulated charity causes them to neglect their own sanctification, or at least to be turned aside from that capital work, which, after all, is the Will of God in their regard. We cannot invert this essential order without loss. Now our duties to God precede our duties to our neighbour. God has a right to our service, a right to our perfect sanctification since He has given us all the means to secure it; His Will is that we should use these same means for the end He proposes to Himself.

During Holy Communion our prayer for certain persons and for certain intentions will be fruitful, according as that Communion gives glory to God and brings profit to ourselves. To multiply Communions with no other object than that of making intercession for our neighbour, or even simply out of custom, is a dangerous proceeding often animadverted upon by the directors of souls, who are well aware of the disorders which this practice may produce. When the Church prescribes Confession and Communion as conditions for gaining a plenary indulgence, is not her immediate aim to place the soul in the state which will enable her to profit by the favours promised? Are not these very favours a clever allurement, an invitation to bring about within ourselves the conditions which must necessarily prepare the way for their reception. In receiving the Holy Eucharist, it is then all important to remember, in the first place, those divine words, "He that eateth My Flesh and drinketh My Blood abideth in Me, and I in him."[25] And again, "Amen, amen, I say unto you, unless you eat the Flesh of the Son of man and drink His Blood, you shall not have life in you."[26]

For those who cannot frequently receive Holy Communion, the practice of the Church assigns feast days in preference to others for receiving the Holy Eucharist; because the celebration of the holy mysteries prepares the soul, by suggesting supernatural thoughts and by predisposing it for divine favours.

We have not ended our enumeration of the helps prepared

---

[25] Qui manducat meam carnem, et bibit meum sanguinem, in me manet, et ego in illo (Joann., vi, 57).

[26] Amen, amen, dico vobis, nisi manducaveritis carnem Filii hominis et biberitis ejus sanguinem, non habebitis vitam in vobis (Joann., vi, 54).

by our Lord for enabling us to attain more securely the end
which He proposes to Himself. As long as we are not confirmed
in grace by the beatific vision we are liable to fall, and our
loving Lord wills to provide for these falls. Adam had been
created in original justice and established in union with God;
we are sinners prone to evil, our falls are frequent. Is there then
no hope of pardon? Is our loss irreparable? We can die a
spiritual death, can we not rise again? Is our eternal life at the
mercy of one weak moment? Alas, if it were so! and it might
have been! But God would not be so severe with His frail
creature. He bids His children forgive one another seventy
times seven times, and then He Himself forgives them times
without number, never allowing today's pardon to be affected
by the foreseen faults of tomorrow. The psalmist points to this
work of infinite mercy when he says: "With the Lord shall the
steps of a man be directed, and he shall like well his ways.
When he shall fall, he shall not be bruised, for the Lord putteth
His hand under him."[27]

The Sacrament of Penance is an exceptional kind of
tribunal. Far from condemning the culprit who acknowledges
his guilt, it acquits him. If the accusation is sincere and contrite,
the sentence is always favourable; and by a prodigy of divine
Omnipotence innocence is restored, and the sinner is justified,
provided he resolves to correct his faults and break with the
occasions of sin. The virtue of the sentence is such that the soul
regains the holiness of its Baptism and the merits that it may
have acquired before its sin, it may also by reason of the
fervour of its sorrow and repentant love leave the tribunal not
only discharged from all guilt, but moreover free from all
penalty. We may truly say that our Lord, in His anxiety for the

---

[27] Apud Dominum gressus hominis dirigentur, et viam ejus volet.
Cum ceciderit, non collidetur, quia Dominus supponit manum suam
(Ps. xxxvi, 23-24).

progress of His loved ones, has broken down all barriers, and has put within our reach every means of cleansing and adorning ourselves and of removing from our path all hindrances to our perfect union with Himself.

In order to enjoy this gracious and unreserved pardon we have only to make up our minds to satisfy the claims of our Baptism, to reject what it condemns and to resolve to live by the laws of our regeneration. Then the work of sanctification takes up its course with renewed forces. But we must own that sometimes our Lord is thought to ask too much; what He so lovingly requires in the Sacrament of Penance is considered too severe, or is partially misunderstood; hence the soul that only half fulfils the conditions lessens within itself the strengthening effect of the Sacrament.

We must also beware of making the whole Sacrament of Penance to consist in a paltry and minute examination of conscience. Scrupulous people, under the empire of servile fear, without sorrow, without firm purpose of amendment, without trust in the sentence pronounced, with a childish fear of forgetting the most trivial circumstances and smallest details, go to receive absolution as a judicial discharge. They go to God, not as a prodigal son to his father, but as a debtor to his exacting creditor, if not as a trembling victim to the executioner. And yet the first words that our Lord taught us to say in our prayer are, "Our Father." Others overlook the divine element in the Sacrament, and occupy themselves too much with the human element, thinking more of the advice which their confessor may give them than of the Sacrament they are receiving. To benefit fully by the grace of the Sacrament it is necessary to enter into God's views and the ends for which the sacred tribunal was instituted.

Finally, in His ardent desire to receive us at once into His arms when we leave this world, God has instituted the Sacrament of Extreme Unction, which is the soul's last means of purification. The Christian may sometimes have committed faults through his senses, whereas he ought to have resolutely broken with the life of the senses. God wills now that all should be perfectly pure, that harmony and beauty should everywhere be restored. For this purpose He gives us the anointing with Holy Oil, the effects of which is to restore, and even to adorn man's whole being, and efface the last traces of sin.

Thus does the divine liberality appear in the world of the Sacraments, where everything is prepared beforehand for man's perfect sanctification. We purposely omit speaking of other less powerful means of grace. What we have said suffices to show that God has arranged all things with a view to man's sanctification; the Sacraments are the most certain, authentic and easy means for bringing it about; God's providence works by them, and His desires call for the perfection of our life.

In beholding this widespread love on the part of God, these ingenious efforts of His inconceivable tenderness, we are reminded of those words of the Prophet Isaias, "And now, O ye inhabitants of Jerusalem and ye men of Juda, judge between me and my vineyard. What is there that I ought to do more to my vineyard that I have not done to it?"[28] On the great day of supreme revelations, when God Himself will place before our eyes this summary of means so tender, so strong, so secure, we shall have no difficulty in understanding the severe reprisals of His justice and of His disregarded love.

---

[28] Nunc ergo, habitatores Jerusalem et viri Juda, judicate inter me et vineam meam. Quid est quod debui ultra facere vineæ meæ, et non feci ei? (Isa., v, 3-4).

CHAPTER VI
Who are they that advance the most rapidly in the spiritual life?

I T will be interesting to ask ourselves now what ways lead most speedily to intimate union with God, even before death gives us entrance "within the veil."[1] This is a useful study, and we can enter upon it without difficulty aided by the holy Scriptures; we shall not attempt to exhaust the subject, but merely to offer some general considerations, which each one can apply to himself.

Those persons attain union with God more promptly and securely who are free from all lofty thoughts and pretensions, who do not aim at making a display, at being learned, witty or men of character—in a word who are perfectly simple. This our adorable Master teaches when He says: "I confess to Thee, O Father, Lord of heaven and earth, because Thou hast hid these things from the wise and prudent, and hast revealed them to little ones."[2] And again, "Amen I say to you, unless you be converted and become as little children you shall not enter into the kingdom of heaven."[3] There can be no doubt that the "kingdom of heaven" thus mentioned in Scripture very often signifies, not only the heavenly Jerusalem, but moreover the highest reach of the spiritual life.

---

[1] Ad interiora velaminis (Heb. vi, 19).

[2] Confitebor tibi, Pater, Domine coeli et terrre, quia abscondisti hæc a sapientibus et prudentibus, et revelasti ea parvulis (Matth. xi, 25).

[3] Amen dico vobis, nisi conversi fueritis et efficiamini sicut parvuli, non intrabitis in regnum coelorum (*Ibid.*, xviii, 3).

There is an obvious connexion between spiritual infancy and the virtue of humility; but since some souls, already wearied with the sorrows and struggles of the Christian life, might be affrighted at not feeling within themselves any freshness or spiritual youth, our divine Lord forestalls these fears and shows these wearied souls how they may renew their youth. He knows well that if some begin with this graceful simplicity, which easily resolves the greatest problems of the spiritual life, others on the contrary end with it, and recover this simplicity only by the total transformation of their nature. Hence to these our Lord says: "Come to Me, all you that labour and are burdened, and I will refresh you. Take up My yoke upon you, and learn of Me because I am meek and humble of heart; and you shall find rest unto your souls, for My yoke is sweet and My burden light."[4]

These are well-known texts, but they require to be carefully studied. Our Lord is speaking to wearied souls, worn out with struggle; He shows them that they also can advance; He promises to be their support, and even proposes Himself as their example and encouragement. "Be not affrighted at your miseries," He says to them; "take up My yoke; do as I did in the midst of My toils upon earth; I was meek and humble of heart. If you imitate My example, you shall find rest to your souls, that is the peace which is the tranquillity of order and a very heaven upon earth when it is firmly established in the soul."

Therefore souls that apply themselves to acquire humility and meekness of heart, taking this attitude towards God, towards their neighbour and towards themselves, advance with giant strides towards their sanctification. "Blessed are the meek,

---

[4] Venite ad me omnes, qui laboratis et onerati estis, et ego reficiam vos. Tollite jugum meum super vos, et discite a me quia mitis sum et humilis corde; et invenietis requiem animabus vestris. Jugum enim meum suave est, et onus meum leve (Matth., xi, 28-30).

for they shall possess the land,"[5] says our Lord. The Psalms also proclaim God's preference for the meek: "He will teach the meek His ways."[6] The Book of Proverbs likewise says: "It is better to be humbled with the meek, than to divide spoils with the proud."[7] Lastly, the great contemplative Moses is thus praised by the Holy Spirit: "Moses was a man exceeding meek above all men that dwelt upon earth.[8]

Meekness, however, and humility are not the only dispositions that touch the heart of our God; true compunction and deep regret for sin are means for advancing rapidly: "Father, I have sinned against heaven and before Thee, I am not now worthy to be called Thy son."[9] And the Father's heart gives way; not only does He grant pardon but He dowers the repentant child with all His wealth. David well understood this tender compassion on the part of God, when he cried out: "A sacrifice to God is an afflicted spirit; a contrite and humbled heart, O God, Thou wilt not despise."[10]

Those again advance more rapidly in the ways of God who, in accordance with the lesson of our Lord Jesus Christ, banish all disquiet and vague forebodings: "Thou art careful, and art troubled about many things. But one thing is necessary."[11] Or

---

[5] Beati mites, quoniam ipsi possidebunt terram (Matth. V, 4).

[6] Docebit mites vias suas (Ps. xxiv, 9).

[7] Melius est humiliari cum mitibus, quam dividere spolia cum superbis (Prov., xvi, 19).

[8] Erat Moyses vir mitissimus super omnes homines qui morabantur in terra (Num., xii, 3).

[9] Pater, peccavi in cœlum et coram te: jam non sum dignus vocari filius tuus (Luc., xv, 21).

[10] Sacrificium Deo spiritus contribulatus: cor contritum et humiliatum, Deus, non despicies (Ps. L, 19).

[11] Sollicita es, et turbaris erga plurima, porro unum est necessarium (Luc., 41, 42).

again: "Be not solicitous therefore, saying, What shall we eat,
or what shall we drink, or wherewith shall we be clothed? For
after all these things do the heathens seek. . . . Be not therefore
solicitous for tomorrow. .... Sufficient for the day is the evil
thereof."[12] St. Paul is urgent in teaching Christians how all
anxiety can easily be cut short: "Be nothing solicitous," he says,
"but in everything by prayer and supplication with
thanksgiving let your petitions be made known to God."[13] And
again he says: "But I would have you to be without solicitude."[14]
St. Peter in like manner says: "Casting all your solicitude upon
Him, for He hath care of you."[15] It would be superfluous to
point out the innumerable passages in which the Holy Spirit
teaches that anxiety and exaggerated forecasting are enemies
of the spiritual life. Our Lord Himself indicated this fatal
tendency as one of the things which stifle the good seed: "And
that which fell among thorns are they who have heard, and,
going their way, are choked with cares .... and yield no fruit."[16]

Those progress rapidly who have a blind confidence in the
goodness of God; they as it were put a constraint upon our
heavenly Father, and bear away His highest favours: "If you
then, being evil, know how to give good gifts to your children,

---

[12] Nolite ergo solliciti esse, dicentes: Quid manudcabimus, aut quid
bibemus, aut quo operiemur? Hæc enim omnia gentes inquirunt. .
.. Nolite ergo solliciti esse in crastinum. . . . Sufficit dici malitia sua
(Matth., vi, 31-34).

[13] Nihil solliciti sitis; sed in omni oratione et obsecratione cum
gratiarum actione, petitiones vestræ innotescant apud Deum
(Philipp., vi, 6).

[14] Volo autem vos sine sollicitudine esse (1 Cor., vii, 32).

[15] Omnem sollicitudinem vestram projicientes in eum, quoniam ipsi
cura est de vobis (1 Pet., v, 7).

[16] Quod autem in spinas cecidit, hi sunt qui audierunt, et a
sollicitudinibus. . . . euntes suffocantur et non referunt fructum
(Luc., viii, 14).

how much more will your Father from heaven give the good Spirit to them that ask Him?"[17] What is this "good Spirit," if not the perfection of charity and the consummation of divine union?"Do not therefore lose your confidence, which hath a great reward."[18]

Only, these words do not refer to a timid and wavering confidence, but to that very same which made holy Job exclaim: "Although he should kill me, I will trust in Him;"[19] or again to that expressed in the psalm: "In Thee, O Lord, have I hoped; let me never be confounded."[20] is David goes so far even as to say that the fulness of heavenly sweetness is reserved for this confidence: "Oh, how great is the multitude of Thy sweetness, O Lord .... which Thou hast wrought for them that hope in Thee";[21] which Jeremias confirms, saying: "The Lord is good to them that hope in Him."[22] Moreover, David shows that this is the path of perfect security, for he assures us that God Himself is the shield of them that hope in Him: "God .... is the shield of all that trust in Him."[23] And Isaias declares that supernatural privileges of highest price are bestowed upon souls that trust: "But they that hope in the Lord shall renew their strength, they shall take wings as eagles, they shall run and not be weary,

---

[17] Si ergo vos cum sitis mali, nostis bona data dare filiis vestris: quanto magis Pater vester de coelo dabit Spiritum bonum petentibus se? (Luc., xi, 13).

[18] Nolite itaque amittere confidentiam vestram, quæ magnam habet remunerationem (Heb., x, 35).

[19] Etiam si occideret me, in ipso sperabo (Job xiii, 15).

[20] In te Domine, speravi, non confundar in æternum (Ps., xxx, 1).

[21] Quam magna multitudo dulcedinis tuæ, Domine. . . perfecisti eis qui sperant in te (Ps., xxx, 20).

[22] Bonus est Dominus sperantibus in eum (Thren., iii, 25).

[23] Deus . . . scutum est omnium sperantium in se (2 Reg., xxii, 31).

they shall walk and not faint."[24] Is not this insuring to
confidence in God, together with the final victory, the most
powerful soarings of contemplation?

It is certain that nothing is more odious and more unjust
than the servile mistrust which makes us doubt of the infinite
goodness of God. We ought to expect everything from the
divine generosity, according to those words of the apostle:"He
that spared not even His own Son, but delivered Him up for us
all, how hath He not also, with Him, given us all things?"[25]
These thoughts are old as the world. By the mouth of Ezechiel
God said: "I will seek that which was lost; and that which was
driven away I will bring back again; and I will bind up that
which was broken, and I will strengthen that which was weak,
and that which was fat and strong I will preserve; and I will
feed them in judgment."[26] Are we not then grievously insulting
God when we ignore His merciful intentions and obstinately
persist in fearing, in spite of this law of confidence? Are we not
wounding our Lord to the quick? Can we be astonished that
Saint Benedict ends the list of his "Instruments of Spiritual
Profession" with these two admirable sentences: "To put his
trust in God," and "Never to despair of God's mercy."[27]

Again, those who covet divine favours must be open-

---

[24] Qui autem sperant in Domino, mutabunt fortitudinem, assument
pennas sicut aquilæ, current et non laborabunt, ambulabunt et non
deficient (Isa., xl, 31)

[25] Si etiam proprio Filio suo non perpercit, sed pro nobis omnibus
tradidit illum: quomodo non etiam cum illo omnia nobis donavit?
(Rom., viii, 32).

[26] Quod perierat requiram, et quod abjectum erat reducam, et quod
confractum fuerat alligabo, et quod infirmum fuerat consolidabo, et
quod pingue et forte custodiam; et pascam illos I judicio (Ezech.,
xxxiv, 16).

[27] Spem suam Deo committere, et de Dei misericordia numquam
desperare (S. Reg., iv, 41, 72).

hearted and generous towards their neighbour. Much more
than we think do we ourselves provide for God the measure of
His graces to us, and often His conduct in our regard is
modelled upon our conduct towards our neighbour: "For with
the same measure that you shall mete withal, it shall be
measured to you again."[28] Severity, dryness, exclusiveness and
selfishness merit for us a corresponding return of severity and
rigour on the part of God. We have proof of this in that
sentence of our Lord which points out what will be the matter
of God's judgment: "Amen I say to you, as long as you did it not
to one of these least, neither did you do it to Me. And these
shall go into everlasting punishment."[29] Whereas charity is the
distinctive mark of the true disciples of Christ, who taught it to
His apostles, saying: "A new commandment I give unto you,
that you love one another as I have loved you, that you also
love one another. By this shall all men know that you are My
disciples, if you have love one for another."[30] It is even to works
of mercy that the prophet attributes the remission of sins:
"Learn to do well: seek judgment, relieve the oppressed, judge
for the fatherless, defend the widow, and then come and accuse
Me, saith the Lord: if your sins be as scarlet, they shall be made
as white as snow."[31]

Love of our neighbour is also the sign of true love: "We

---

[28] Eadem quippe mensura, qua mensi fueritis, remetietur vobis (Luc.,
vi, 38).

[29] Amen dico vobis, quamdiu fecistis uni ex his fratribus meis
minimis, mihi fecistis (Matth., xxv, 40).

[30] Mandatum novum diligatis invicem. In hoc cognoscent omnes
quia discipuli me estis, si dilectionem habueritis ad invicem (Joann.,
xiii, 34-35).

[31] Discite benefacere: quærite judicium, subvenite oppresso, judicate
pupillo, defendite viduam, et venite et arguite me, dicit Dominus; si
fuerint peccata vestra ut coccinum, quasi nix dealbabuntur (Isa., I,
15-18).

know that we have passed from death to life because we love the brethren."[32] "He that loveth his brother abideth in the light, and there is no scandal in him."[33] St. Paul will have this charity exercised at one's own cost. "Bear ye one another's burdens," he says, "and so you shall fulfil the law of Christ."[34] But that which throws the clearest light upon all this teaching is the very word of our Saviour Himself. "And not for them only do I pray," He says, "but for them also who through their word shall believe in Me; that they all may be one, as Thou, Father, in Me, and I in Thee: that they also may be one in us."[35] How then can any one that breaks unity enjoy the blessings accruing from this prayer, which is the one only source of all sanctification?

Once more, those walk with a more rapid step who willingly and perseveringly despoil themselves of all that they have and of all that they are. "So likewise every one of you that doth not renounce all that he possesseth cannot be My disciple"[36]—a conclusion which our Lord again expresses thus: "If a man will contend with thee in judgment and take away thy coat, let go thy cloak also unto him."[37] This facility in parting with what we possess marks the detachment indispensable for

---

[32] Nos scimus quoniam translati sumus de morte ad vitam, quoniam diligimus fratres (1 Joann., iii, 14).

[33] Qui diligit fratrem suum, in lumine manet, et scandalum in eo non est (*Ibid.*, ii, 10).

[34] Alter alterius onera portate, et sic adimplebitis legem Christi (Gal., vi, 20).

[35] Non pro eis autem rogo tantum, sed et pro eis qui credituri sunt per verbum eorum in me: ut omnes unum sint, sicut tu Pater in me, et ego in te, ut et ipsi in nobis unum sint (Joann., vii, 20, 21).

[36] Sic ergo omnis ex vobis, qui non renuntiat omnibus quæ possidet, non potest meus esse discipulus (Luc., xiv, 33).

[37] Et qui vult tecum judicio contendere et tunicam tuam tollere, dimitte ei et pallium (Matth., v. 40).

one who would rise on the wings of the spirit. It is besides the law for the athlete: "And every one that striveth for the mastery refraineth himself from all things."[38]

Finally, they run a quick race who arm themselves with courage, and who brave all obstacles: "Who then shall separate us from the love of Christ? Shall tribulation? or distress? or famine? or nakedness? or danger? or persecution? or the sword? . . . But in all these things we overcome because of Him that hath loved us."[39] These violent ones carry away the kingdom of heaven by assault; they have a right to that promise of the Apocalypse: "To him that overcometh I will give the hidden manna, and will give him a white counter, and in the counter a new name written, which no man knoweth, but he that receiveth it."[40] This mysterious food and this hidden name is the great secret which God communicates to the soul when it fias attained perfect charity and the consummation of its union with the heavenly Bridegroom.

---

[38] Omnis autem qui in agone contendit, ab omnibus se abstinet (1 Cor., ix, 25).

[39] Quis ergo nos separabit a caritate Christi? Tribulatio? An angustiæ an fames? An nuditas? An periculum? An persecutio? An gladius? . . . Sed in his omnibus superamus propter eum, qui dilexit nos (Rom., viii, 35-37).

[40] Vincenti dabo manna absconditum, et dabo illi calculum candidum: et in calculo nomen novum scriptum, quod nemo scit, nisi qui accipit (Apoc., ii, 17).

CHAPTER VII
The Remote Preparation for Prayer

HE GREAT interest of man's life is then, as we have been striving to show, his advancement to the highest degree of the spiritual life. We think it, therefore, useful to examine in detail the most sure means of reaching that height; not that we can create in ourselves that which only the Holy Spirit can give, but that we may prepare His way and strive to establish in our souls those dispositions which He ordinarily requires as conditions for attaining divine union.

For this purpose, we shall read with profit what the ancient fathers thought of perfection, and what means they considered best for its attainment: "The whole scope of the monastic life," says Cassian, "its highest perfection, consists in a constant and uninterrupted perseverance in prayer, and in preserving, so far as human frailty will permit, peace of soul and purity of heart. To attain this most precious good all the efforts of our body and all the aspirations of our mind should be directed; and there are between these two things, namely, prayer and perfection, close and necessary relations. The whole edifice of the virtues is only raised to attain the perfection of prayer, and if it is not crowned with prayer, which unites and binds all the parts together, it will neither be solid nor lasting. Without the virtues, it is impossible to acquire this peaceful and continual prayer, and without this prayer, the virtues, which are its foundation, will not reach their perfection."[1]

---

[1] Cassian, Coll., ix, cap. Ii.

Prayer is then the secret sanctuary in which God unites Himself to our souls; but prayer must be prepared for by purity of life, according to the advice of the wise man: "Before prayer prepare thy soul, and be not as a man that tempteth God."[2] This condition can surprise no one. We cannot deceive the eye of God, who searches the heart and the reins; we can keep nothing secret from Him, "But all things are naked and open to His eyes to whom our speech is."[3] The hour of prayer is that in which the soul, being more attentive to God, is also more fit to respond to His action; but during prayer she meets her habitual imperfections, and the effects of her many external distractions. Each of these is an obstacle to her intercourse with God. Our Lord frequently awaits these moments of intimacy to punish or to reward our external acts according as they have deserved. St. Benedict well knew all these secrets of the spiritual life when, seeking to form in his monks the spirit of prayer, he gave them the counsel: "To observe every hour the actions of his life."[4]

In this the holy patriarch summed up the teaching of the ancients, as we find it in Cassian: "We must build up this edifice of all the virtues, and preserve our minds from all kinds of distractions, that they may become, little by little, accustomed to the contemplation of God and divine things. Whatever occupies the mind before prayer will necessarily present itself to our thoughts in the time of prayer. We must, therefore, put ourselves beforehand into those dispositions which we wish to have during prayer. The impressions of words and acts that have gone before will recur again whilst we are in the midst of our spiritual exercises; these recollections will make sport of us,

---

[2] Ante orationem præpara animam tuam, et noli esse quasi homo qui tentat Deum (Eccli., xviii, 23).

[3] Omnia autem nuda et aperta sunt oculis ejus, ad quem nobis sermo (Heb., iv, 13).

[4] Actus vitæ suæ omni hora custodire (S. Reg:, iv, 48).

and cause us to be angry or melancholy, if we were so before. The desires and thoughts that engaged our minds will also return, and to our confusion, will make us fall back into distraction or even foolishly laugh at a ridiculous word or action."[5] We recognize in these practical lessons three instruments of good works mentioned in the Rule of St. Benedict, "Not to love much talking; not to speak vain words or such as move to laughter; not to love much and dissolute laughter."[6]

We must then, if we would develop within us the spiritual life and obtain the gift of prayer, not only know our faults and combat them, but moreover banish vain preoccupations, repress the turmoil of our many idle thoughts, and all that savours of levity and instability of mind; we must mortify curiosity—that is the desire of knowing, seeing and hearing—all which things distract the soul by pouring it out upon external things, and causing it to lose all relish for what is spiritual. The admirable law of silence established in religious orders is intended for no other purpose than to force the soul to recollection, and to withdraw it little by little from the life of the senses. But we can easily understand that this law of external silence would profit little if the soul did not labour to rule the imagination; the peril would be all the greater for being less visible. The ancient fathers had far less experience of the wanderings of the imagination, but nowadays they must be taken into serious account.

Education in our times is rarely strong and manly. Children are allowed to grow up in ignorance and moral idleness; hence their piety is too often nothing but mere sentiment—a sort of misty and vague dreaminess—which is death to the spirit of

---

[5] Cassian, Coll, ix, cap. iii.

[6] Multum loqui non amare; verba vana aut risui apta non loqui; risum multum aut excussum non amare (S.Reg. iv,53-55).

prayer. Besides this many Christians, after devoting themselves with zeal to good works, are taken up with childish and frivolous amusements. Why then should they be astonished that they are not at once set free from these useless dreams when they come to prayer, and that they cannot without pain and effort apply their minds to the mysteries of our holy faith? How can they expect that a recollected spirit will fall upon them unawares?

The imagination is closely linked with the senses, and if it is not mastered and curbed we can never hope to have that pure prayer of which Cassian speaks: "The soul raises itself in prayer according to the degree of its purity. The more it withdraws from the sight of material and terrestrial things, the more is it purified and sees Jesus Christ interiorly, either in the humiliations of His life, or in the majesty of His glory. . . . They alone can contemplate His divinity with a most pure eye, who turn away from base and earthly thoughts and works to ascend with Him the high mountain of solitude, where, free from the tumult of passions, and rid of all vices, they contemplate by the light of their faith and from the height of their virtue the glory and beauty of His countenance, which the pure of heart alone may see."[7]

Thus a soul which desires to advance in the spirit of prayer and to obtain union with God, should strive to banish vain and useless thoughts, and to apply herself, as far as she can, to walk in the presence of God. This again is the teaching of St. Benedict: "To know for certain," he says, "that God beholdeth him in everyplace."[8] And this should be true of the recreation hours as well as of the silence of the cell, whilst reading and whilst doing our manual labour, which act the fathers considered a help to the spirit of prayer. "For," says Cassian,

---

[7] Cassian, Coll., x, cap. vi.

[8] In omni loco Deum se respicere, pro certo scire (S Reg. iv, 49)

speaking of the Eastern monks, "it is difficult to say whether it is in order to meditate better that they occupy themselves unceasingly in manual work, or whether it is by this assiduity in labour that they acquire so much piety, knowledge and light."[9]

This again is the reason of our continuous occupations in the monastic life. They are a help to union with God; for manual labour, regulated by obedience, is like a firm and immovable anchor which steadies the levity of the mind, whilst leaving it free to soar up to God.

With regard to intellectual work, God forbid that it should ever become a distraction for the religious, and withdraw him from the divine presence! It is given to us not to satisfy curiosity or to flatter pride, but to consecrate our intellect as well as our heart entirely to God. We must seek only God in the books we read; and the study of His works, whatsoever they may be, must ever invite us to exclaim with the psalmist: "How great are Thy works, O Lord! Thou hast made all things in wisdom."[10] Which of us would not be content to say with the Apostle: "For I judged not myself to know anything among you but Jesus Christ, and Him crucified."[11]

And indeed this is not a lessening of true science, but rather its greatest height and perfection. The ancient fathers desired to have this kind of supernatural science, and it is what St. Benedict wished to form in his children by what he calls "holy reading." Cassian also thus recommends it: "It is impossible for a soul that is not pure to attain the gift of spiritual science. Employ therefore every care that your study may not become

---

[9] Cassian, Instit. lib. ii, cap. xiv.

[10] Quam magnificata sunt opera tua, Domine! Omnia in sapientia fecisti (Ps., ciii, 24).

[11] Non enim judicavi me scire aliquid inter vos, nisi Jesum Christum, et hunc crucifixum (1 Cor., ii, 2).

to you, instead of the means by which you may acquire the
light of spiritual science and the glory which is promised to
those that obtain it, the instrument of eternal perdition through
the vanity and presumption which it would create in you."[12]

Who has not been struck by the words of Ecclesiastes?
After draining the cup of profane knowledge, he owns, sadly,
in the end: "He that addeth knowledge, addeth also labour."[13]
"Of making many books there is no end, and much study is an
affliction of the flesh."[14]

But though intellectual intemperance is dangerous, it is
useful and even necessary to cultivate the mind by study,
"Willingly to hear holy reading."[15] "We must read
unremittingly," says Cassian, "and commit the holy Scriptures
to memory. This continual meditation will produce a double
fruit. First of all, when our minds are occupied with these holy
readings, they will necessarily be freed from all bad thoughts,
and secondly, if whilst labouring to learn the Scriptures off by
heart, we do not always understand them, later on, when
disengaged from exterior things we meditate upon them in the
silence of the night, we shall penetrate into them more deeply,
and discover hidden meanings that we had not been able to
grasp during the day, and that God reveals sometimes even
during sleep.

"When this study has renewed our heart, the holy Scripture
will appear to us under quite a new aspect, and its beauty will
go on increasing in proportion as we make progress; for the
holy Scripture is understood by each one according to his
dispositions. It seems earthly to the carnal, and divine to the

---

[12] Cassian, Coll., xi v, cap. x.

[13] Qui addit scientiam addit et laborem (Eccli., i, 18).

[14] Faciendi plures libros nullus est finis; frequensque meditatio,
carnis afflictio est (Eccles. xii, 12).

[15] Lectiones sanctas libenter audire (S. Reg. iv, 56).

spiritual; so that they who at first only saw it enveloped in profound obscurity cannot afterwards sufficiently admire its splendour, nor bear, undazzled, its great light."[16] St. Paul teaches the same truth to the Corinthians: "Now we have received not the spirit of this world, but the Spirit which is of God, that we may know the things that are given us from God. Which things also we speak, not in the learned words of human wisdom, but in the doctrine of the Spirit, comparing spiritual things with spiritual. But the sensual man perceiveth not these things that they are of the Spirit of God; for it is foolishness to him, and he cannot understand, because it is spiritually examined."[17]

Therefore everything in the spiritual life ought to lead the soul to occupy herself with the realities of faith, that being nourished with this divine element her life may by little and little become heavenly. But this is not all; and we fully agree with the ancient fathers who said: "He who prays only when he is upon his knees prays very little; but he who, while on his knees, allows his mind to wander prays not at all."[18] This brings us to speak of a practice universally recommended by the masters of the spiritual life, namely, "ejaculatory prayer." The Fathers attached great importance to these frequent, short aspirations towards God as being well suited to form the spirit of prayer. Cassian, in his "Institutions," says: "They think that it is better to make short prayers and to repeat them more frequently. By multiplying these prayers we unite ourselves

---

[16] Cassian, Coll, xiv, cap. x, xi.

[17] Nos autem non spiritum hujus mundi accepimus, sed Spiritum qui ex Deo est, ut sciamus quæ a Deo donata sunt nobis; quæ et loquimur non in doctis humanæ sapientias verbis, sed in doctrina Spiritus, spiritualibus spiritualia comparantes. Animalis autem homo non percipit ea quæ sunt Spiritus Dei: stultitia enim est illi, et non potest intelligere: quia spiritualiter examinatur (I Cor, ii, 12-14).

[18] Cassian, Coll, x, cap. xiv.

more intimately to God, and by making them short we better escape the darts which the devil hurls against us, particularly at that time."[19] And again: "We should make short prayers, but frequent, lest, if they are long, the enemy should have time to cast distractions into our heart."[20] Hence, according to the teaching of these holy men, short prayer is more easily kept pure because it is free from distraction, and these rapid darts from the heart are very efficacious for promoting union with God, and they are far preferable to a prolonged and dreamy prayer.

The Psalms, which are the form and type of all prayer, give us numberless examples of these short and expressive aspirations. The verse, "O God, come to my assistance—*Deus in adjutorium meum intende* was very familiar to the ancient Fathers, and, later on, was St. Catharine of Sienna's favourite prayer, as "*Misericordias Domini in æternum cantabo*—The mercies of the Lord I will sing for ever," was St. Teresa's. But there is no need to lay out any plan for ourselves; we must follow with docility the whisperings of the Holy Spirit and the leanings of our own souls.

Thus the soul is not only able to preserve a sense of the divine presence during the whole day, but to entertain herself sweetly with God—either in heart only, or with heart and mouth—and this without any manual or mental work being able to distract her from Him. The soul which is faithful to this practice of ejaculatory prayer may believe that she is coming nigh to the *semper orare* of the Gospel. She will find therein a great help for silencing the passions, repressing too great activity about external things, and overcoming spiritual idleness. In this way she will accustom herself to live in intimacy with God, as St. Jerome taught the holy virgin

---

[19] Cassian, Instit., lib. ii, cap. x.

[20] Cassian, Coll, ix, cap. xxxvi.

Eustochium: "Always keep within thy chamber, always rejoice with thy Spouse within. When thou prayest, thou dost speak to the Spouse; when thou readest, He speaks to thee."[21] We find the same in another form in the legend of St. Hugh, Abbot of Cluny: "If he was silent, he was always with the Lord; if he spoke, it was always in the Lord or of the Lord."[22] The supernatural life grows in this way hour by hour, so to say, and increases to the perfection of charity, which is holiness.

Nevertheless such is the frailty of human nature that these efforts to form within ourselves the spirit of prayer would be quite insufficient, were the soul not to reserve some moments each day for self-examination as to her dispositions and her faults. If it is pernicious to be constantly occupied with self and to turn all mental prayer into examination of conscience, it is equally pernicious, especially in the case of beginners and of thoughtless people who have not yet mastered their evil tendencies, never to observe what goes on within them in order to judge and correct their faults. This negligence may greatly impede the soul's progress. "I have thought on my ways," says the Prophet, "and turned my feet unto Thy testimonies."[23]

Self-examination is an ancient practice, based upon sound reason. The holy king Ezechias made use of it. "I will recount to Thee all my years," he says, "in the bitterness of my soul."[24] It is not, however, any whatsoever examination of conscience. It is made before God, in the light of the graces received from His

---

[21] Semper te cubiculi tui secreta custodiant, semper tecum Sponsus ludat intrinsecus. Oras, loqueris ad Sponsum; legis ille tibi loquitur (S. Hieron., Epist. ad Eust.).

[22] Silens quidem semper cum Domino; loquens autem semper in Domino, vel de Domino loquebatur? (Vita S. Hug., cap. i.)

[23] Cogitavi vias meas, et converti pedes meos in testimonia tua (Ps. cxviii, 59).

[24] Recogitabo tibi omnes annos meos in amaritudine animæ meæ (Isa. xxxviii, 15).

goodness, as on the threshold of eternity; it produces a complete surrender of ourselves into our Father's hands, and fills the soul with humble confidence, making her cry out: "O Lord, if man's life be such, and the life of my spirit be in such things as these, Thou shalt correct me, and make me to live."[25]

When the soul judges herself before God without excuse, without exaggeration, and places herself in her Saviour's hands, this act alone causes her to find grace and pity. Covered with her sins, the soul appears before Him like that poor woman whom the Pharisees brought before our Saviour and accused. In her shame she could say nothing to defend herself. "Woman, where are they that accuse thee? Hath no man condemned thee? Who said: No man, Lord. And Jesus said: Neither will I condemn thee. Go, and now sin no more."[26] Does it not seem that the sovereign Holiness was disarmed before this sinner, who by her silence judges herself?

It is of the utmost importance, therefore, for the sanctification of the soul, that at least once a day she should examine herself, and see not only of what sins she has been guilty, but moreover what are her imperfections and secret tendencies.

This is a sure means of obtaining self-knowledge and of foiling the devil's artifices, for he has no better allies than our own inattention and thoughtlessness. It is the way to repair our daily losses by loving contrition, to obtain abundant graces, and finally to bring about the continual amendment of our life. St. Benedict could not overlook this important practice. He thus recommends it: "With tears and sighs daily to confess his past evils to God in prayer, and to amend those evils for the time to

---

[25] Domine, si sic vivitur, et in talibus vita spiritus mei, corripies me, et vivicabis me (Isa., xxxviii, 16).

[26] Mulier, ubi sunt qui te accusabant? Nemo te condemnavit? Quæ dixit: Nemo Domine. Dixit autem Jesus: Nec ego te condemnabo; vade, et jam amplius noli peccare (Joann., viii, 10, 11).

come."[27] And the Psalmist renders the same thought in these words: "My soul is continually in my hands, and I have not forgotten Thy law."[28] Scrupulous persons however should make this examination with the heart rather than with the head, otherwise it will not profit them. It should create confidence and a firm purpose of amendment, not fretfulness and discouragement. It should also be brief and limited to the appointed time. Some souls cannot turn to God without falling at once into self-examination. This is a disastrous tendency, which ruins the spirit of prayer and hinders all development of the spiritual life. In every case the examination should conclude with sincere sorrow and a firm, courageous and calm resolution to do better for the future.

Generally speaking the soul's acts are stronger in proportion as they are prompt and energetic, leaving no time for dreaminess. The slowness of many people is but disguised idleness, vain subtlety, the very opposite of spiritual operations. We need resolution and confidence in God to advance; and if to analyse is a necessity for our slow reason, we must beware of pushing analysis and the discussion of ourselves to such an excess that they deprive the soul of all confidence in God, of all stability, leaving her a prey to perpetual and pusillanimous wavering.

Nevertheless, giddy, impressionable and inconstant persons should examine themselves with greater leisure and attention, giving a practical tone to their resolutions, otherwise their best impulses will vanish into thin air. It is not sufficient to have a general and vague good will to serve God and to sanctify our souls; we must make up our minds as to what we really will do, resolve upon it clearly, and follow it up strenuously to the very

---

[27] Mala sua præterita cum lacrymis vel gemitu quotidie in oratione Deo confiteri, et de ipsis malis de cætero emendare (S. Reg., iv, 58).

[28] Anima mea in manibus meis semper, et legem tuam non sum oblitus. (Ps., cxviii, 109).

end, all which is impossible without serious self-examination.

Examination of conscience, thus understood, will be the best preparation for the Sacrament of Penance. When practised daily, it will dispense the soul who is preparing for Confession from those interminable searchings which some persons make before their accusation, as though everything consisted in discovering their faults and mentioning every minute detail about them; whereas the conceiving of supernatural sorrow and the preparing to receive pardon have also to be taken into consideration. Happy they who, full of faith, of fervour, of regret and of good resolution, approach this Sacrament, thirsting to obtain that perfect charity which redeems the penalty while it effaces the guilt of sin. Such as these will speedily attain to that consummate purity which is the object of their desires, and union with God will soon become their habitual state.

This is the end to which holy Church is ever tending: to make up for the insufficiency of our expiation, and after inviting us to the frequent reception of the Sacraments, she still further opens with great, liberality the treasury of her Indulgences. The reason of this is that she longs to see all things restored through Christ in our souls; and as long as there remains any obstacle between them and God, she suffers as from an irregular and constrained state. One would think that she was for ever repeating to herself: "Blessed are the clean of heart, for they shall see God."[29] Her maternal heart will find no rest, no joy, till our souls, having become pure as crystal, will be apt to receive and to reflect the rays of the uncreated light.

And even then the most holy Bride of our Lord will not suffer her children ever to lay aside the spirit of penance which is necessary for them to the end of their pilgrimage here below. Each year she brings back her children, even the perfect among

---

[29] Beati mundo corde, quoniam ipsi Deum videbunt (Matth. v, 8).

them, to the solemnity of the Lenten fast. Those in fact who have attained perfection are never fixed in the fulness of the good, the true and the beautiful while they are yet on earth; and it is to them that may be applied the admirable teaching of St. Denis regarding the heavenly Spirits: "Piety permits us to say that in the angelic hierarchies the less noble intelligences are purified by the light which God sends them concerning things till then hidden from their sight; that is to say, when He calls them to a more perfect knowledge of the divine secrets, and correcting the ignorance in which they are actually plunged, He causes them to rise, by means of the superior Spirits, to the glory of a more profound and luminous intuition."[30]

Thus it is with the souls that God already satiates with His fulness. They have no longer to expiate their own faults; but as long as they are upon earth they can, by the labour of penance, be admitted to a higher possession of the divinity, and purify themselves evermore and more, in the sense that they pass to a more excellent good, following the counsel of the apostle: "Be zealous for the better gifts."[31]

---

[30] Hier. Eccl. cap. vi.

[31] Æmulanimi charismata meliora (i Cor. xii, 31).

CHAPTER VIII
The Treatise on Prayer given by Our Lord Jesus Christ.

BY prayer man is brought into relation with God; therefore this duty was laid upon him from the very beginning, and it is evident all through the Old Testament what an important place prayer has in the life of man.

When our divine Lord came into this world to teach us all truth, he brought us new light upon the subject of prayer, which is the great means of attaining union with God, and He gave us the example of it in His most holy life. We find Him consecrating at one time whole nights to prayer, at another fixed hours of the day. He prays before working His miracles, and before choosing His twelve apostles. With a loud voice He gives thanks to His Father, He recollects Himself within Himself; in fact, He is the shining example of a life devoted to the most perfect prayer. But not content with giving us the example, He moreover imparted to His apostles a precise teaching and left them the divine method of prayer.

On one occasion, as St. Luke relates, when our Lord had concluded His prayer, one of His disciples drew nigh, and said: "Lord, teach us to pray, as John also taught his disciples. And He said to them: When you pray say: Father, hallowed be Thy name, Thy kingdom come. Give us this day our daily bread. And forgive us our sins, for we also forgive every one that is indebted to us. And lead us not into temptation."[1] We see clearly from the simple question of the apostle that, even in the old law, the prophets gave their disciples regular instructions on the subject of prayer, and possibly little rivalries arose between the different schools. They sought a master in the art, for no doubt it had become evident that souls profit much by the experience of one already versed in prayer, and are spared much groping in the dark and many mistakes.

St. Matthew, in his Gospel, does not mention the question of the disciple, but he gives us the whole of the Lord's prayer, and the Church has chosen his more complete text as her formula. Moreover, this evangelist transmits to us the precious teaching on preparation for prayer with which our Lord accompanied the *Pater noster*.

The first danger that our Master points out is ostentation or vanity—faults too common in prayer: "When ye pray ye shall not be like the hypocrites, that love to stand and pray in the synagogues and corners of the streets that they may be seen by men. Amen, I say to you, they have received their reward."[2] Prayer is in itself a meritorious act, but it must be animated by purity of intention to have its proper efficacy: if it is sullied with human motives, it will be null or of very little good. It is only just that in his familiar intercourse with God, man should banish every foreign thought and preoccupation.

Our Lord next says: "But thou, when thou shalt pray, enter into thy chamber, and having shut the door, pray to thy Father

---

[1] Domine, doce nos orare, sicut docuit et Joannes discipulos suos. Et ait illis: Cum oratis, dicite: Pater, sanctificetur nomen tuum. Panem nostrum quotidianum da nobis hodie. Et dimitte nobis peccata nostra, siquidem et ipsi dimittimus omni debenti nobis. Et ne nos inducas in tentationem (Luc., xi, 1-4).

[2] Cum oratis, non eritis sicut hypocritæ, qui amant in synagogis, et in angulis platearum stantes orare, ut videantur ab hominibus: amen dico vobis, receperunt mercedem suam (Matth. vi, 5).

in secret; and thy Father, who seeth in secret, will repay thee."[3] Hence, in the first place, the conditions which our Saviour requires are that we should enter into our private dwelling place, that we should shut the door, that we should recollect ourselves in the presence of God, and that we should banish all distracting thoughts. The soul can then humbly address herself to Him, whom, with good reason, she calls her Father, since she has received the spirit of adoption, and she can speak to Him "in secret." Plainly this "secret" is something more than the material solitude created round about her by the "closing of the door"; it means that mysterious darkness of faith—a darkness which is brighter than the day—in which we pray to God, our Father. In this prayer of pure and simple faith the soul receives her reward, and rises securely to God. "We pray in our chamber", says Cassian, "when we banish from our heart the tumult of our thoughts and anxieties, in order to offer our prayer to God in the 'secret' of love. We 'close the door' when we close our lips in order to pray in silence to Him who hears the heart much more than the words. We 'pray in secret' when we make known our petitions to God with our whole heart and soul, without letting our enemy know what we are asking; for we pray in silence not only that our brethren may not be distracted by our groans and cries, and thus be prevented from praying themselves, but also to hide our intentions from the demons, who attack us especially during prayer."[4]

To pray to our Father "in secret" also means seeking God in the depths of our soul, in that secret dwelling place prepared within us by the holy Sacrament of Baptism. This impulse towards the depths of the soul is one of the first impressions that we receive when we begin to forsake the life of the senses

---

[3] Tu autem, cum oraveris, intra in cubiculum tuum, et clauso ostio, ora Patrem tuum in abscondito: et Pater tuus qui vidit in abscondito, reddet tibi (Ibid, vi, 6).

[4] Cassian, Coll. ix, cap. xxxv.

and to be "strengthened by the Spirit unto the inward man."[5]
Then, instead of seeking God outside, and in symbols and
images, the soul enters within herself, there to find Him. St.
Benedict, and all the ancients, favoured the repression of
external demonstrations in prayer.

St. Cyprian had already taught to the ardent Christians of
his Church this wise reserve: "But let our speech and petition,
when we pray, be under discipline, observing quietness and
modesty. Let us consider that we are standing in God's sight.
We must please the divine eyes both with the habit of body and
the measure of voice. For, as it is characteristic of a shameless
man to be noisy with his cries, so, on the other hand, it is fitting
to the modest man to pray with moderated petitions. Moreover,
in His teaching, the Lord has bidden us to pray in secret—in
hidden   and   remote   places,   even   in   our   very
bedchambers—which is best suited to faith, that we may know
that God is everywhere present, and hears and sees all, and in
the plenitude of His majesty penetrates even into hidden and
secret places.

"Nor need He be clamorously reminded, since He sees
men's thoughts . . . and this, Anna, in the First Book of Kings,
who was a type of the Church, maintains and observes, in that
she prayed to God not with clamorous petition, but silently and
modestly, within the very recesses of her heart. She spoke with
hidden prayer, but with manifest faith. She spoke, not with her
voice, but with her heart, because she knew that thus God
hears; and she effectually obtained what she sought, because
she asked it with belief."[6]

St. Teresa's teaching is exactly the same as that of the
ancient fathers, and thus we see that the latter ages of the
Church are like unto the first.

---

[5] Virtute corroborari per Spiritum ejus in interiorem hominem (Eph.
iii, 16).

[6] S. Cypr. De Orat. Dom., nn. 4, 5.

But let us return to our divine Master, and learn from Him how to avoid other excesses in our prayer; "And when you are praying speak not much, as heathens. For they think that in their much speaking they may be heard. Be not you therefore like to them, for your Father knoweth what is needful for you before you shall ask Him."[7] Unlike the pagan, the Christian knows whom he is addressing; he must avoid in his prayer that superabundance of words which betrays ignorance of the divine Majesty. To escape this error the divine Master gives His disciples the formula of all our prayers: "Thus therefore shall you pray: 'Our Father who art in heaven, hallowed be Thy name. Thy kingdom come. Thy will be done on earth as it is in heaven. Give us this day our supersubstantial bread. And forgive us our debts, as we also forgive our debtors, and lead us not into temptation. But deliver us from evil. Amen.'"[8]

All prayers, all petitions which do not fall under the head of one or another of these petitions of the Pater noster will fail to be acceptable to God. We must, therefore, study closely this admirable formula of prayer. Divinely composed, it contains not only the secret of all prayer, but moreover the secret of our transformation into God. It is like a diapason, to which our soul must be attuned, that we may render to our Lord the glory which is due to Him; for it was not our Lord's intention to give us merely a set form of words, but rather to deposit a living and effectual prayer in the very depth of our souls.

---

[7] Orantes autem nolite multum loqui, sicut ethnici; putant enim quod in multiloquio suo exaudiantur. Nolite ergo assimilari eis; scit enim Pater vester quid opus sit vobis, antequam petatis eum. Sic ergo vos orabitis (Matth., vi, 7-9).

[8] Sic ergo vos orabitis: Pater noster qui es in coelis, sanctificetur nomen tuum. Adveniat regnum tuum. Fiat voluntas tua, sicut in coelo et in terra. Panem nostrum, supersubstantialem da nobis hodie. Et dimitte nobis debita nostra, sicut et nos dimittimus debitoribus nostris. Et ne nos inducas in tentationem. Sed libera nos a malo. Amen. (Matth., vi, 9-13).

Hence the great solemnity with which, in the fourth week of Lent, this formula was given to the catechumens when, as the time of their Baptism drew near, they came to the Church to receive, together with the holy Gospels and the Rule of Faith, the Lord's Prayer and the Law of Prayer. Why should we be astonished that the fathers delighted in commenting on this prayer? Tertullian thus speaks of it: "In summaries of so few words, how many utterances of the prophets, the gospels, the apostles! How many discourses, examples, parables of our Lord are touched upon! How many duties are simultaneously discharged! The honour of God in the title of 'Father,' the testimony of lively faith which asks for the glory of His name, the offering of obedience which sighs after the accomplishment of His will; the exercise of hope which calls for the coming of His kingdom; the petition for life in the daily bread; the full avowal of our sins in the prayer for forgiveness; the remedy against temptations in the request for divine protection. What wonder! Only God could teach us how He wished us to pray to Him. Therefore the religious rite of prayer, ordained by Himself and animated by His own Spirit when it issued from His divine mouth, ascends by its own prerogative into heaven, commending to the Father what the Son has taught, touching the heart of the Father by the words of the Son. Since however the Lord, the forseer of human necessities, said separately, after delivering His rule of prayer: 'Ask, and ye shall receive'; and since there are petitions which are made according to the circumstances of each individual, our additional wants have the right—after beginning with the legitimate and customary prayers, as a foundation—of rearing an outer superstructure of petitions, yet with remembrance of the [Master's] precepts."[9] St. Cyprian comments upon and enlarges the same thoughts. Like Tertullian he shows that everything is contained in the sublime prayer which the Word of God Himself has taught us. To be

_____

[9] Ter. De Orat. Dom., ix, x.

fully convinced of this, we have only to read their treatises on
the *Pater noster.* They show clearly that in the Church the laws
of prayer have ever been the same. St. Augustine, in his letter
to the holy widow Proba, gives a like testimony: "If you go over
all the prayers that are in the sacred Scriptures, you will, I
believe, find nothing that cannot be comprised and summed up
in the petitions of the Lord's Prayer. Therefore, in praying, we
are free to use different words, but we must ask the same
things; in this we have no choice."[10]

Lastly, Cassian says: "The most perfect and sublime prayer
is that inspired by the contemplation of God and the glowing
fire of charity when the soul, dissolved in love of her Creator,
speaks tenderly and familiarly with Him as with a father. The
prayer which Jesus Christ has taught us shows by its first
words, *Pater noster,* that we should apply ourselves earnestly to
the attainment of this disposition."[11] It is superfluous to recall
how, in the sixteenth century, the seraphic reformer of Carmel,
in her "Way of Perfection," makes use of the *Pater noster.*

Following the example of so many venerable authors, we
would, in our turn, add a few words to show how completely
the *Pater noster* contains the rule of perfection as well as the
rule of prayer. For if it begins with the words *Pater
noster*—because those who are saying it have received the Spirit
of adoption, and it is of them our Lord says: "I have manifested
Thy name to the men whom Thou hast given Me out of the
world"[12]—it is none the less true that practically as regards our
perfection, the last petition of the prayer comes first. In fact,
according as this prayer works its effect in our souls,
germinates so to say, it begins by delivering us from evil; then
it obtains that we be not tempted in a dangerous manner, as our

[10] S. Aug. Epist. cxxx, cap. Xii.

[11] Cassian, Coll. ix, cap. xviii.

[12] Manifestavi nomen tuum hominibus, quos dedisti mihi de mundo
(Joann, xvii, 6).

Lord says: "Pray that ye enter not into temptation."[13]

If we are strictly faithful, this prayer soon obtains for us the full and entire pardon of our sins, on condition that we practise the second commandment, which is like unto the first, since it is the external proof and certain pledge that we are accomplishing it. Then it unites us to God by obtaining for us the supersubstantial Bread of eternal Truth, either under the form of doctrine, or under the appearances of that Bread, which in truth is the Body of the Lord. The divine will is then accomplished in the soul, on earth as it is in heaven; the kingdom of our Lord Jesus Christ is established and the Father's name is truly glorified by the creature thus restored and remade. Cassian expresses the same thought, when he says: "The aim of every monk and the perfection of his heart tends to continual and unbroken perseverance in prayer,"[14] till at last this mysterious prayer transforms the soul itself and puts it in possession of the incomparable inheritance, which the single word "Our Father" implies.

Moreover, this sublime prayer contains a very noble mention of the three divine Persons, for the first petition is addressed particularly to the eternal Father, the second to the Incarnate Word, and the third to the divine Paraclete, who gathers together the members of Christ's mystical Body into that marvellous unity for which our Lord prayed at the Last Supper, "That they may be one, as We also are one."[15] After this mention of the three divine Persons in their relations with us, comes the petition for union with God; for communion with Him either by the Holy Eucharist or by the holy Scripture; and lastly the fifth, sixth and seventh petitions seem to refer to the Unitive, the Illuminative and the Purgative Life, and the whole ends with "Amen," a word which belongs to time and to

---

[13] Orate ut non intretis in tentationem (Malth. xxvi, 41).

[14] Cassian, Coll. ix, cap. Ii.

[15] Ut sint unum, sicut et nos unum sumus (Joann., xvii, 22).

eternity.

There is no form of prayer more excellent than this. The Church puts it on the lips of her priests in the very midst of the cloud, when standing face to face with God in the divine mysteries. Hence we can have no difficulty in appreciating that profound passage of Cassian, which refers to the highest stage of the spiritual life: "The prayer taught and recommended by our Lord contains in truth all perfection. Yet it raises those that are faithful to it to a still more sublime state, of which we have already spoken, for it conducts them to that glowing and burning prayer known only to a few, which cannot be explained because it surpasses the conception and intelligence of man. This prayer is formed by no sound of the voice, by no movement of the tongue, by no utterance of words; the soul enlightened by a heavenly light uses no human language, but, as an abundant fountain, she overflows with affections, and raises herself to God in an ineffable manner, saying so many things all at once that when she returns to herself she can neither express them in words nor recall them in thought. Our Lord gave us the example of this prayer when He retired alone upon the mountain, or when He prayed in silence and watered the ground with His Blood in the agony of His incomprehensible ardour."[16]

---

[16] Cassian, Coll, ix, cap. xxv.

CHAPTER IX
Should Mental Prayer be made with Method or Without Method?

HE GENERIC expression "mental prayer" signifies, as we understand it, all communication of the soul with God, all elevation of the heart towards Him, that is free, personal and not restricted to any determined liturgical form. Thus understood, individual prayer has multifarious shades, degrees without number; but it must nevertheless obey fixed and unchanging laws based upon the relations that God has created between Himself and man.

Nowhere has the Creator established, nor can He establish anything without order: "Thou hast ordered all things in measure and number and weight."[1] Divine love itself, free from all outward constraint—for what is more free than love?—makes the soul acknowledge, when it has reached perfection, that its whole course has been regular and orderly. "He set in order charity in me."[2] There is perfect harmony in the highest regions of the spiritual life, and there is an admirable method in the ways that lead to them. Hence the truth and meaning of these words of the Book of Esther: "So going in she passed through all the doors in order, and stood before the king, where he sat."[3]

It is principally in the writings of the ancient masters of the spiritual life and the fathers that we find the description of this

---

[1] Omnia in mensura, et numero, et pondere disposuisti (Sap., xi, 21).

[2] Ordinavit in me caritatem (Cant., ii, 4).

[3] Ingressa igitur cuncta per ordinem ostia, stetit contra regem, ubi ille residebat (Esth., xv, 9).

spiritual order; an order without the restraints of system; an order ruled by strong and unchangeable laws, which are not limits but rather the determining conditions of energy and the most supple activity. "Contemplation without preparation or without rules leads but to illusion. When we are imbued first of all with the principles of the fear of God, then cleansed, and as it were spiritualized, we may without peril raise ourselves to the heights. For where fear reigns, obedience to the law of God is found; and where there is obedience, there is the body mortified and brought low, so that it ceased to be as a heavy cloud, obscuring the light of the soul and preventing it from beholding clearly the splendour of the divine rays."[4] "Let us note well," said Dom Gueranger in his familiar conversations, "that the science of the Christian life is a determined and definite science. Therefore we must not rest satisfied with repeating conventional phrases or with multiplying sentimental formulas; it is by labour, and not by dreaming and excitement, that we must learn the secrets of a science which has its axioms, its deductions and its certain rules. All must be drawn from divine sources, that this science may be truly that of the spiritual life in the Christian Church."

Order is the handmaid of the Holy Spirit; but order is no more a system than disorder is liberty, such liberty at least as Christianity acknowledges, and we know no other. Hence the relations of the soul with God in mental prayer are subservient to laws, which are at once both order and liberty.

If then by "method" we are to understand the rules and axioms of a man or of an epoch, we say with Dom Gueranger:

---

[4] Effrenata enim contemplatio in præcipitia quoque fortasse nos impulerit; verum ut timoris rudimentis imbuti et purgati, atque, ut hoc verbo utar, attenuati, in altum efferamur. Ubi enim timor est, illic quoque mandatorum observatio: ubi autem mandatorum observatio, illic etiam carnis, quæ nubis cujusdam instar, animæ lumen obscurat, nec divini radii splendorem pure intueri sinit, purgatio est (St. Gre. Naz., Or. In S. Lumina, cap. viii).

"God preserve us from men of system and ready-made ideas."[5] If methods of prayers have been drawn up by Saints, and have been praised by the Church, or consecrated by Christian usage, they deserve our respect; criticism will be silent, and souls who for good reasons prefer not to follow these methods will carefully guard against putting aside, together with the methods themselves, those general principles which are the necessary conditions of prayer, founded on the universal teaching of the Church. For on these matters the Church has received a doctrinal deposit, which St. Denis called a secret and sacerdotal tradition—secret in his day because it was for the baptized only. This deposit, contained in the holy Scriptures and the writings of the fathers and holy doctors, is the method which we look upon as laid down for all.[6] Monastic spirituality recommends no particular system. It is strongly bound to the traditional teaching of the Church, and to that alone. Thus with us absence of method can signify only freedom from human rules, and never disorder and the absence of intelligent culture. There is a just medium in this wise balance of liberty and rule, the keeping of which calls for something more than great prudence; it needs the guidance of the Spirit of God Himself.

Man, being a pilgrim on earth journeying towards his heavenly country, may not waste his time in idleness. Even in the state of innocence, when God first placed Adam in the beautiful garden of paradise, it was not merely that he might walk about and admire that glorious creation which had come forth all fresh, pure and well-ordered from the hand of the Creator, but that he might "dress it and keep it."[7] There, however, work was but a delightful occupation, an intelligent cooperation with God's designs in creation, and as such it was

---

[5] Instit., lib. ii. p. 112.

[6] De Coel., Hier., cap. ii.

[7] Ut operaretur et custodiret illum (Gen., ii, 15).

honourable to man, whom God indeed freely created, but whom He will not reward without efforts of his own. In the mystic and well closed garden of the Canticle of Canticles, where dwells the regenerated human race, in the person of the sacred bride, we have again a picture of industry. From the earliest dawn of spring souls are on the watch for flowers; here they are catching the little foxes that destroy the vines, there they are gathering in the fruits and storing up the harvest; in a word the fertile earth is being turned to profit for the glory of the King of Peace.

But since the fall of our first parents the easy work of the earthly paradise has become changed into labour which is always hard and sometimes even bloodstained. The earth brings forth thorns and thistles; and the soil of man's heart is no exception to this law of punishment. The supersubstantial Bread of the divine Word is given to us only in the sweat of our brow; for it is the most dangerous of illusions to expect the soul of man to produce salutary fruits unless it is well tilled and cultivated with great pains. Of course the labourer will not pretend that he can give the germs a fruitfulness which only the Creator Spirit can impart; neither will he think that any artificial heat can supply for the rays of the Sun of Justice, or that a few drops of brackish water from the hollow of his hand can take the place of the dew from on high; but his work is wisely to till the soil, to sow in season that he may reap in due time, and to remove the parasitic weeds that stifle the good grain.

But it may perhaps be asked, if you dismiss with a stroke of the pen the accompanying help of methods ready to hand, are you not afraid of leaving the Christian soul to go at haphazard, and to pray as it were at random? Our answer in the first place is that all the children of the Church have the science of their Mother in the sacred liturgy, which contains the most perfect method of prayer, the most traditional, the best ordered, the most simple, and the one which leaves the greatest scope to the liberty of the Holy Spirit.

This is the reason why our fathers seem never to have thought of tracing out any human method for religious souls. They thought it sufficient to make use of the hierarchical and divinely-established mode according to which truth reaches us. "For," says St. Denis, "it is a general law established by infinite Wisdom that divine graces are given to inferior beings by the ministry of superior natures."[8] Therefore every faithful soul aspiring to a life of prayer and union with God came and placed himself under the guidance of a master; the veterans only, now become masters, ever ventured to walk without a guide. The Rule of St. Benedict maintains this tradition when speaking of the novices: "And over him," it says, "let such senior be deputed as is skilful in gaining souls, who will watch over him with anxious care and attention . . . let him have told unto him all the hard and rough roads by which one goeth unto God."[9]

It is, therefore, indispensable to have a guide in the ways of God, and an enlightened guide. "It behoves him to be learned in the divine law."[10] But this is not the teaching of St. Benedict only, it comes directly from the one great Master by excellence: "Let them alone," He says, "they are blind, and leaders of the blind. And if the blind lead the blind, both fall into the pit."[11] St. Teresa's esteem of learning in directors of souls is well known; and if experience is joined to learning, there will result from these combined elements—namely, learning, God's action, the liturgical sense and the maturity of experience—a living method by means of which any ignorant and simple soul may be

---

[8] De coel., Hier., cap. viii.

[9] Et senior ei talis deputetur, qui aptus sit ad lucrandas animas, et qui super eum omnino curiose intendat et sollicitus sit. Præcidentur ei omnia dura et aspera, per quæ itur Deum (S. Reg. cap. lviii).

[10] Oportet eum esse doctum in lege divina (Ibid., cap. lxiv).

[11] Sinite illos: cæci sunt, et duces cæcorum: cæcus autem si cæco ducem præstet, ambo in foveam cadunt (Matth., xv, 14).

guided, even unknown to herself and without any danger, to the highest union with God, and this by a way as perfectly well-ordered as it is free from all human system.

CHAPTER X
The Divine Office and Mental Prayer

OD created man to have fellowship with Him, and to contract a bond of love and intimacy which will he completed and perfected in heaven. Meanwhile is it not the principal concern of the present life to bring about within ourselves, by our own efforts aided by grace, the conditions of that perfect union, and to endeavour, as we can do, to live already as we shall live in eternity.

But can we do this? Yes, without any doubt. The sin of our first parent did not break completely the sweet intimacy of the earthly paradise. God did not cease to communicate Himself to men, and they might still treat with His divine Majesty. The promise of a Redeemer immediately followed the fall, and man was thus reinstated in several of his supernatural privileges in virtue of the foreseen merits of his Saviour. But since the accomplishment of the mysteries of redemption we must own that this intimacy with God has taken far larger proportions. Servants have become friends and brethren; and to the spirit of bondage and fear which reigned in the old law has succeeded the spirit of adoption whereby we cry: "Father, Father."[1]

Prayer, which sums up the relations of the the soul with God in its state as wayfarer *(viator)*, is consequently a subject well worth the attention of all who know for what end they were created. Therefore it will be useful briefly to set forth the general forms of prayer, were it only to show the perfect unity

---

[1] Abba, Pater (Rom. viii, 15).

of the divine plan, in the many and various ways that may lead the spirit to union with God.

The soul of man may, under two forms of prayer, treat with its Lord—Liturgical prayer regulated by the Church, and individual prayer. In itself there can be no doubt that the first form far surpasses the second in dignity, authority, comprehensiveness and power. A little explanation will suffice to make this evident.

The official and social homage rendered by the Church militant to God, Father, Son and Holy Ghost—that whole group of spoken formulas, of chants and ceremonies which is, as it were, the necessary accompaniment of the eternal Sacrifice—constitutes the most noble portion of divine worship, which is the essential tribute of adoration, thanksgiving, praise and impetration.

Even amid the figures of the old law, the importance of that prayer, the words of which were for the most part inspired by God, the general forms of which were fixed by the Church, was not overlooked; and it would be almost impossible to bring forward the many passages of Scripture in which the Holy Spirit asserts God's rights in regard of this. Moses attaches blessings from on high to the fidelity of the people in observing not only the commandments of God but even the smallest details of His worship: "Keep the precepts of the Lord thy God, and the testimonies and ceremonies which He hath commanded thee. . . . that it may be well with thee: and going in thou mayest possess the goodly land, concerning which the Lord swore to thy fathers."[2] The Book of Ecclesiasticus, when praising men of renown, mentions in particular their solicitude for the worship rendered to the true God.[3] Finally Esther, when

---

[2] Custodi præcepta Domini Dei tui, ac testimonia et ceremonias quas præcepit tibi . . . ut bene sit tibi, et ingressus possideas terram optimam, de qua juravit Dominus patribus tuis (Deut., vi, 17, 18).

[3] Eccli, xliv.

seeking to draw down the divine mercy, lays great stress on this decisive argument: "They design," she says, "to change thy promises and destroy thy inheritance, and shut the mouths of them that praise thee, and extinguish the glory of thy temple and altar."[4] Our Lord, during the whole of His life on earth, showed by His example the importance of public and social prayer. His frequent visits to Jerusalem had no other end than this; and the exactness with which He fulfilled every, even the least detail of the Mosaic Law shows clearly what place the prayer of the Church should hold in our esteem and practice. The early Christians in their turn gave abundant evidence that our divine Lord came not to abolish the rites of the Synagogue, but to fulfil what was figurative in them, and to bring to His Father adorers in spirit and in truth. The Epistles and the Acts of the Apostles tell us what was the custom of the early Christians and what place social prayer held among them. Later on the fathers handed down the tradition of the importance of liturgical prayer and gave us in their writings the very forms which it took at different periods. Holy Church also proves well enough what is the mind of the Holy Spirit who rules and animates her, by obliging all her clergy to the recitation of the Divine Office.

Finally, the holy Gospel gives us some severe words of our Lord regarding the Jews, and in so doing it teaches us how greatly God has at heart the purity of the official homage which He expects from His creatures. Quoting the Prophet Isaias, our Saviour says: "This people honoureth me with their lips; but their heart is far from me. And in vain do they worship me,

---

[4] Volunt tuæ mutare promissa et delere hæreditatem tuam, et claudere ora laudantium te, atque exstinguere gloriam templi et altaris tui (Esth., xiv, 9).

teaching doctrines and commandments of men."[5] Now on the lips of our Divine Master this reproach has a special tone of gravity; it is addressed to souls tainted with Pharisaism, to those who make everything consist in mere external worship which gives unto God—and that with great show—what is least in man.

Our Lord complained of this mere material and therefore deceitful worship, wherein the lips only utter words while the mind and the heart are not in accord with them. This kind of lying is the more odious as it is addressed to Him before whom "all things are naked and open." Hence, it called for the watchful care of our Saviour, who came to restore all things for His Father's glory. In vain will the Pharisees offer a counterfeit worship with servile exactness and the perfection of external form; they cannot deceive the divine Majesty: "Is this house then, in which My name hath been called upon, in your eyes become a den of robbers? I, I am He: I have seen it, saith the Lord."[6] Therefore our Lord, who came to fulfil all justice, takes up the words of His prophet when He casts the buyers and sellers out of the temple, saying to them: "It is written: My house shall be called the house of prayer; but you have made it a den of thieves."[7]

This house of prayer is principally the soul, which is vowed by her state to the worship of God; she cannot fully satisfy her obligation without uniting in one and the same act both vocal and mental prayer. St. Benedict expresses this perfectly in these

---

[5] Populus hic labiis me honorat, cor autem eorum longe est a me. Sine causa autem colunt me docentes doctrinas et mandata hominum (Mattii. xv, 8).

[6] Numquid ergo spelunca latronum facta est domus ista, in qua invocatum est nomen meum in oculis vestris? Ego, ego sum; ego vidi, dicit Dominus (Jerem. vii, 11).

[7] Scriptum est: Domus mea domus orationis vocabitur; vos autem fecistis illam speluncam latronum (Matth. xxi, 13).

few words: "That our mind concord with our voice."[8] These
words are in reality a summary of the whole teaching of the
ancient fathers on mental prayer. With this in mind, we can
read the chapters of St. Benedict's Rule "On the discipline of
Psalmody" and "Of the reverence of Prayer," where the holy
patriarch insists, above all, on the interior dispositions which
should accompany this sacred psalmody, and shows clearly
what attentive preparation our fathers thought it necessary to
make that they might worthily perform the "Work of God."
Their whole life was devoted to it; their whole observance was
centred in it.

For a considerable length of time in fact the two kinds of
prayer of which we are speaking were conjoined, and it will be
useful to refer here to the liturgical customs which prevailed
before St. Benedict's time that we may better understand the
language of the ancient fathers. It appears evident that in the
early Church the public prayer was interrupted at certain times,
especially after the psalms, to give free scope to prayer without
any set form; the soul spoke intimately to God, and God
sometimes by inspiration revealed Himself to the soul. The
ridiculous apings of Protestant sects in these latter times must
net prejudice us against admitting what is historically true of
the first ages of the Church.

It is also to this kind of extemporaneous prayer, so in
keeping with the ancient style when the first Christians who
were favoured with supernatural gifts lent themselves with
docility to God's working in them, that certain passages of the
first Epistle to the Corinthians refer. They are difficult to
understand in our present way of acting. This is what the
Apostle says: "So you also, forasmuch as you are zealous of
spirits, seek to abound unto the edifying of the Church. And
therefore he that speaketh by a tongue, let him pray that he
may interpret. For if I pray in a tongue, my spirit prayeth, but

---

[8] Mens nostra concordet voci nostræ (S. Reg., cap. xix).

my understanding is without fruit. What is it then?

I will pray with the spirit; I will pray also with the understanding. I will sing with the spirit; I will sing also with the understanding. Else if thou shalt bless with the spirit, how shall he that holdeth the place of the unlearned say "Amen" to thy blessing? Because he knoweth not what thou sayest. For thou indeed givest thanks well, but the others are not edified."[9]

We see from this passage that the faithful who had received the gift of tongues, of prophecy, of interpreting the Scriptures, were allowed at times to speak in the Church, and to communicate to the assembly of Christians the lights they had received; but they were themselves to be judged by those who had the gift of discernment of spirits. Among all these gifts St. Paul frankly owns his preference for that of prophecy; but he numbers them all as follows: "How is it then, brethren? when you come together, every one of you hath a psalm, hath a doctrine, hath a revelation, hath a tongue, hath an interpretation: let all things be done to edification."[10] He wishes that all be done with order, wisdom, decorum, without any confusion, and for this he gives admirable lessons of prudence. In view of this he points out in particular that the spirits of the prophets are subject to the prophets, and that there is in the use of these supernatural gifts neither overpowering pressure nor

---

[9] Sic et vos, quoniam æmulatores estis spirituum, ad ædificationem Ecclesiæ quærite ut abundetis. Et ideo qui loquitur lingua, oret ut interpretetur. Nam si orem lingua, spiritus meus orat, mens autem mea sine fructu est. Quid ergo est? Orabo spiritu, orabo et mente: psallam spiritu, psallam et mente. Cæterum si benedixeris spiritu, qui supplet locum idiotæ, quomodo dicet, Amen, super tuam benedictionem, quoniam quid dicas nescit? Nam tu quidem bene gratias agis, sed alter non ædificatur (1 Cor., xiv, 12-17).

[10] Quid ergo est, fratres? Cum convenitis, unusquisque vestrum psalmum habet, doctrinam habet, apocalypsim habet, linguam habet, interpretationem habet: omnia ad ædificationem fiant (1 Cor., xiv, 26).

loss of liberty: the Holy Spirit is never immoderate. In the same place the Apostle forbids women to raise their voice in the Church, either because they have no place in the regular hierarchy of the Church or perhaps also because the weaker sex is more exposed to mistake dreams of the imagination for true inspirations, and by so doing more easily to fall a victim to delusion.

Why not stop for a moment here to point out the word *Benedictio*, which St. Paul uses when speaking of this semi-liturgical extemporization, to which the people answered "Amen"? According to documents recently discovered it is certain that it is what we now call the Collect, which the Church has definitely fixed, and thus taken away the occasion of those abuses which would inevitably have arisen if liberty had been left to the spirit of each. It is easy to see in all the ancient writers that when certain moments were given to personal extemporization in the midst of the liturgical service, this prayer had necessarily to be short; otherwise there would have been danger of vanity, empty discourse and the assumption of airs of importance; and these were the abuses against which the masters were anxious to guard.

Let us hear St. Augustine in his letter to Proba: "Wherefore it is neither wrong nor unprofitable to spend much time in praying if there be leisure for this without hindering other good and necessary works to which duty calls us, although even in the doing of these, as I have said, we ought, by cherishing holy desire, to pray without ceasing. For to spend a long time in prayer is not, as some think, the same thing as to pray with much speaking. Multiplied words are one thing, longcontinued warmth of desire is another. For even of the Lord Himself it is written that He continued all night in prayer, and that His prayer was more prolonged when He was in an agony; and in this an example is given to us by Him, who is in time an intercessor such as we need, and who is with the Father eternally the hearer of prayer.

"The brethren in Egypt are reported to have very frequent prayers, but these are very brief and, as it were, sudden and ejaculatory, lest the wakeful and aroused attention, indispensable in prayer, should by protracted exercises either vanish or lose its keenness. And in this they themselves show plainly enough, that just as this attention is not to be continued unto weariness, so if it is well sustained there is no need suddenly to interrupt it. Far be it from us either to use much speaking in prayer or to refrain from prolonged prayer, if fervent attention of the soul continues. To use much speaking in prayer, is to employ a superlluity of words in asking a necessary thing; but to prolong prayer is to have the heart throbbing with continued pious emotion towards Him to Whom we pray. For in most cases prayer consists more in groaning than in speaking, in tears rather than in words. But He setteth our tears in His sight, and our groaning is not hidden from Him who made all things by the Word, and who does not need human words."[11]

It is thus that St. Augustine wards off intemperance of speech in prayer. Cassian in his turn gives rules of discretion with reference to the prayers that follow the Psalmody:

"When the solitaries meet together to celebrate the Offices, all keep profound silence, and in that multitude of brethren, he alone is heard who rises to recite the Psalms; it seems as though there was no one at all in the church. At the end of the prayer especially there is no sighing, no noise; no talking troubles the assembly, nor drowns the voice of the priest who recites the prayer."

Thus from this quotation we see that there is mention of three distinct parts: the Psalmody, the Prayer and the conclusion made by the priest. Cassian next proceeds to give some reasons why this free kind of prayer should end briefly

---

[11] Epist. cxxx.

saying:

"Those, on the contrary, who pray in a noisy manner and show little fervour are accounted guilty of a double fault. They make prayer a profanation by offering it to God negligently, and moreover by their noise they trouble their neighbours, who otherwise would perhaps pray with more recollection. Therefore our Fathers recommend a prompt end of prayer, lest by prolonging it we should be unable to keep up attention. We must make haste in order to secure our fervour from the snares of the devil. . . . For this reason, the masters of the spiritual life thought it better to make short prayers and repeat them more frequently. By multiplying these prayers we attach ourselves more intimately to God, and by making them short we the better avoid the darts which the devil hurls against us more particularly at that time."[12]

Hence St. Benedict, laying down this teaching still more precisely, says in his Rule: "And therefore prayer should be short and pure, save perchance one be led to lengthen it from the affection of an inspiration of divine grace. But in the monastery let the prayer be very short, and as soon as the superior has given the signal, let all rise together."[13]

With his usual discretion the holy patriarch cuts short all the abuses which might find their way into prayer made in common. But he had not the slightest idea of asserting that what we nowadays call mental prayer might be curtailed to a few moments; for in his mind this attention of the soul to God is the very law of our existence. In the great schools of the contemplative life it was thought that man should be unceasingly occupied with divine things, in order to be

---

[12] Cassian, Instit., lib. ii, cap. x.

[13] Et ideo brevis debet esse et pura oratio; nisi forte ex affectu inspirationis divinæ gratiæ protendatur. In conventu tamen omnino brevietur oratio, et facto signo a Priore, omnes pariter surgant (S. Reg., cap. xx).

thoroughly affected by them.

Now private or mental prayer, though lower in dignity, has this advantage over social prayer, that it can be uninterrupted; it can be offered to God at all times and in all places, in sickness and in health, by day and by night. There can however be no advantage in making a jealous parallel between these two forms of Catholic prayer, or in making them stand alone in a kind of rivalry; we fail to see how they can either harm or exclude each other. Happy they who unite both in one common love! Let each keep its respective place in the practice and esteem of the children of the Church. In the king's palace, the pomp of court ceremonial is indispensable to enhance the royal dignity; but it does not forbid the outpourings of tender love and friendship. Thus our great King and Lord of lords has a right to the splendid service of a royal court, but at the same time He wishes to find tender devotedness in the hearts of His subjects, love in His bride, filial piety in His children, and fraternal affection in those whom He honours with the name, friends. He would read in the heart of the very last of His courtiers not a servile fear inducing Him to perform with mere external exactitude His duties in the palace, but a love which exalts those duties and causes them to be fulfilled with the most delicate care. We are well aware that in private sources the soul may find food for mental prayer; but it is no less true that the Divine Office will ever be the principal and richest food of contemplation. And how could it be otherwise if on this subject we believe the words of the Apostle: "For we know not what we should pray for as we ought; but the Spirit Himself asketh for us with unspeakable groanings."[14]

How can it be that a soul prepared and formed by the Holy Spirit should not know better than any other how to converse with God in the intimacy of her heart returning as she does to

---

[14] Nam quid oremus, sicut oportet, nescimus: sed ipse Spiritus postulat pro nobis gemitibus inenarrabilibus (Rom. viii, 26).

her solitude laden like a bee with honey from so many flowers? How can she be ignorant of the right language in which to address the Divine Majesty, when she enters into the secret chamber of her heart, all replenished with the Divine Word. What is contemplation in its highest form but the opening out of the beautiful affirmations which the prayer of the Church puts upon our lips? When a soul borrows her expressions from human language, she will never find any words that more exactly convey tile truths she has contemplated than the forms of liturgical prayer, lending themselves, as they do, with equal ease to the lispings of the soul beginning to seek God and to the enraptured outpourings of the soul that has found Him. It is needless therefore to make contrasts between liturgical prayer regulated by the Church, and mental prayer as it takes its free and varied course; the former cannot be perfect without the latter, and the latter gains its strength from the former and leans securely upon it. The Church does not cripple the soul nor weaken her tendency to God. She fixes and regulates the forms of official prayer, and then leaves souls at liberty in their personal intimacy with God; she excludes nothing here below that can prepare the way for divine union, and hesitates not to find even in physical beauty a precious help for raising us to the one true source of all beauty. Not indeed that the spirit of prayer can ever resemble the vague and purely æsthetic emotions which sometimes seize upon the soul in presence of the beauties of the Liturgy; even unbelievers may have impressions such as these, but we simply mean to say that the Church makes use of all the natural forces which she finds in the soul in order to elevate it to God.

"Whence," asks Dom Gueranger, "did the holy Doctors of the early ages and the venerable Patriarchs of the desert acquire their spiritual knowledge and tender devotion, of which they have left us such treasures in their writings and their works? It was from those long hours of psalmody, during which truth, simple yet manifold, unceasingly passed before the eyes of their soul, filling that soul with streams of light and love." According to the ancient practice what they called meditation and attentive reading of the Scriptures followed the prayers said in the oratory, and every one will admit that this looks very like what we nowadays call mental prayer. A few examples will show this more clearly. Cassian says: "The solitaries join private vigils to those imposed by the Office, and they apply to them with even greater care, in order to preserve the purity they have acquired by prayer and to gain by their meditations in the night that strength and vigilance which ought to be their safeguard during the day."[15] "They also join manual labour to their vigils that idleness may not make them a prey to sleep, and they do not interrupt it any more than their meditation. They exercise equally the faculties of the soul and of the body in order to unite the efforts of the exterior man to those of the interior man."[16] This meditation, which fills up the intervals between the Divine Office, is preserved by St. Benedict as a precious tradition: "As to the time that remains after the vigils," he says, "let it be spent in the study of the Psalms and Lessons, by such of the brethren as may have need thereof."[17] Of course this does not mean a dry exercise of the memory, but a work of the mind and heart, a work in which the soul, fed upon the holy Scriptures and supernatural truths, becomes more fit to celebrate the work of God. Thus light is thrown upon the Rule of St. Benedict by the constant custom of the ancient Fathers, who all devoted to meditation the time that followed the vigils.

Plainly, therefore, mental prayer, as we understand it nowadays, is the indispensable preparation for worthily

---

[15] Cassian, Instil, lib. ii, cap. xiii.

[16] Ibid.,xiv.

[17] Quod vero restat post vigilias, a fratribus qui Psalterii vel lectionum aliquid indigent meditationi inserviatur (S. Reg., cap. viii).

celebrating the Divine Office and for rendering to God the homage of perfect praise. In it the soul takes her attitude, as it were, prepares and drills herself to fulfil perfectly the four great ends of the Sacrifice of Praise; in it again, she tunes her instrument, so to say, that when the hour comes it may vibrate in perfect harmony to the glory of the Father, Son and Holy Ghost. For in order rightly to celebrate the Divine Office, it is not enough to have a general intention to apply our minds to it, we must also bring actual attention to the great work, and this the soul cannot either gain or preserve unless she has made progress in the spirit of prayer and lost the habit of dissipation. It is in this way that the exercise of mental prayer fixes and steadies the soul for the time of the Divine Office.

What we here assert is not a mere opinion. The preparatory prayer which the Church appoints to be said before the Divine Office, shows clearly what dispositions she expects to find in the hearts of those whom she deputes to sing the divine praises, when they stand before God: "*Ut digne, attente, ac devote hoc officium recitare valeam*—That I may worthily, attentively and devoutly recite this Office." And we are taught in the same prayer to beseech our Lord to cleanse our heart not only from vain and wicked thoughts—*vanis perversis*—but also from thoughts foreign to the purpose—*alienis cogitationibus*; to enlighten our understanding, intellectual *illumiua*, to kindle our affections, affectum *influmvia*, by which words we ask directly for the grace of contemplation. The Church, therefore, counts upon her children bringing to the Divine Office the dispositions requisite for contemplation, that they may offer to God a living homage and not a mere external worship.

Thus, by a double current, which consists in praying mentally the better to celebrate the Divine Office, and seeking in the Divine Office the food of mental prayer, the soul gently, quietly and almost without effort arrives at true contemplation. Practically these two forms of prayer can never either stand against each other or be separated in those who are vowed by their state to the contemplative life.

It is by the use of these several means, combined together and supporting one another, that the soul raises herself day by day to God. This progress was well known to the ancients: "When by the charms of harmony," says Saint Denis, "the song of the sacred truths has prepared the powers of our soul for the immediate celebration of the Sacred Mysteries, and when it has subdued them so to say, borne along by this music, down to the cadence of an absorbing divine transport, and has put us in unison with God, with our brethren and with ourselves, then what the holy Chants expressed in brief, and shadowed forth by figures, the reading of the holy Scriptures will worthily develop in descriptions and narratives more ample and more clear. Then we behold all things tending to one perfect unity under the influence of one only Spirit."[18]

---

[18] Hier., Eccl., cap. iii, 5.

CHAPTER XI
On Meditation

NDER the general term "Meditation" we comprise every form of mental prayer in which the soul, by the labour of reflection and reasoning, raises herself to God. Though it contains only the first elements of prayer, meditation is one of the surest means of entering upon a spiritual life.

In that admirable rule of holy living, Psalm cxviii, one thought is constantly recurring: "Unless Thy law had been my meditation, I had then perhaps perished in my abjection.[1] Thy testimonies are wonderful: therefore my soul hath sought them.[2] My eyes to Thee have prevented the morning, that I might meditate on thy works."[3] Scripture abounds with texts such as these, proving the importance of meditation. The first Psalm makes man's happiness consist in meditation on the law of God: "On His law he shall meditate day and night . . . and shall bring forth fruit in due season."[4] St. Paul, speaking to his disciple Timothy of the Sacrament of Holy Orders, which he has received, gives this counsel: "Meditate upon these things, be wholly in these things: that thy profiting may be manifest to

---

[1] Nisi quod lex tua meditatio mea est, tunc forte periissem in humilitate mea (Ps. cxviii, 92).

[2] Mirabilia testimonia tua; ideo scrutata est ea anima mea (Ibid., 129).

[3] Prævenerunt oculi mei ad te diluculo, ut meditarer eloquia tua (Ps. cxviii, 148).

[4] In lege ejus meditabitur die ac nocte . . . . et fructum suum dabit in tempore suo (Ps. i, 2, 3).

all."[5] To go still further back, it is related in the Book of Genesis
that Isaac, son of the free woman, went out into the field on the
eve of his marriage to meditate near the mysterious well, called
"Of the Living and the Seeing." This well was a symbol of the
laborious way by which grace was obtained in the Old Law and
of its comparatively sparing measure. It contrasts strongly with
that river whose torrent rejoiceth the city of God. "And he was
gone forth to meditate in the field, the day being now well
spent."[6]

Reflection is a law of our very nature. Reflection, that is to
say natural meditation, is necessary when a man wishes to
undertake any work whatsoever; he must steady his thoughts,
weigh them well, and put them in order. Meditation is
moreover a means of rousing strong feelings. David
experienced this when he said: "My heart grew hot within me:
and in my meditation a fire shall flame out."[7] If this is the
process by which our thoughts take shape and become
powerful in the purely natural order, why should we not
employ this faculty to apprehend the truths which God has
deigned to reveal, and to imprint them deeply on our hearts.
What more holy subject of reflection than God's mysteries?
What more noble use of the human intellect and will than to
look into and to comprehend the Good, the Beautiful and the
True.

Moreover, it would be a strange error to suppose that all
souls could turn their thoughts from vanities, and without
labour and using violence rid themselves of the tumult of
external things. One of the deepest traces of original sin is this

---

[5] Hæc meditare, in his esto: ut profectus tuus manifestus sit omnibus
(1 Tim., iv, 15).

[6] Et egressus fuerat ad meditandum in agro, inclinata jam die (Gen.,
xxiv, 63).

[7] Concaluit cor meum intra me, et in meditatione mea exardescet
ignis (Ps., xxxviii, 4).

very weakness of the intelligence which rebels against the light and prefers darkness to it, so much so indeed that unless the will by force arrests the unstable mind and applies it with perseverance to divine things, there is every reason to fear that the spiritual life will take very little root within us.

"Meditation," said Dom Gueranger, "has a twofold object: to bring back to the mind truths well known but too much forgotten; to draw them out of the darkness and silence in which they are sleeping, and to give these truths a power of action which they can have only when recalled to mind and reflected upon. Meditation consists, therefore, in recollecting ourselves and considering attentively that supernatural truth, the impression of which has grown weak, and no longer sufficiently rules our lives to stamp them with its character and seal. As long as the soul has not become familiar with supernatural truths, or as often as she feels herself becoming less impressed by them and less powerfully spurred on, meditation, or a return to it, will be absolutely necessary. As we cannot see unless we look, so it is only by means of meditation that the soul either gains or regains the truth.

"Experience shows clearly that when the mind works, its steady and orderly reflection gives back to the intelligence matter which had been forgotten; so also meditation on the supernatural truths has the power to restore our conviction of them even after a long period of disregard and forgetfulness."

In was in this sense that the Fathers spoke of meditation: "Prayer," says St. Ambrose, "is the ordinary food that we should give to our souls, because this food, being digested by constant meditation, supports and feeds the soul, as the manna from heaven heretofore strengthened the body."[8] St. Augustine also in explaining the Psalms insists upon meditation: "We exhort you, beloved, that what by hearing, ye store, so to speak, in the stomach of your memory, that, by again revolving and

---

[8] De Cain et Abel, lib. II, cap. vi.

meditating, ye in a manner ruminate."[9] And elsewhere the holy
Doctor proposes the example of David: "The prophet," he says,
"was conversing in the secret place of his own heart. But let
him declare to us what he was doing there. . . . This man was
examining his spirit, and was speaking with that same
spirit—that is to say, he was questioning himself, was
examining himself, was judging himself. . . . He was rejoicing
at the mercies of the Lord and exulting in the remembrance of
His works."[10]

On this subject it is scarcely necessary to quote any more
from the Fathers; however it is important to bring forward the
teaching of Cassian, as it sums up the tradition of the great
contemplatives of old, who presided over schools of perfection
and holiness.

"The most elementary principles of a profession," says
Cassian, "facilitate its beginnings, and enable us easily to reach
its highest degree of perfection. A child could never pronounce
syllables without first knowing its letters, and how could he
read fluently who could scarcely put words together? Or how
could one become skilful in rhetoric, or philosophy, who had
not mastered the rules of grammar? So likewise the sublime
science which teaches us how to unite ourselves to God, has
certain fundamental principles which will be a sure
groundwork whereon to erect the spiritual edifice of the
highest perfection. It seems to us that the first of these
principles consists in the remembrance and thought of God, and
then in the means for fixing this remembrance and thought in
our minds. Is not all perfection herein contained? We would,
therefore, know what these means are of forming some
conception of God, and having Him ever present to our minds,
so that if we sometimes lose sight of Him we may be able to

---

[9] St. Aug. In Ps., cxli.

[10] *Ibid.*, in Ps., lxxvi.

recall His divine presence immediately and without difficulty."[11]
The holy solitary, the Abbot Isaac, to whom Cassian was speaking, then gave a perfect lesson of meditation on the verse: *Deus, in adjutorium meum intende,* showing that by means of one single verse of a Psalm the soul can become recollected in God, and thus avoid that fickleness and inconstancy which these venerable men looked upon as a great danger in the spiritual life. Let us once more borrow from them the exact picture of these wanderings of the imagination in prayer: "Scarcely do we begin to think on some verse of a Psalm, than it immediately and insensibly escapes us, and we wonder how we can so easily roam from place to place in holy Scripture; as soon as we begin to apply, and before we have apprehended what we were reflecting upon, the memory has hurried to another passage, and we lose all the fruit of our meditation. Thus the mind runs from one subject to another, and skips from Psalm to Psalm, from the Gospels to the Epistles, from the Epistles to the Prophets, and from the moral to the historical parts of Scripture. It does nothing but wander, without any fixed purpose, through the whole extent of the sacred volume. It can retain nothing, reject nothing by choice. It meditates on nothing, penetrates into nothing. It runs lightly over a subject, without being able to relish the inward meaning, or to produce and assimilate any holy thoughts. Thus always roving, always unstable, always distracted, the soul resembles an intoxicated person, even during the Divine Office, and is incapable of discharging its duties rightly. For instance, when we pray, we are thinking of some Psalm or some reading; if we chant a Psalm, something else not at all connected with it will rush into the mind; if we read, we are distracted by dwelling upon what we have done, or upon what we have to do, and thus we are the sport of chance, without rule or any means of fixing our will

---

[11] Cassian, Coll., x, cap. viii.

and retaining what we should wish to meditate upon."[12]

The wound is plainly discovered just as we know it after the lapse of so many ages; and here in part is the answer of the Abbot Isaac: "Three things arrest the wanderings of the mind: watching, meditation and prayer. An assiduous application to these exercises will render the soul firm and immovable. This result, however, cannot be obtained without manual labour."[13] Thus we learn from Cassian that our Fathers made a distinction between prayer and meditation, and that our mind should be intent upon some one thing in meditation, and not be carried away by a variety of thoughts. It is well known that the mind shows greater power when it reduces many notions to unity and simplicity, than when it wastes itself lightly in a multitude of thoughts.

The ancients prescribed this method, especially for beginners, as we may infer from the advice of the holy Abbot Paphnutius to the generous penitent Thais: "Sitting and looking towards the east, frequently repeat this one prayer: 'Thou, who hast created me, have mercy on me.'"[14] After three years God made known by a miracle that this short prayer had been so pure as to bring about the perfect cleansing of the venerable penitent, and now the virgins themselves were preparing her adornments.

From these examples we see clearly that, although meditation is a discourse of the mind, a summary of considerations intended to impress truth upon the heart and to develop the love of God, it must not be a work of the understanding only, such as the composition of a sermon or the drawing up of a learned theological thesis. Nothing could be

---

[12] Cassian, Coll, xiv, cap. xiii.

[13] Ibid., cap. xiv.

[14] Tantummodo sedens contra Orientem respice, hunc sermonem solum frequenter iterans: Qui plasmasti me miserere mei (Vita S. Thaidis, cap. ii).

farther from the purpose than this kind of meditation, which will gratify vanity rather than foster the love of God. For self is mirrored in these high thoughts, and the soul takes delight in her own sublimity; of all other illusions this is the most dangerous, since there can be no true prayer without humility, which is the purity of the mind, just as chastity is that of the body. The devil himself, with exaltation of mind, knows how to meditate on divine things, he could give lessons in it even to men of genius; but this very meditation intoxicates him with pride: "By the multitude of thy merchandise, thy inner parts were filled with iniquity; thou hast sinned, and I cast thee out from the mountain of God."[15]

Meditation on divine things is then a certain cure for the wanderings of our mind. Therefore all true meditation will have for its object to give back the light of divine truths and to make them sink deeper into our hearts. As light, however, never exists without heat, this greater hold of truth will increase within us the fire of love.

We have already pointed out that the Fathers of old recommended their disciples, when meditating, to avoid a multiplicity of thoughts, plainly proving that true meditation is not an offspring of curiosity, but occupies itself humbly with the simplest truths, because these afford no matter for vain, subtle inquiry, and more easily carry the soul to God. Here we are reminded of that comprehensive lesson of perfection given to St. Catharine of Sienna by our Lord Himself in these few words: "I am He who is: thou art she who is not."

It follows from what has been said thus far, that we must use meditation properly socalled only until we have gained a firm and lasting hold upon supernatural truths. No one should ever forget that meditation is intended to fill up a deficiency in our souls, and to conquer our natural inattention; and that if it

---

[15] In multitudine negotiationis tuæ repleta sunt interiora tua iniquitate,et peccasti; et ejeci te de monte Dei (Ezeeh. xxviii, 16).

is very important to make use of it when necessary, it is childish to persist in it when no longer needed.

It is necessary as long as the truths of faith are not deeply impressed upon the soul; it ceases to be so, at least continually, when the gift of piety so works within us that without any difficulty we relish holy things, and when the mind retains them present and active by an attention that no longer wanders. Were the soul in these conditions to continue the use of meditation she would run the risk of stifling within herself the true spirit of prayer, which does not consist in reasoning but in the affections. She would resemble a person seeking a light and continuing to strike with the steel when the stone had already given the spark, thus risking to extinguish it again. It is necessary to strike the stone as long as it does not give a spark, but it is unwise to continue a superfluous labour beyond all limit.

We repeat, meditation must always tend to inflame the heart; but if the heart warms up without much meditation on divine truth, we must dwell peacefully in this affection for it is true prayer and the end of all meditation. There is folly in seeking a thing found and in pursuing an end which has been reached.

Experience, however, suggests a remark which must find its place here. Side by side with those persons who, without any merit on their part, are by a special grace, and from the very beginning drawn to prayer without passing through meditation, there are others who, even naturally, are unfit for this exercise. In consequence of a lively imagination and a certain levity and want of steadiness, they are almost incapable of fixing their mind upon any subject whatever. In vain would they persist in trying to meditate; were they to succeed, it would be mere human labour and a kind of philosophical work. How then will they employ their time? On this point St. Teresa, who was not able to meditate, gives excellent advice which we shall quote farther on. But what is most important of all is that they should not lose courage, thinking that because they are not able to meditate therefore they are unfit for mental prayer. There are indeed various other means of rendering the soul attentive to divine things and of fixing the heart upon them. Thus for example, making many acts of the virtues of which we stand most in need; making intercession for the Church, for our neighbour and for ourselves; reciting some vocal prayer very slowly, and gently fixing our attention upon it.

Many persons ask what are the best subjects for meditation. This is a question of some importance, especially for beginners in the spiritual life, as it may happen that not having chosen a fixed subject, caprice becomes mistress of their prayer, and they waste their time skipping from one thing to another, which is the ruin of all self-control. Masters of the spiritual life have often advised preparation over night of the subject for meditation. It is an excellent practice, especially for persons unaccustomed to recollection and the exercise of the presence of God.

But having in a general way touched upon this subject, it seems almost impossible to give any precise rule for the choice of our meditations. Each soul has its own aptitudes and needs; and these are not the same at all times. We pray differently when we are in joy or in sorrow, in fervour or in discouragement, in consolation or in trial. One person can with ease gather up his thoughts and apply his mind to the mysteries, another can arrest his attention only by some pious imagination, such as picturing a place, a scene and, as it were, the external and sensible part of the mysteries. A few lines suffice for one, more is necessary for another. Some souls have a special attraction for one mystery—and we must take heed of disapproving of this—while others feel the need of following the liturgical cycle and uniting themselves even in private prayer, with its successive phases. In all this there is no law, no general system to be adopted; each must seek light from those who have mission and authority, and submit his drawings to them.

There is no need to vary the subjects of our prayer; we have found that the ancient Fathers thought that a single verse of a Psalm was sufficient to feed the soul for many years. St. Teresa suggests another very simple and profitable way of prayer: "You already know," she says, "that before beginning your prayer you must first of all examine your conscience, then say the *Confiteor*, and make the sign of the Cross. This being done try at once, my daughters, since you are alone to find a companion, but what companion is preferable to the Divine Master? . . . Think not that I ask you to make long meditations upon this Divine Saviour, to reason much, to produce great and subtle considerations; simply gaze at Him, if you can do no more keep for at least a few minutes the eye of your mind fixed upon your Spouse. Who can hinder this?"

The seraphic Mother suggests as a means for recollection the keeping a picture of our Lord before our eyes, or the reading a spiritual book in our own tongue; and elsewhere she observes: "The words of the Gospel always led me to recollection better than any other works, however well they might be written, especially when they were not by authors thoroughly approved, for then I felt no desire to read them."[16] In point of fact the holy Scriptures will always have a special power to cleanse our souls, to nourish them and to raise them to God.

But, it will be said, does it not often happen that in spite of all efforts, in spite of all contrivances, the hour of prayer comes, and the soul is devoid of feeling and empty of thought? What use is there in continuing an exercise in which we are only wasting our time? Christian soul, this is a snare of the devil; the enemy of man dreads above all things fidelity in prayer, and he seeks by every possible means to discourage us from doing a work in which the very least particle of success is an immense

---

[16] *Way of Perfection*, xxii.

gain. Our perseverance and assiduity in meditation, even in the midst of the aridities of which we are speaking, will always have the advantage of making us practise the humility of the Canaanitish woman who, when she was seemingly rejected by our Lord, cried out: "Yea, Lord; for the whelps also eat of the crumbs that fall from the table of their masters."[17] Now, who can ever read without emotion the answer of the Lord, who had thus tried her: "O woman, great is thy faith; be it done to thee as thou wilt."[18]

May not then the King of heaven leave His servant at the gate of His palace without doing him an injustice, and are we right in at once forsaking the post assigned to us in order to undertake some other work of our own liking that we think more useful? The soldier on watch at the king's gate may neither read nor speak; he is under strict discipline, and seemingly inactive and useless. Round about him some are occupied in business, others in pleasure; and he has nothing to do but to play his profitless part. But his simple presence is a homage rendered to his sovereign. What would be said if, under the specious pretext that the king had never invited him into his presence, he were to refuse his service? Yet the humble sentinel of the King of heaven may hope that one day, even before eternity dawns, his patience and perseverance will touch the heart of the Divine Master and win the intimacy of his Lord.

Again we have heard reflections such as these: "But we see sometimes persons very regular in their mental prayer, and yet it is evident that even after years of fidelity they have made no progress beyond what is absolutely commonplace." Such an example proves too much, and therefore proves nothing; in the same way numbers of persons daily receive Holy Communion, and yet remain very imperfect. Can we on this account argue

---

[17] Etiam, Domine: nam et catelli edunt de micis, quæ cadunt de mensa dominorum suorum (Matth. xv, 27).

[18] O mulier, magna est fides tua: fiat tibi sicut vis (Ibid., 28).

against the Holy Eucharist? The most powerful means of sanctification may through our own fault become sterile.

Meditation only does not make us perfect; still it is a means of withdrawing us from the life of the senses. But if we desire to advance in prayer we ought to join with it a generous struggle against our faults. We can scarcely conceive how much our progress in prayer depends upon our gaining of virtue; but we must add that meditation only will not suffice for everything. Some souls will never reach the perfection of virtue unless they seek strength in a higher kind of prayer. This is expressly pointed out in the Psalm lxxxiii: "Blessed is the man whose help is from Thee: in his heart he hath disposed to ascend by steps, in the vale of tears, in the place which he hath set. For the lawgiver shall give a blessing; they shall go from virtue to virtue."[19]

What we have said of meditation is almost superfluous here. Arguments are not needed when we speak to souls aspiring after contemplation, who, on that very account, cannot be faithful except on condition of living entirely by prayer and attention to divine things. Only let them consent from the beginning to make efforts and to be faithful, and a special grace, a particular help will soon raise them above themselves and free them, without much delay from the slow and painful ways of meditation.

---

[19] Beatus vir, cujus est auxilium abs te, ascensiones in corde suo disposuit, in valle lacrymarum, in loco quem posuit. Etenim benedictionem dabit legislator, ibunt de virtute in virtutem (Ps., lxxxiii, 6, 7, 8).

CHAPTER XII
That Mental Prayer is especially indispensable for the Spouses of Christ

SOULS who have heard the voice of the Holy Spirit inviting them to a close alliance with the Son of God, stand in need of mental prayer more than all others; for the call which they have received and the life which they have vowed necessarily imply mental prayer. "Hearken, O daughter," says the psalmist, "and see, and incline thy ear: and forget thy people and thy father's house."[1] In these words we have a summary of the effects which that contact with God, only found in prayer, should work in the human soul. These effects are the enabling that soul to listen with attention, to open her eyes to the sovereign Beauty, and to incline her heart to exact and courageous fidelity in all the duties of her state of life. "And the King shall greatly desire thy beauty."[2] Then the King will bend down, He will take full possession of this daughter of men, to make her His own for ever by causing her to become a sharer of His throne of glory.

A soul consecrated to God is in truth like one of those maidens sprung of royal blood who, in former times, was taken beforehand into the country and family of her future spouse. What then took place, we know from the Book of Esther. What attentions were lavished! How careful was the search for everything necessary to prepare the bride; for her contemplated

---

[1] Audi filia, et vide, et inclina aurem tuam, et obliviscere populum tuum et domum patris tui (Ps. xliv, 11).

[2] Et concupiscet Rex decorem tuum (Ps. xliv, 12).

union! What solicitude on her part to guess the tastes of the king! And when the union is accomplished, with what exactitude does not the queen accommodate herself to all the minutest customs of that court, and to the sanctioned ceremonial, humbly waiting till the king deigns to summon her into his presence! During this period of expectation, how constantly is she preoccupied with the fear of giving displeasure, how ardently desirous is she of securing her king's favour.

Is not this a picture of the life in a monastery of virgins? All are espoused to the King of kings, but all have not yet free access to Him. They must first become initiated into the ways of the royal court, they must study the character and the tastes of their Spouse, and entirely conform to them, that they may please their Lord, and may be allowed in due time to enjoy intimacy with Him.

The dignity of sovereigns seems ordinarily to require that their marriages should be celebrated by proxy. Consider then what is and what should be the legitimate curiosity of a princess irrevocably united to a powerful prince whom she has never seen; what inquiries, what efforts does she not make to find out what he is like, what he loves, and what he wishes.

Do we not here see an outline of the part that prayer must take in the contemplative life? For if by virtue of her consecration, the religious soul is irrevocably united, though only by proxy, to the King of kings and Lord of lords; if she knows through the holy Scriptures and the teaching of the Church the nobility and the beauty of her Lord, still she has never been with Him face to face. He has sent her many messages and incomparable tokens of His love. Like Rebecca, she has received from the hands of Eleazer the earrings of faith, the bracelets of the divine commandments.[3] She is enriched with His grace; already Baptism and Confirmation have

---

[3] Gen. xxiv, 47.

bedecked her "as a bride adorned with her jewels."[4] The demon contemplates with jealous and angry envy this bride clad in her glittering attire: "She clothed herself with the garments of her gladness, and put sandals on her feet, and took bracelets and lilies and earlets and rings, and adorned herself with all her ornaments."[5] Yes, men and the very devils look upon souls consecrated to God as truly espoused to the divine King.

What then would men say of those who in so noble a position should scarcely ever think of their Spouse, or of His kingdom, or of His interests or of those who form His court, but should content themselves with observing in His regard the strict rules of etiquette? Seeing them so disposed, no one could help thinking that if they truly loved their King, their heart would make them more anxious to know Him better. Yet this is the picture of a soul consecrated to God and having no desire for mental prayer and meditation; she seems indifferent about her Lord, as though she were in no hurry to know Him.

The Church, the mistress of divine love, gives her, in the Advent Liturgy, a very different example; that liturgy admirably expresses the sentiments of the soul at its first entrance upon the spiritual life. There we find most careful preparation, zealous zeal to banish everything that could offend the eyes of the Lord who is coming; diligent search for all that can please Him. There again we find the purification of penance, together with all the anxiety of a loving fear which the Holy Ghost inspires. Finally, we find ardent, generous and burning desires which, by making straight God's paths, hasten the hour of the King's happy coming.

Again, meditation is, with respect to the soul, like the dialogue between Rebecca and the faithful servant who came to

---

[4] Quasi sponsam ornatam monilibus suis (Isa., lxi, 10).

[5] Induit se vestimentis jucunditatis suæ, induitque sandalia pedibus suis, assumpsitque dextraliola, et lilia et inaures, et annulos et omnibus ornamentis suis ornavit se (Judith, x, 3).

propose to her the nuptials with Isaac. Nothing disheartens the bride elect; neither the long waiting, nor the difficulties of the journey, nor the dangers she may encounter: "*Vadam*, I will go,"[6] she says, "I will follow the Holy Spirit—the Divine Eleazer." And she starts off at once, but before reaching the end of her journey how many conversations must she have had about that longed for goal, and about the spouse whom she was to meet there?

The day will dawn at last when she will come into the presence of Isaac, even before reaching the house of the nuptials; but she will then be veiled. All this is mysteriously symbolic of what our destinies are to be. Yes, before meeting the Bridegroom, the bride is unveiled—she speaks freely with Eleazer about the Eternal Truth; but if, already in this life, leaving behind all images and figures, she meets the Spouse Himself, she quickly takes her veil and covers herself, for though she is in presence of her Lord, her eyes cannot behold Him: "Clouds and darkness are round about him."[7] But better, better far is it to be with Him, though without sight, than to contemplate the most vivid images of His beauty.

It is thus that after having gone forth to meet the soul whom He has chosen, after having stooped to her, after having found in her an ardent desire for Him, a constant watchfulness for Him, the heavenly King, in His turn, fulfils in her regard all the promises contained in the Rite of the Consecration of Virgins. He raises her up to Himself and grants her, as far as may be in this life, the experience of eternal good things. Then, also, she becomes more powerful over the Heart of God; her prayer is at once more elevated and universal. Henceforth she embraces in her petitions the interests of her Spouse in all their universality; for the Holy Spirit addresses every consecrated soul in the words of Mardochai to Esther: "Think not that thou

---

[6] Gen., xxiv, 58.

[7] Nubes et caligo in circuitu ejus (Ps., xcvi, 2).

mayest save thy life only, because thou art in the king's house, more than all the Jews: for if thou wilt now hold thy peace, the Jews shall be delivered by some other occasion: and thou and thy father's house shall perish. And who knoweth whether thou art not therefore come to the kingdom, that thou mightest be ready in such a time as this?"[8]

In point of fact, in order to escape death, it is not enough to be in the king's house; the queen cannot disown her race, she must labour to save it if she desires to secure her own safety. Here lies the whole secret of a vocation higher than that of other men; if the soul thus chosen for divine espousals either shrink back or shut herself up in cold egotism, God will easily find another fulcrum, other souls more generous and faithful, to whom He will confide the carrying out of His work. Do not these threatening words point to the decline of religious Orders? The members having failed in their mission, God, as a punishment for their failure, at last deprives them of their ancient appenage, and bestows it upon more fervent souls.

But the true Esther does not fail in her duty. Prepared by fasting and prayer she goes to the King, and finds favour in His eyes. "What wilt thou, Queen Esther? What is thy request? If thou shouldst even ask one half of the kingdom, it shall be given to thee."[9] And the most prudent princess, whose ambition is unlimited and who knows the power of love, beseeches her lord that he would deign to come and sit at her table: "If it please the king, I beseech thee to come to me this day, and

---

[8] Ne putes quod animam tuam tantum liberes, quia in domo regis es, præ cunctis Judæis; si enim nunc silueris, per aliam occasionem liberabuntur Judæi, et tu, et domus patris tui, peribitis. Et quis novit utrum idcirco ad regnum veneris, ut in tali tempore parareris? (Esth., iv, 13, 14).

[9] Quid vis, Esther regina? Quæ est petitio tua? Etiam si dimidiam partem regni petieris, dabitur tibi (Esth., v, 3).

Aman with thee to the banquet which I have prepared." [10]

Let us take notice that Esther invites the king to come to her, and that she does not ask to go to him: it is a figure of the present life, during which the soul aspires to possess her Lord already before her entrance into eternity. It is to a banquet that she invites Him, with the determination of inebriating Him with the wine of love and of not allowing the presence of her enemy Aman to hinder her from so doing. Thus, even here on earth, the demon has no power to hinder from true contemplation a soul generously devoted to God; all his vain efforts simply make his own condemnation the heavier. Aman's presence does not prevent the holy inebriation of the king, nor his ineffable complacency in the bride who has won his heart. Esther is not intimidated nor silenced nor impeded in her designs; nothing comes of Aman's presence but a more shameful fall and a more humiliating defeat for the enemy.

All this is what happens on earth whenever a Spouse of our Lord, faithful to her vocation and using all the means of sanctification which she has in her power, intervenes to make intercession for the salvation of souls, this being the fruit, the pledge and the reward of her union with our Lord Jesus Christ.

---

[10] Si regi placet, obsecro ut venias ad me hodie, et Aman tecum, ad convivium quod paravi (*Ibid,* v, 4).

CHAPTER XIII
Our external enemies and our Angelic Protectors

IFE on earth is but a passing trial intended for our merit, that is to say, to furnish us with the means of giving to God a pledge of our faithfulness. We must not seek in it anything stable, perfect or final, nor be astonished to meet with certain stumbling blocks on our way. Besides the weaknesses to which all creatures are subject, and the special dangers resulting from the fall of our first parents, we have also to conquer an antagonist who is very strong, very crafty and full of hatred. It is of him that it behoves us to speak, as of the external enemy of our salvation.

To deny that there is a devil is impossible, for the holy Scriptures everywhere prove his existence and action. But we must at least know him in order to combat him well, to unmask and overcome him; this is God's own victory while at the same time it is ours.

Lucifer—this is the name of his original splendour—was by God created in magnificence, and according to the Prophet Ezechiel, with a perfect impress of the divine likeness: "Thou wast the seal of resemblance, full of wisdom and perfect in beauty."[1] Destined to be filled with the very fulness of God, "thou wast in the pleasures of the paradise of God;" clothed with all gifts of nature and of grace, as with a priceless garment to enhance his beauty, Lucifer's creation was like a feast full of harmony: "Thou a cherub stretched out, and protecting, and I

---

[1] Tu signaculum similitudinis, plenus sapientia et perfectus decore (Ezech., xxviii, 12).

set thee in the holy mountain of God, thou hast walked in the midst of the stones of fire. Thou wast perfect in thy ways from the day of thy creation, until iniquity was found in thee."[2]

So then, in this creature so high, so perfect, iniquity was found, although no external agent had provoked him to revolt. But his heart was lifted up, saying: "I am God, and I sit in the chair of God in the heart of the sea."[3] Under these mysterious words a well-founded tradition admits that God made known to Lucifer His design of creating the human race and of exalting one of its members to hypostatic union with the Second Person of the Holy Trinity. At this revelation of the mystery of the Incarnation Lucifer contemplated himself, and pride burst forth from the depths of his splendid being; he could not endure that any other creature than himself should contract so close a union with God, and refusing to obey the divine command made known to us by St. Paul, "And again, when he bringeth in the first-begotten into the world, he saith: And let all the angels of God adore him,"[4] he set himself in revolt against God and in hatred of the privileged race.

Chastisement followed the revolt; and he who protected all the rest in the amplitude of his power was hurled down from the holy mountain, and the Lord said to him: "I will bring forth a fire from the midst of thee to devour thee, and I will make thee as ashes upon the earth in the sight of all that see thee."[5]

---

[2] Tu cherub extentus et protegens, et posui te in monte sancto Dei, in medio lapidum ignitorum ambulasti. Perfectus in viis tuis a die conditions tuæ, donec inventa est iniquitas in te (Ezech. xxviii, 14, 15).

[3] Deus ego sum, et in cathedra Dei sedi in corde maris (Ezech. xxviii, 2).

[4] Et cum iterum introducit primogenitum in orbem terræ, dicit: Et adorent eum omnes angeli Dei (Heb., I, 5).

[5] Producam ergo ignem de medio tui, qui comedat te, et dabo te in cinerem super terram in conspectu omnium videntium te (Ezech., xxvii, 18).

Drawing after him many legions of angels, who formed his cursed army and his dark empire, Lucifer could find no rest but in an insatiable desire to frustrate God's designs and thwart His plans; whereas the glorious Michæl and his faithful phalanxes, acquiescing in the eternal decrees, strove to second with all their burning charity that work by excellence, the Incarnation of the Word.

But it is well to sketch precisely the appearance of Lucifer, now become Satan. Sisara is one of his types, by the burning thirst which, being pursued by the Hebrews, he experienced, and which brought about his ruin, for entering the tent of Jahel for refreshment, he was killed by the hand of this valiant woman. Goliath describes better still his infernal physiognomy. He is a giant, so strong and powerful is his nature; but the Scripture gives him the only epithet that befits him, *Vir spurius*. He abuses his strength, and thinks to conquer by terror. The one who is to overcome him is young and delicate; he is the last in his family, a little one, and scarcely counting among his brethren; yet when in presence of the giant and hearing his threats he resolves to fight him. But refusing ordinary armour, and despising human means, he places his confidence in God only, and is content with a little stone out of the brook to overthrow him whose strength defied the most valiant.[6]

In the Book of Judith Satan appears under the figure of Holofernes. Here again it is brute force persuaded that nothing can stand against it; but overcome by beauty, it is taken in the snare, as the holy widow of Bethulia sings in her immortal Canticle: "Her sandals ravished his eyes, her beauty made his soul her captive, with a sword she cut off his head."[7] Thus it is that the demon, while striving to capture the race, adorned with grace and beauty for the eternal nuptials, is himself ruined; and

---

[6] 1 Reg., xvii.

[7] Sandalia ejus rapuerunt oculos ejus, pulchritudo ejus captivam fecit animam ejus; amputavit pugione cervicem ejus (Judit xvi, 11).

it is a woman, proclaimed *Benedicta a Deo suo*,[8] that strikes the mortal blow.

Again, Aman is a type of the enemy of mankind who has sworn its ruin. Esther, to whom it is said: "Thou shalt not die; for this law is not made for thee, but for all others"[9]—Esther obtains favour for her people and the death of Aman. She triumphs and saves those belonging to her, not by the sword, but by her unrivalled beauty.

In all these figures we see Satan, though strong, powerful and formidable by nature, always overcome by the weak, the unarmed, provided that they put their confidence in God. In fact we clearly see that by the weakest instruments our Lord takes pleasure in overthrowing his pride to humble him the more.

This combat is indeed willed by God; the glory accruing to Him from it has a special relish, as we gather from the first chapters of the Book of Job. There it is not beauty, nor the sword, nor the sling that triumphs over the enemy; it is suffering and patience, carried even unto heroism. Therefore God seems desirous of rewarding Job's fidelity, even before giving him back his possessions, by allowing him to see the enemy against whom he had been fighting in his trials, and by revealing to him under the mysterious form of two monsters, Behemoth and Leviathan, the extent of Satan's infernal power, God brings them before Job, saying: "Behold Behemoth, whom I have made with thee."[10] He is a mere creature, like thyself, in spite of his extraordinary terrifying power. Created in the beginning, he was once God's masterpiece; but since his fall any one may easily lay hold of him. And so of Leviathan, the monster of pride, as Behemoth is the monster of brutality. Man

---

[8] Benedicta a Deo suo (Judith xiii, 23).

[9] Non morieris; non enim pro te, sed pro omnibus hæc lex constituta est (Esth. xv, 13).

[10] Ecce Behemoth, quem feci tecum (Job xl, 10).

has received power to bring him low, according to God's word: "Will he make many supplications to thee, or speak soft words to thee?" "Lay thy hand upon him: remember the battle, and speak no more. Behold his hope shall fail him, and in the sight of all he shall be cast down."[11]

While despising this monster the Holy Spirit reveals his terrible nature, adding by way of conclusion: "There is no power upon earth that can be compared with him who was made to fear no one. He beholdeth every high thing, he is king over all the children of pride."[12] This description of Satan's power can neither disconcert nor surprise the servants of God. By nature they are very much inferior to him, but their superiority by grace gives them incomparable advantages over him, and their union with God communicates to them a supernatural force capable of withstanding the whole power of hell.

Moreover this power is limited; our soul is a sanctuary guarded by the will, and no one by violence can enter there. The father of lies cannot act directly upon the superior part of our soul; he can affect it only by a kind of reverberation. His temptations tell only upon the sensitive part, which part he basely strives to turn to profit in order thus to trouble the understanding and the will.

Hence in our Lord's temptation, to which we shall return in detail, Satan seeks to stir up the three vulnerable sides of man which St. John thus points out: "For all that is in the world, is the concupiscence of the flesh, the concupiscence of the eyes

---

[11] Numquid multiplicabit ad te preces, aut loquetur tibi mollia? . . . Pone super cum manum tuam; memento belli, nec ultra addas loqui. Ecce, spes ejus frustrabitur cum, et videntibus cunctis præcipitabitur (Job xl, 22, 27, 28).

[12] Non est super terram potestas quæ comparetur ei, qui factus est ut nullum timeret. Omne sublime videt. Ipse est rex super universes filios superbiæ (Job xli, 24, 25).

and the pride of life, which is not of the Father but is of the world."[13] In our Divine Lord the devil could find no auxiliary; but for us the danger lies much less in the attacks of the enemy than in our own infirmity. However furious may be his assaults, he is extremely weak when he no longer finds anything to take hold of within.

It is therefore of primary importance that the rupture between us and Satan should be complete, and that the soul should become his resolute antagonist. Conciliation with him is out of the question; we must either conquer or become the victim of that enemy whom our Lord treated as a murderer: "He was a murderer from the beginning, and he stood not in the truth, because truth is not in him. When he speaketh a lie, he speaketh of his own, for he is a liar, and the father thereof."[14]

When the Church begins to exercise her action upon a human being, her first care is to snatch him from the tyranny of Satan, in virtue of the power she has received from her Head, and to burst asunder the bonds which by original sin have been twined round the creature. The strong formula of the exorcisms are so important that if Baptism has been administered in haste, it is required, in supplying the ceremonies of this Sacrament, that the exorcisms should be used, in spite of the inversion of order that it causes, when the regeneration has once taken place. The Church moreover wishes that the baptized Christian should by his sponsors make a solemn promise to renounce the devil with all his works and pomps—a promise from which he can never free himself without committing either perjury or apostasy. It is only on this condition that the soul can be

---

[13] Quoniam omne quod est in mundo concupiscentia carnis est, et concupiscentia oculorum, et superbia vitas; qua; non est ex Patre, sed ex mundo est (i Joann, ii, 16).

[14] Ille homicida erat ab initio, et in veritate non stetit, quia non est veritas in eo: cum loquitur mendacium, ex propriis loquitur, quia mendax est a pater ejus (Joann., viii, 44).

regenerated and made a child of God.

Knowing this, why should we be astonished that the Church forbids, under the severest penalties, all voluntary communication with Satan? But on the other hand how can we explain the fact that Christians, who have no wish to apostatize, should nevertheless yield to an unhealthy curiosity, and under futile pretexts, in which levity vies with ingratitude, should presumptuously make experiments which are as hurtful to their health of body as they are detrimental to their health of soul. This strange conduct marks a total absence of the Christian sense, and it cannot possibly be justified by love of science.

The Church, while transmitting to all her ministers, from the Order of Exorcists, the power which she has received against Satan, does not without a positive mandate permit them to use this power, so well does she know the danger of coming in contact with the demons.

The infraction of these rules, which we would willingly call hygienic, is punished in many ways. The enemy takes care to reward the curiosity of the disobedient by an unexpected loss of balance, a loss which is at once both the necessary preliminary and the consequence of these practices, by strange illnesses, disorders of the brain and suicidal tendencies—evils which are by no means rare in these our days. All this is the outcome of voluntary intercourse with the demon, even when such intercourse is looked upon as nothing more than an experiment for arriving at the knowledge of a hidden and not fully defined power. The Church, on the contrary, in her maternal anxiety for our true interests, beseeches God in her beautiful collect for the seventeenth Sunday after Pentecost, that we may be delivered from all unwholesome intercourse: "Grant to Thy people, we beseech Thee, O Lord, to avoid the defilements of the devil, and with a pure mind to follow Thee, the only God."[15]

But there are combats with the demon which St. Paul points out as inevitable; they are involuntary on our part, and decreed by God for a salutary end: "For our wrestling is not against flesh and blood, but against principalities and powers, against the rulers of the world of darkness, against the spirits of wickedness in the high places. Therefore take unto you the armour of God, that you may be able to resist in the evil day, and stand in all things perfect."[16] For these struggles we have the requisite grace, and temptation is one of the means of attaining glory: "God hath tried them, and found them worthy of Himself."[17] God wishes to be the object of man's election and choice before bestowing His own beatitude upon him; the soul must have said at her own cost: "My Beloved is white and ruddy, chosen out of thousands."[18]

Temptation is not a consequence of the first fall, for Adam did not escape it in the state of original justice. It is even customary with the demon to rage most cruelly against the most beautiful and pure; hence making his way into the "Garden of delights," and contemplating our first parents in the splendour of their fresh beauty, he could find no rest till he had brought about their ruin.

Therefore, taking the woman by surprise, he said to her: "Why hath God commanded you, that you should not eat of

---

[15] Da quæsumus Domine populo tuo diabolica vitare contagia, et te solum Deum pura mente sectari.

[16] Quoniam non est nobis colluctatio adversus carnem et sanguinem, sed adversus principes et potestates adversus mundi rectores tenebrarum harum, contra spiritualia nequitiæ, in coelestibus. Propterea accipite armaturam Dei, ut possitis resistere in die malo, et in omnibus perfecti stare (Eph., vi, 12, 13).

[17] Deus tentavit eos, et invenit illos dignos se (Sap., iii, 5).

[18] Dilectus meus candidus et rubicundus, electus ex millibus (Cant., v, 10).

every tree of Paradise?"[19] In his first words the enemy shows his spirit of contention and pride: "*Cur?*—Why?" He calls God to account for what He had ordained, seeking to provoke in Eve's heart ungrateful curiosity and inordinate desire. The snare was a gross one. If Eve had been generous, she would have answered, like the leader of the heavenly hosts: "Quis ut Deus?—Who is like unto God?" But she consented to parley with the enemy, whose audacious language ought to have repulsed and disgusted her. The demon, feeling the advantage he has so speedily gained, profits by it to lie boldly: "No, you shall not die the death. . . . You shall be as gods, knowing good and evil."[20]

To be as gods! Such was the enviable lot reserved for man through his brotherhood with the Messias, and this was the very thing that the demon would hinder by his lies, when he deceived our first mother. But neither human weakness nor satanic malice could frustrate the divine plan. God foreknew all: "I will put enmities between thee and the woman, and thy seed and her seed: she shall crush thy head, and thou shalt lie in wait for her heel."[21] The demon's apparent success has but created a new abyss between himself and man, and prepared the way for his own irremediable ruin. In vain will his persevering efforts prevail to bring about revolt and corruption through successive generations; the divine plan will take its course. At the moment foreseen from all eternity, the miry flood of defilement will be stopped in its course; and by miraculous preservation, the Virgin, the Woman predestined to crush the

---

[19] Cur præcepit vobis Deus ut non comederetis de omni ligno paradisi? (Gen., iii, 2).

[20] Nequaquam morte moriemini . . . et eritis sicut dii, scientes bonum et malum (Gen., iii, 4, 5).

[21] Inimicitias ponam inter te et mulierem, et semen tuum et semen illius; ipsa conteret caput tuum, et tu insidiaberis calcanco ejus (Gen. iii, 15).

dragon's impure head will rise up all radiant and immaculate. Satan had thought to subject to his empire every member of the execrated race, and behold, the very one whom it concerned him most to strike secretly escapes.

In vain has the enemy been watching for four thousand years all the avenues by which the Lord might come, heaping up rottenness and poison, in order to repulse supreme holiness; behold God is made man: *Verbum caro factum est et habitavit in nobis.*[22] He comes so humbly, so prudently, that the mystery escapes the notice of the fallen cherub: "For while all things were in quiet silence, and the night was in the midst of her course, Thy almighty Word leapt down from heaven from Thy royal throne, as a fierce conqueror into the midst of the land of destruction."[23]

The life of the Word on earth ran its course of thirty years in silence and mystery, as it had begun; then for our consolation, the Son of man began His public life by allowing the demon to approach His adorable Person; he made use of those perfidious insinuations by which he had most frequently succeeded in dragging men into the abyss of hell.

There again Satan betrays himself by his own words. Every detail of this immortal page of the Gospel must be examined. In the first place, here as always, God permits the temptation and appoints its place, its extent and its duration: "Jesus was led by the Spirit into the desert, to be tempted by the devil."[24] The three Evangelists who speak of the temptation are unanimous in saying that Jesus was impelled by the Holy Spirit. We are

---

[22] Joann., I, 14.

[23] Cum enim quietum silentium contineret omnia, et nox in suo curso medium iter haberet, omnipotens sermo tuus et coelo, a regalibus sedibus, durus debellator in mediam exterminii terram prosilivit (Sap., xviii, 14, 15).

[24] Jesus ductus est in desertum a Spiritu, ut tentaretur a diabolo (Matth. iv, i).

never given up at random to the blind rage and power of our enemy. He who is the Creator of angels and of men is the supreme regulator of the struggle, and according to the promise of His Apostle: "God is faithful, who will not suffer you to be tempted above that which you are able: but will make also with temptation issue, that you may be able to bear it."[25] This truth of faith is our strength.

We learn another lesson from our Lord's temptation; it is that the demon chooses the moment when his experience and high intelligence lead him to presume that we are most vulnerable. This is one of his cowardly tricks, which our Lord discloses to us. St. Luke says that, after fasting forty days and forty nights, our Lord was hungry. The tempter knew this circumstance, just as he can by observation know many details of our lives; and he wished to find out whether he was treating with an ordinary man by provoking Christ's sensible appetite: "If thou be the Son of God, command that these stones be made bread."[26] But instead of finding a frail man, Satan strikes against the deep treasury of Eternal Wisdom and without unveiling the mystery which shrouds Him, Jesus borrows from Holy Scripture the answer against temptation: "It is written, not in bread alone doth man live, but in every word that proceedeth from the mouth of God."[27] Our Lord has no need to answer whether He is the Son of God, nor to work a miracle; it suffices for the demon to know that man can conquer sensuality by grace, which leads him to seek a higher life. Adam had suffered himself to be conquered by sensuality, it was fitting that the new Adam should break this charm and free us from it by an

---

[25] Fidelis autem Deus est qui non patietur vos tentari supra id quod potestis; sed faciet etiam cum tentatione proventum, ut possitis sustinere (1 Cor. x, 13).

[26] Si Filius Dei es, duc ut lapides isti panes fiant (Matth., iv, 3).

[27] Scriptum est: non in solo pane vivit homo, sed in omni verbo quod procedit de ore Dei (Matth., iv, 4).

astounding victory.

The tempter, though repulsed, did not lose hope, but setting our Lord upon the pinnacle of the temple made a new trial: "If Thou be the Son of God, cast Thyself down, for it is written: That He hath given His angels charge over Thee, and in their hands they shall bear Thee up, lest perhaps Thou dash Thy foot against a stone."[28] Here the demon hypocritically quotes the Scriptures, but after the fashion of heretics, he corrupts the true meaning. Never are the demons more dangerous and more obstinate than when they set themselves up as doctors. The Man God makes no answer to this false and lying science, but, without discussing and without even satisfying the secret curiosity of His adversary, He says: "It is written again: Thou shalt not tempt the Lord thy God."[29]

The more clearly Jesus of Nazareth manifested His sovereign wisdom and His sovereign holiness, the more the tempter was devoured by the desire of bringing Him under his power. But in His merciful goodness to us our Lord suffered the monster, blinded by his irrepressible pride, to proceed. Therefore, showing all the kingdoms of the earth and the glory thereof, as though they were his lawful possession and not the fruit of his rapine, the demon had the audacity to say to our Lord: "All these will I give Thee, if falling down Thou wilt adore me."[30]

This, in point of fact, was the object towards which Satan had always tended, in directing his efforts against individuals or against nations, and his success caused our Lord Himself to

---

[28] Si Filius Dei es, mitte te deorsum. Scriptum est enim: Quia Angelis suis mandavit de te, et in manibus tollent te, ne forte offendas ad lapidem pedem tuum (Matth., iv, 6).

[29] Rursum scriptum est: Non tentabis Dominum Deum tuum (Matth., iv, 7).

[30] Hæc omnia tibi dabo, si cadens adoraveris me (Matth., iv, 9).

name him "the prince of this world."[31] The Messias was to be adored as the Son of God, and he—Satan—purposed to arrogate to himself this honour. A summons such as this is always the last word in the devil's enterprises. But our Lord, without divulging mysteries, for His hour was not yet come, answered with almighty authority: "Begone, Satan, for it is written, the Lord thy God shalt thou adore, and Him only shalt thou serve."[32] "And all the temptation being ended, the devil departed from Him for a time."[33]

Our Lord had for ever struck down the power of hell, had laid open its intrigues, and obtained for His own devoted servants a special grace of strength which should enable them to sing with the royal Psalmist: "Blessed be the Lord my God, who teacheth my hands to fight and my fingers to war."[34] Their security was, moreover, to proceed from that formal assurance of their Divine Master: "In the world you shall have distress; but have confidence, I have overcome the world."[35]

From our Lord's conduct towards the enemy we must gather another lesson, which will be most useful for our guidance in the struggle. In time of temptation men must not slop to parley with the demon; a few short words from holy Scripture, a few energetic interior acts suffice. If we engage in long conversation, Satan, who is cleverer than we are, will find a hundred reasons for drawing us over to his side.

In one special circumstance related in the Gospel this

---

[31] Princeps hujus mundi (Joann, xii, 31).

[32] Vade, Satana, scriptum est enim: Dominum Deum tuum adorabis, et illi soli servies (Matth. iv, 10).

[33] Et consummata omni tentatione, diabolus recessit ab illo usque ad tempus (Luc. iv, 13).

[34] Benedictus Dominus Deus meus, qui docet manus meas ad proelium, et digitos meos ad bellum (Ps. cxliii).

[35] In mundo pressuram habebitis; sed confidite, ego vici mundum (Joann, xvi, 33).

vigorous way of acting is brought before us. The Apostle St. Peter had just made his magnificent confession of the Divinity of his Master, and had received, as the reward of his faith, the power of the keys; then, on hearing our Saviour speak of His coming Passion, he yielded for a moment to a diabolical suggestion, and said: "Lord, be it far from Thee, this shall not be unto Thee."[36] Put our Lord, seeing the enemy behind His apostle, did not hesitate harshly to repulse tile author of the temptation without noticing the intervening person: "Go behind Me, Satan, thou art a scandal unto Me; because thou savourest not the things that are of God, but the things that are of men";[37] thus teaching us to repel temptation even when it is concealed under an unusual and beloved form. This made the glorious Patriarch St. Benedict say in his Rule: "Presently by the remembrance of Christ to put away any evil thoughts which may enter into his heart and to dash them against Christ."[38]

Therefore from what has been said, let us draw the conclusion that when temptation is violent and sudden, it must be resisted promptly and energetically. But it does not always take this form and the danger is not less, when the enemy, taking advantage of our levity and sloth, softly and gently insinuates his temptations. As a preservative against these our Lord said to His apostles: "Watch ye, and pray that ye enter not into temptation. The spirit indeed is willing, but the flesh is weak."[39] Watchfulness and prayer are the arms which prevent the temptation from entering; for if by the help of our torpor it succeeds in creeping in, it has already become master of the

---

[36] Absit a te, Domine; non erit tibi hoc (Matlh. xvi, 22).

[37] Vade post me, Satana, scandalum es mihi, quia non sapis ea quæ Dei sunt, sed ea quæ hominum (Matth. xvi, 23).

[38] Cogitationes malas cordi suo advenientes mox ad Christum allidere (S. Reg., cap. Iv, 50).

[39] Vigilate et orate, ut non intretis in tentationem. Spiritus quidem promptus est, caro autem infirma (Matth., xxvi, 41).

position almost before we are aware of its presence. Watchfulness is the sentinel of the soul warning her of approaching danger, while prayer keeps the heart closely united to God, our true Tower of strength. If Peter had kept close to his Master, he would never have denied Him; but he followed from afar: "But Peter followed afar off."[40] A soul that does not pray follows our Lord afar off, and she is always in danger.

Hence later on the Prince of the Apostles will tell his convert Christians to "be sober and watch, because the devil, as a roaring lion, goeth about, seeking whom he may devour. Whom resist ye, strong in faith."[41] The imagery is of striking energy. As long as the lion is young it roams about the wilderness, and finds abundant prey; but when it grows old it can no longer wander so far, and hence in the dark hours of the night it comes prowling round inhabited places, seeking a more easy prey. Woe betide the man or the beast that ventures outside the walls! He is at once spied by the monster lying in wait, seized, mercilessly dragged into the forest and devoured. Faith is our defence, because it makes us cling to God, and anchors us fast to the Rock which is Christ, where we are in perfect safety.

It is well to observe that the enemy is very seldom allowed to take us by surprise. In spite of his powerful intelligence, in spite of his experience, his acquired knowledge and his keen observation, the darkness in which he moves often causes him to be deceived. Nevertheless, if he succeeds once, we may be sure that he will return by the same way: "When an unclean spirit is gone out of a man, he walketh through places without water, seeking rest; and not finding, he saith: I will return into

---

[40] Petrus sequabatur a longe (Luc., xxii, 54).

[41] Sobrii estote et vigilate, quia adversarius vester diabolus tamquam leo rugiens circuit, quærens quem devoret: cui resistite fortes in fide (1 Pet., v, 8, 9).

my house whence I came out. And when he is come, he findeth it swept and garnished. Then he goeth and taketh with him seven other spirits more wicked than himself, and entering in they dwell there. And the last state of that man becomes worse than the first."[42] Our Lord did not speak these words to discourage us, but to urge us to strengthen our weak point, which is sure to be first attacked, and which the demon is well acquainted, with having already gained an entrance by that way. If he find this door, hitherto open to him, now well closed, he will make a great uproar there; he will prowl about, and force hard; he will bring up reinforcements in order to gain his ground. Let him do as he likes and let us put in practice that teaching of the apostle St. James: "Be subject therefore to God, but resist the devil, and he will fly from you."[43]

It is a certain and most consoling truth that nothing in the world has power to snatch us from God: "For I am sure that neither death, nor life, nor angels .... nor any other creature shall be able to separate us from the love of God, which is in Christ Jesus our Lord,"[44] says the Apostle who had often had occasion to experience it. But our certainty increases notably from the fact that we lay aside the works of darkness to put on the armour of light. We cannot too often repeat that the enemy's whole strength depends chiefly on our own connivance, as St. Austin says: "He can bark, he can entice, he

---

[42] Cum immundus spiritus exierit de homine, ambulat per loca inaquosa, quærens requiem; et non inveniens dicit: Revertar in domum meam unde exivi. Et cum venerit, invenit eam scopis mundatam et ornatam. Tunc vadit, et assumit septem alios spiritus secum, nequiores se, et ingressi habitant ibi (Luc., xi, 24-26).

[43] Subditi ergo estote Deo; resistite autem diabolo, et fugiet a vobis (Jac., iv, 7).

[44] Certus sum enim, quia neque mors, neque vita, neque angeli .... neque creatura alia poterit nos separare a caritate Dei quæ est in Christo Jesu, Domino nostro (Rom. viii, 28-39).

can bite only those that will to be bitten."[45] If in all circumstances we are careful to cover ourselves with the shield of faith we become invulnerable: "In all things taking the shield of faith, wherewith you may be able to extinguish all the fiery darts of the most wicked one."[46]

We may notice that proud, obstinate characters that are harsh towards their neighbours, lend themselves to the enemy by a kind of affinity, and give him a hold; whereas he has a horror of humility, of wise condescension, and of kindness. In no other way did the most amiable Virgin Mary, Mother of God, escape his malice; hence she sings: "He hath scattered the proud in the conceit of their heart. . . . And hath exalted the humble."[47] One might say that Satan is so inflated with monstrous pride that he is absolutely incapable of grasping whatever is delicate and little. In the like manner poverty of spirit and abnegation, by despoiling us not only of all things, but of our very selves, make it impossible for the enemy to lay hold of us. For as in olden time the wrestler during the games laid aside his garments for the contest, the better to escape his adversary, so the soul, truly stripped of all things by renouncement and brought to perfect simplicity, easily preserves herself from the demon, who has no longer anything by which to hold her.

The atmosphere in which Satan enfolds himself, which goes before and follows him, is composed of trouble, melancholy and darkness, of which he is the "prince." We may say that he lives in sadness, whilst serenity, peace, supernatural joy cultivated within us as a virtue, repel him, just as the dawn of morning

---

[45] Latrare potest, sollicitare potest, mordere omnino non potest, nisi volentem (Aug. *De Civit. Dei*, lib. XX, cap. viii).

[46] In omnibus sumentes scutum fidei, in quo possitis omnia tela nequissimi ignea exstinguere (Eph. vi, 16).

[47] Dispersit superbos mente cordis sui . . . et exaltavit humiles (Luc., i, 51, 52).

light puts to flight the birds of the night. Satan loves violent things, all that is pushed to extremes, even in good; his preferences are all for excess. The axiom, *In medio stat virtus*, seems made to combat him; measure, that which the Ancients prized so highly and called discretion, breaks up all his force and brings him down; moreover, it is for this reason that in the Scriptures we are so frequently recommended to be sober.

The demon seeks as much as possible to destroy the equilibrium in our nature, which indeed is composite, but which was created in order and full of harmony and beauty; for having once established disorder, he knows that he can with more chance of success hazard a battle. This is what we see in the Gospel, where it would seem that our Lord begins the cure of all the sick presented to Him by casting out a diabolical influence, as being the root of the malady that He is going to cure. Evidently there are sicknesses which have another origin; but we cannot deny that, on account of the Word Incarnate, the demon hates our bodies almost as much as he hates our souls, and when he does not succeed in destroying these bodies, he brings upon them all the evils that he possibly can.

We must also be persuaded of the fact that when Satan does not succeed in making us commit a fault he contents himself with hindering good. He derives more satisfaction from a single venial sin committed by a soul consecrated to God than from many crimes committed by persons upon whom he has some claim. Who does not remember the legend of the demon carried in triumph because he had succeeded in making a monk commit a slight fault? We must make up our minds to fight "by the armour of justice on the right hand and on the left,"[48] that is to say by practising virtues seemingly the most opposite. It is in the same sense that St. Paul again says: "For the weapons of our warfare are not carnal, but mighty to God unto the

---

[48] Per arma justitias a dextris et a sinistris (2 Cor. vi, 7).

pulling down of fortifications."[49]

As a general rule, the demon's influence is to be feared almost more than his positive temptations. The enemy's tactics consist in hiding himself behind thoughts which do not seem positively bad. He creates a vague feeling of sadness and discouragement; the soul does not perceive then that some one far different from the Spirit of God is inspiring her thoughts, judgments and appreciations, and if she has not yet learnt to know herself and to rule her passions, she will be especially liable to be dragged before long into the commission of grave sins.

The demon, moreover, delights in urging some persons to practise indiscreet mortifications, while he inspires others to take exaggerated care of their health. He falsifies our judgment by phantoms and mirages; he skilfully groups round about us a number of disagreeable circumstances, such as want of tact in our neighbours, awkwardnesses and the like; he creates misunderstandings, and scatters with a lavish hand discord and poisoned words; he wearies us out in the pursuit of mistaken tracks, and when we are completely exhausted he presents the real snare into which he has all along been intending to draw us.

In all temptations of this kind the demon's aim is to bring about a state of illusion, a kind of hallucination tending to put the soul in a false position, to induce her to do unfortunate acts which, without in themselves being culpable, may have disastrous consequences. In all these things Satan's object is to impede what is good, or what is better, by heaping up against God's designs obstacles which will cause great loss of time, and the removal of which will need great effort. He loves to retard God's works, to lessen them, yea, even to cause their failure through the very persons who were predestined to bring them

---

[49] Nam arma militias nostras non carnalia sunt, sed potentia Deo ad destructionem munitionum (2 Cor. x, 4).

about and who, thanks to his clever, insidious and captious influence, are the very ones to destroy them, even before they have been assaulted by a single real temptation. This is what the Holy Spirit puts before us in the following words: "For the bewitching of vanity obscureth good things, and the wandering of concupiscence overturneth the innocent mind."[50] This bewitchment is the work of one whom it behoves us boldly to face, in order to know him well and to constrain him to throw off the mask.

Our diabolical enemies are of every character and of varied force. There are those who simply annoy like flies; they are wearying, but they are not terrible; and there are those that are very dangerous, very tenacious and very wicked. They take upon themselves to meddle with science, cases of conscience, philosophy, theology and exegesis. They turn to interest the "pride of life—superbia vitæ and puff up the man with whom they measure their strength. Really, it would seem that they are skilfully selected according to the souls with which they have to fight. This is perhaps the meaning of those lines in the hymn of a Confessor:

> Calcavit hostem fortiter,
> Superbum ac satellitem.

But whether strong or weak, whether powerful or insignificant, without our connivance they can only help us to gain merit and promote our sanctification, if we are simple as doves and prudent as serpents.[51]

To brave this terrible enemy without relying upon God's strength is dangerous presumption; to have an excessive fear of him is want of faith and pusillanimity. We must neither see the demon everywhere, nor deny his existence; and since all the

---

[50] Fascinatio enim nugacitatis obscurat bona, et inconstantia concupiscentiæ transvertit sensum sine malitia (Sap., iv, 12).

[51] Estote ergo prudentes sicut serpentes, et simplices sicut columbæ (Matth., x, 16).

means of our sanctification are arms wherewith to combat him, and all that leads to holiness crushes him at our feet, we owe it to God to despise this monster from all the height, not of our personality, but of our Baptism.

Satan's tremendous pride is like that of Nabuchodonosor, who gave orders that, at the sound of trumpet and of flute, all under penalty of death should fall down and adore his statue. Such injunctions however blustering they may be, will not trouble those who follow the Apostle's advice to the Ephesians: "Give not place to the devil."[52] Do not in anything yield to him, give him no place, and as far as you can, ignore him completely, for the kind of contempt to which he is most sensible is an utter disregard of his orders, of his threats and of his uproars. The fathers of the desert were well acquainted with the plan of despising this lover of fuss and noise; and St. Teresa, after having prayed for the grace of always seeking her rest in God, adds: "Then I shall have nothing but contempt and disdain for all the demons, and they will be afraid of me. I do not understand those fears which cause us to exclaim: "The demon, the demon," when we can say: "O God, O God."[53]

We do not pretend to have exhausted this important subject; moreover it was requisite to limit ourselves to the most ordinary struggles which souls may have to maintain against the enemy. In the higher regions of the spiritual life the combat assumes a somewhat different aspect, and Satan, meeting an adversary who has become more spiritualized, throws off the mask, and shows himself more in all his ferocity and repulsive ugliness. But beginners need not be uneasy; so long as the devil can rely upon their bad habits as upon his secret correspondents enabling him to act in the soul, he contents himself with employing his most simple manoeuvres. When he can no longer hope for this concurrence and for the success of

---

[52] Nolite locum dare diabolo (Eph. iv, 27).

[53] Life of St. Teresa, xxv.

his weaker agents, then only does he rush to the assault with the superior demons and risk a struggle of spirit against spirit. When we come to speak of the purified soul that has become one with God, the explanation of this kind of trial will find its proper place.

We cannot conclude this chapter without saying a word on the heavenly spirits who take part in all our combats as friends and brethren; for we have not only the help of grace in our temptations, but God has commanded also His angels to watch over us "lest we dash our foot against a stone."[54]

Devotion to the holy angels is therefore an efficacious means for encouraging ourselves against that exaggerated terror of the devil with which our pusillanimity would inspire us. It is also a debt of justice and gratitude towards those blessed spirits who help us with so great solicitude. Their nature, equal to that of our enemies, has over these latter all the superiority which the supernatural order confers upon them. We shall never know all that we owe to their wise and fraternal love, nor how precious to us is their pure and blessed influence.

The Book of Tobias, which was written to make known some of these consoling secrets, also expresses the gratitude with which the witnesses of such great services were filled: "What can we give him sufficient for these things?"[55] said Tobias to his son. For in point of fact the archangel Raphæl, while fulfilling his mission, had not neglected to give material as well as spiritual help, watching with equal care over the goods of those committed to his charge, as over their souls and bodies, and strenuously defending them against the assaults of the demon.

And so it is with us through God's infinite goodness. The holy angels ward off material dangers, they suggest good inspirations and holy thoughts prolific in virtuous deeds.

---

[54] Ne forte offendas ad lapidem pedem tuum (Ps. xc, 12).

[55] Quid illi ad hæc poterimus dignun dare? (Tob. xii, 3).

Finally, when they carry our prayers before the throne of God,
they join their own supplications with them: "When thou didst
pray with tears, and didst bury the dead .... I offered thy prayer
to the Lord."[56] Also in the Apocalypse we read: "And another
angel came, and there was given to him much incense, that he
should offer of the prayers of all saints upon the golden altar,
which is before the throne of God. And the smoke of the
incense of the prayers of the saints ascended up before God
from the hand of the angel."[57] These words, as well as many
other passages of holy Scripture, teach that the holy angels
present our prayers to God, and transmit to men, who are
aspiring resolutely after an interior life, many lights which will
lead them to union with God. Jacob's vision of the mysterious
ladder reaching from earth to heaven, upon which angels were
descending and ascending, is an example of this. The Lord
Himself leaning upon the top of this ladder spoke to Jacob, who
when he awoke exclaimed in rapturous wonder: "Indeed the
Lord is in this place, and I knew it not."[58]

Might we not often repeat the same words, for we are
surrounded by the divine world, by the angelic world, and we
take no heed of it? It is good therefore for us to reanimate our
faith, and to call to mind the good things which we possess, as
also our helps on all sides. By this means we shall be enabled to
advance more joyfully in the spiritual life—feeling ourselves
supported and encouraged, as in very truth we are. Our
progress towards divine union is not an isolated one; many
companions escort us, help us and communicate to us the lights

---

[56] Quando orabas cum lacrymis, et sepeliebas mortuos ... ego obtuli
orationem tuam Domino (Tob., xii, 12).

[57] Et alius angelus venit . . . et data sunt illi incensa multa, ut daret
de oratibus sanctorum omnium super altare aureum, quod est
ante thronum Dei. Et ascendit fumus incensorum de oratibus
sanctorum de manu angeli coram Deo (Apo., viii, 3, 4).

[58] Vere Dominus est in loco isto, et ego nesciebam (Gen., xxviii, 16).

which they themselves receive direct from God.

This angelic intervention in the work of our purification, illumination and sanctification is brought before us in Scripture in the person of the Prophets. Was not Isaias among others the object of a mysterious purification by the ministry of a Seraphim, who revealed to him that the purity of spirits, whatever it may be, consists in a participation in the light and holiness of God? As St. Denis says: "God radiates upon inferior natures through superior natures; and to say all in one word, it is by the ministry of the highest powers that He comes forth from the depths of His adorable obscurity."[59]

Hence we can understand the unquestionable advantage souls aspiring to the Unitive life may gain by cultivating an intimacy with the heavenly spirits, either by thinking of them or by praying to them. The angels are as magnets drawing us to God, who is the powerful cause of all things, and the mysterious force which governs beings, which encompasses them and keeps them within due limits. They feel honoured in serving us for the sake of our Lord Jesus Christ, whose brethren we are, and whom they adored, loved and served during His mortal life as the cause of their first victory.

The mystery of the Incarnation is ever the reason of the continual struggle between the powers of darkness who would drag us into the abyss, and the heavenly powers who aim at transporting us into the never-failing light; but once again we cannot too strongly express how unequal these forces are, and also how easily our will, which is always seconded by grace, can obtain the victory. For the battle of which our earth is the theatre has all the elements of success which are found in heaven, where Michæl and his angels fight against the dragon and his agents; but these latter are the weaker: "And the great dragon was cast out, the old serpent, who is called the devil and Satan, who seduceth the whole world; and he was cast unto the

---

[59] Hier., Coeles., xiii.

earth, and his angels were thrown down with him. And I heard a loud voice in heaven saying: Now is come salvation and strength and the kingdom of our God, and the power of His Christ, because the accuser of our brethren is cast forth, who accused them before our God day and night."[60]

These combats in which we are so marvellously upheld are not, however, the only difficulties of our present life. God in other ways puts us to a further test, in order not to crown us until we have legitimately fought and until the work of our restoration is accomplished in Christ.

---

[60] Et projectus est draco ille magnus, serpens antiquus, qui vocatur diabolus et satanas, qui seducit universum orbem, et projectus est in terram, et qui seducit universum orbem, et projectus est in terram, et angeli ejus cum illo missi sunt. Et audivi vocem magnam in coelo, dicentem: nunc facta est salus, et virtus, et regnum Dei nostri, et potestas Christi ejus, quia projectus est accusator fratrum nostrorum, qui accusabat illos ante conspectum Dei nostri die ac nocte. (Apoc., xii, 9, 10).

CHAPTER XIV
Of the Interior Trials which form the Soul's First Purification

HE CONDITIONS under which our pilgrimage on earth must be accomplished expose all men to a certain amount of suffering and trial, which none can entirely escape. It is not merely the fact of the primeval fall and the necessary laws of expiation that subject us to many evils; the Christian has also to fill up in his flesh, according to the bold expression of St. Paul, what is wanting to the Passion of our Lord: "For which cause we faint not; but though our outward man is corrupted, yet our inward man is renewed day by day. For that which is at present momentary and light of our tribulation worketh for us above measure exceedingly an eternal weight of glory."[1] Writing to the Romans the Apostle from another point of view sets forth the same teaching: "And if sons, heirs also: heirs indeed of God, and joint heirs with Christ: yet so if we suffer with Him, that we may be also glorified with Him. For I reckon that the sufferings of this time are not worthy to be compared with the glory to come, that shall be revealed in us."[2]

Let us listen also to the prince of the apostles: "Greatly

---

[1] Propter quod non deficimus; sed licet is, qui foris est, noster homo corrumpatur, tamen is qui intus est renovatur de die in diem; id enim, quod in præsenti est momentaneum et leve tribulationis nostræ, supra modum in sublimitate æternum gloriæ pondus operatur in nobis (2 Cor., iv, 16, 17).

[2] Si autem filii, et hæredes, hæredes quidem Dei, cohæredes autem Christi, si tamen compatimur, ut conglorificemur. Exisitimo enim quod non sunt condignæ passiones hujus temporis ad futuram gloriam, quæ revelabitur in nobis (Rom., viii, 17, 18).

159

rejoice if now you must be for a little time made sorrowful in divers temptations: that the trial of your faith, much more precious than gold which is tried by the fire, may be found unto praise and glory and honour at the appearing of Jesus Christ, whom having not seen, you love; in whom also now, though you see Him not, you believe."[3]

Side by side with these general reasons, which make trial and sorrow necessities for all men, the holy Scriptures speak of special and, in some sort, privileged laws, which guide our Lord in the distribution of suffering. We know that there are sufferings which are a glory to man, sufferings which are not a chastisement: "Afflicted in few things, in many they shall be well rewarded, because God hath tried them and found them worthy of Himself."[4] Who does not remember that dramatic scene with which the Book of Job opens; the Lord boasting of the fidelity of His servant, says to the enemy: "Hast thou considered My servant Job, that there is none like him in the earth, a simple and upright man, and fearing God and avoiding evil? And Satan answering, said: Doth Job fear God in vain? Hast Thou not made a fence for him, and his house, and all his substance round about? . . . But stretch forth Thy hand a little and touch all that he hath, and see if he blesseth Thee not to Thy face. Then the Lord said to Satan: Behold, all that he hath is in thy hand: only put not forth thy hand upon his person."[5]

---

[3] In quo exsultabitis, modicum nunc si oportet contristari in variis tentationibus: ut probatio vestræ fidei, multo pretiosior auro quod per ignem probatur, inveniatur in laudem, et gloriam, et honorem, in revelatione Jesu Christi, quem cum non videritis, diligitis; in quem nunc quoque non videntes creditis (1 Pet. I, 6-8).

[4] In paucis vexation multis bene disponentur, quoniam Deus tentavit eos, et invenit illos dignos se (Sap. iii, 5).

[5] Numquid considerasti servum meum Job, quod non sit ei similis in terra, homo simplex et rectus ac timens Deum, et recedens a malo? Cui respondens Satan, ait: Numquid Job frustra timet Deum? Nonne tu vallasti eum, ac domum ejus, universamque substantiam per

And after a terrible enumeration of evils, the sacred text concludes: "In all these things Job sinned not by his lips, nor spoke he any foolish thing against God."[6]

Holy Tobias also was struck with blindness at the very moment when he was exercising heroic fidelity to God's law: "Now this trial the Lord therefore permitted to happen to him, that an example might be given to posterity of his patience, as also of holy Job. For whereas he had always feared God from his infancy, and kept His commandments, he repined not against God because the evil of blindness had befallen him; but continued immovable in the fear of God, giving thanks to God all the days of his life."[7] And when in their folly his friends mocked at his good works, he answered them: "Speak not so, for we are the children of saints, and look for that life which God will give to those that never change their faith from Him."[8]

Let us take notice how, in the light of faith, the trials of this life lose their terrible aspect. It seems as if the Holy Spirit would raise us above ourselves and inure us to war, by showing us the magnificence of the end to which we are tending. These trials are called by St. Paul "momentary and light"; the Book of

---

circuitum? . . . Sed extende paululum manum tuam, et tange cuncta quæ possidet, nisi in faciem benedixerit tibi. Dixit ergo Dominus ad Satan: Ecce universa quæ habet in manu tua sunt; tantum in eum ne extendas manum tuam (Job I, 8-12).

[6] In omnibus his non peccavit Job labiis suis neque stultum quid contra Deum locutus est. (Ibid., 22).

[7] Hanc autem tentationem ideo permisit. Dominus evenire illi, ut posterisdaretur exemplum patientiæ ejus, sicut et sancti Job. Nam cum ab infantia sub semper Deum timuerit, et mandata ejus custodierit, non est contristatus contra Deum quod plaga cæcitatis evenerit ei. Sed immobilis in Dei timore permansit, agens gratias Deo omnibus diebus vitæ suæ (Tob., ii, 12-14).

[8] Nolite ita loqui; quoniam filii sanctorum sumus, et vitam illam exspectamus quam Deus daturus est his qui fidem suam numquam mutant ab eo (Ibid., 17, 18).

Wisdom mentions the elect as "afflicted in few things," God seeming desirous of preventing us Christians from appearing doleful and victimized by giving us the sure hope of good things to come: "In every gift show a cheerful countenance, and sanctify thy tithes with joy."[9] God tries us only to correct, to heal and to save us; is it not just that we should receive from His fatherly hand with submission and calm serenity what He judges necessary for our sanctification?

There are also trials of another order; though not coming from external causes, they are yet not the interior trials of which we purpose to speak. They are the annoyances arising from our own physical or moral or intellectual weaknesses. Such a one is moved to impatience in consequence of a sanguine temperament or to sadness by a certain natural melancholy. All this is a source of trial which fidelity in God's service can sanctify and make meritorious. The same holds good with regard to certain defects, such as awkwardness, dulness or the like, which may be of immense profit to a soul that is truly humble, generous and perfectly resigned to receive everything from God's hand, confessing that she can lay claim to nothing.

Our very imperfections are a cause of suffering to us, but they are also a means of reform and correction when we do not cling to these defects. It is said that the most painful sting of the hornet is cured immediately if the insect can be killed and crushed upon the wound, for it carries within itself an antidote which is thus applied at once. It is by a like process that a very sensitive person may conquer his susceptibility and heal the wound by the very things that would have poisoned it, if he does but turn this sensitive disposition into an occasion of practising frequent acts of humility. Some one else is a lover of ease and comfort, and would be either dainty in point of food

---

[9] In omni dato hilarem fac vultum tuum, et in exsultatione sanctifica decimas tuas (Eccli xxxv, 11).

or over-particular about his personal convenience; but he generously falls in with the common life, and thus his natural imperfection is but an occasion of victory and merit.

We would say the same of intellectual weaknesses. To some persons a bad memory or slowness of wit, or little aptitude for study is a cause of suffering; but they resign themselves gently and humbly to be inferior to others because such is the will of God; here again is abundant matter for sanctification and an excellent cure for many illusions. In fact one thing which experience and divine light clearly show is that God always chooses for us the life which is best. In all those circumstances which do not come under our own control, why say: "If I were in such a place, I should be more recollected. ... If I had not such an employment, I should be more charitable. . . . Without this obstacle I should be more humble"? All these desires and many others of the kind are but idle dreams, and attempts to shelter our scant fidelity under the false idea of what we should be if circumstances were more to our liking.

The special trials of which we here intend to speak are of another character, and it is very important to have clear ideas about them. He who wishes to lead a truly spiritual life in order, even in this world, to attain union with God, places himself by these very aspirations, by these higher ambitions, upon a new ground. He resembles the sons of Zebedee who urged their mother to ask our Lord for a special place for them in His kingdom. Our Lord in His answer, "You know not what you ask,"[10] does not reproach them. He rather instructs them by those profound words. Might He not answer the same to each of us when there is question of spiritual good things? The sequel shows clearly the intention of our Divine Master.

"Can you drink the chalice that I shall drink?"[11] In the first

---

[10] Nescitis quid petatis (Matt., xx, 22).

[11] Potestis bibere calicem, quem ego bibiturus sum? (*Ibid.*, xx, 22).

place, our Lord asks this question of those who wish to be more closely united to Him than others. Now this "chalice" is nothing else than the interior trials of which we are treating. They caused our Lord Himself, in spite of His ardent desire to save us, to exclaim: "My soul is sorrowful even unto death; stay you here, and watch with Me."[12] James and John were then present, and they might have heard our Lord adding: "My Father, if it be possible, let this chalice pass from Me. Nevertheless not as I will, but as Thou wilt."[13] And yet there were no executioners present—there was no cross; our Lord was overwhelmed with a suffering that came entirely from His inmost soul.

The sons of Zebedee, who were sleeping during these dolorous hours, had heretofore answered generously: "*Possumus*—We can."

What an example for us, and also what an encouragement to trust ourselves to the loving Heart of our Saviour! For the Apostles were not faithful in the Garden of Olives; they could not watch even one hour with their Master. Thus we also are often courageous when the chalice is far off, and very cowardly when it comes nigh to our lips; but God in His unspeakable patience, waits for us and takes up again our foundation work.

In sufferings of this kind we must take care not to excite our Lord's compassion before His work is completed. There can be no mistake about it, certain graces which God gives to the soul are not necessary for salvation, but they must be obtained at a price. If we were to make too many difficulties, it might happen that, to spare our weakness, our Lord would let us fall back into a lower way. This, to the eye of faith, would be a terrible and irreparable misfortune.

But it may be said, What does it matter since that person

---

[12] Tristis est anima mea usque ad mortem; sustinete hic et vigilate mecum (Matth., xxvi, 38).

[13] Pater mi, si possibile est, transeat a me calix iste; verumtamen non sicut ego volo, sed sicut tu (*Ibid.*, 39).

will save his soul? True, but our understanding can never appreciate the superiority of a soul that might become the rival of the Cherubim or the Seraphim over one that can be assimilated only to the lower hierarchies. False modesty or the love of mediocrity cannot lawfully influence us in these matters.

We will therefore show when and how these trials appear, in what they consist and how the soul must behave herself in order not to impede God's action, and, by not impeding it, be enabled to advance.

Generally speaking interior trials do not come in the first stage of the spiritual life. In the beginning, God ordinarily draws souls by means of sensible consolations, similar to those mentioned in the first two chapters of the Canticle of Canticles. There all is serene, fresh and joyful as the dawn. If our Lord hides Himself, the soul still hears Him or at least sees Him "looking through the windows, looking through the lattices."[14] No trace of suffering appears as yet. But scarcely is that soul well established like a true dove in the cleft of the rock—that is to say, rooted in faith—than her Lord requires her to catch the little foxes and to destroy those thousand little passions which will persist in springing up again.

Soon a harder road opens out before her. At the very moment when she is more than ever inflamed with joy and consolation, and when her will is entirely given up to her Lord, behold He disappears. "In my little bed by night I sought Him whom my soul loveth: I sought Him, and found Him not."[15] It is in the very midst of the repose she was enjoying that the soul perceives that her Lord has gone. However she thinks it cannot really be so, and that she will soon discern His presence again.

---

[14] Respiciens per fenestras, prospiciens per cancellos (Cant, ii, 9).

[15] In lectulo meo per noctes, quæsivi quem diligit anima mea: quæsivi illum, et non inveni (Cant., iii, 1).

Finding however that the silence and solitude are indeed too real she sets out in search of Him, and her search is in vain. "I will rise," she says, "and will go about the city: in the streets and the broad ways I will seek Him whom my soul loveth. I sought Him, and I found Him not."[16] What a close search in mental prayer, in vocal prayer, in reading, in holy conversation! And the Lord does not show Himself, though the soul ceases not to love Him. Yea, she loves Him more purely than before, since she loves Him not merely for the joy of His presence.

Then she questions the watchmen—that is to say, those who are her guides: "Have you seen Him whom my soul loveth?"[17] But what can they answer? If it is our Lord's will to hide Himself, He will not let them know where He is, and they will have no power to change His way of acting. Therefore only when she has passed them by a little—when she has mortified the desire of too human a help—does our Lord show Himself again: "When I had a little passed by them I found Him whom my soul loveth. I held Him; and I will not let Him go, till I bring Him into the house."[18] How simple is this poor little one to think that she will hold Him so fast after her hard trial, that He will never again escape from her! Her inexperience makes her think that there has been some fault on her part, for she does not yet know the ways of God.

But another time the Lord, on His return, knocks at the door; and the soul, delaying perhaps too much in the sweetness of her devotion, fears that she will have to resume certain occupations from which she was glad to have been set free; in fact, she shows a certain love of self, such as heretofore our

---

[16] Surgam, et circuibo civitatem; per vicos et plateas quæram quem diligit anima mea; quæsivi illum, et non inveni (*Ibid.*, 2).

[17] Num quem diligit anima mea vidistis? (Cant., iii, 3).

[18] Paululum cum pertransissem eos, inveni quem diligit anima mea: tenui eum: nec dimittam donec introducam illum in domum (*Ibid.*, 4).

Lord either overlooked or excused. When at last she rises she finds that her Lord has passed on. "I sought Him, and found Him not; I called, and He did not answer me."[19] He now seems to have departed farther than on the first occasion. Prayer itself becomes difficult; the soul knows not whether she is heard by God.

She asks where her Lord is; she is answered by ill-treatment. Everything in her daily occupations becomes painful to her; they "take away her veil"—that is, her personality. Our Lord no longer tolerates a thousand imperfections which before He seemed to overlook. But in this anxious and painful state she is, without herself being aware of it, to be of great use to others. "I adjure you, O daughters of Jerusalem, if you find my Beloved, that you tell Him that I languish with love."[20] She does not think it necessary to name the person she is seeking; she thinks every one must know Him well enough. But by this very fact she provokes a question to which she gives a most ample reply; and before long, when her Lord returns, she will be able to present to Him those "daughters of Jerusalem" who, being inflamed with the desire of knowing Him, had sought Him with her.

We can but refer in a general way to these two passages of the Canticle which describe so admirably the trials of which we have spoken, and which are the means God uses to purify the soul in its inferior faculties. These sufferings are very different from those arising from our faults and imperfections, from cowardice or tepidity, or even from physical temperament; and nearly always they can be recognised by very clear signs.

Thus, while the soul no longer experiences either relish or consolation in the things of God, she finds none in human

---

[19] Quæsivi, et non inveni illum; vocavi, et non respondit mihi (Cant., v, 6).

[20] Adjuro vos, filiæ Jerusalem, si inveneritis dilectum meum, ut nuntietis ei quia amore langueo (Ibid., 8).

things; because God's intention is to purify her by weaning her from all satisfaction, and by putting obstacles in the way of any clinging to created things, whereas, if the dryness came from imperfections and faults, the soul would find a momentary joy in external distractions, and would succeed in satisfying her cravings outside of God.

Another feature of these trials is that, while they last, the thought of God is habitually accompanied by anxiety and a kind of painful solicitude. The soul sometimes also imagines that she is no longer serving God, but is rather going back because she feels no more relish for divine things. But this suffering proves precisely that her state does not arise from tepidity, since the character of tepidity is to have no anxiety about God's absence.

It is almost impossible that trials of this kind should not appear very early in the spiritual life, and they are a sign of the real advancement of a soul which our Lord is following up with special care. By their means He purifies her, transforms her, and prepares her for the enjoyment of graces which are truly excellent by raising her above the life of the senses: "The cause of this aridity," says St. John of the Cross, "is that God transfers to the spirit the good things and forces of the senses."[21]

Now it is very important not to hinder God's action, but with all our power rather to second it. Some souls will rarely experience these trials, and never for more than two or three days together; others will be under their empire for long weeks, entire months and even for years. All depends upon the good pleasure of our Lord, who alone knows our needs, as also what He intends to accomplish in us. Those who are forgetful of themselves, will pass sometimes with a light foot through these painful stages, how hard soever they may be; but those who cling too much to spiritual comfort will find them very severe,

---

[21] The Obscure Night, I, ix.

and indeed they are doubly so to them. These sufferings resemble somewhat the fire of purgatory, which burns only what it is intended to burn: a perfectly pure soul would pass through untouched.

While these trials last it is very important not to relax anything of our spiritual exercises under plea of unworthiness, and not to diminish our frequentation of the Sacraments. Far from shortening our private prayer, it would be well, after the example of our Lord, who in the hour of His agony "prayed the longer," to prolong it a few minutes. We must also be very generous in the practice of virtue, and hold fast to that exact fidelity which we imposed upon ourselves when we were drawn by sensible grace, for this is the only way of seconding the divine action. This requires great courage; for the more the soul tries to approach God, the more her sufferings increase; whereas, in other sufferings the soul can find consolation in flying to God for refuge.

It is, therefore, passively that the soul suffers in the trials which we have described, and this shows their high character, even when other sufferings of a lower kind may sometimes mingle with them; for we cannot too often repeat that in these matters strict categories and classifications must not be sought for. The science of the spiritual life, like every other science, has its laws; but experience soon shows that precise and exact classifications exist only in books, and that God's liberty, the multifarious working of external causes, the very different ways in which souls receive and make fruitful the grace of God, and also the uprisings of our evil nature, modify so greatly the features of each soul that the history of their supernatural life cannot be reduced to absolutely exact definitions.

CHAPTER XV
Of Contemplation

OD created man to know Him, to love Him and to serve Him, and thus to gain eternal life. There is a close link between these three acts; and, taken together, they lead to union with God—to that union which, as we have already said, every creature gifted with intelligence ought constantly to have in view as his one great end and aim, in order to cooperate with God's designs in the creation of man. Love begets perfection in the service of God: "If you love me, keep my commandments;"[1] but love is itself the offspring of knowledge: "I will not now call you servants: for the servant knoweth not what his lord doth."[2] One of the severest reproaches our Lord ever spoke to His disciples was this: "So long a time have I been with you: and have you not known me?"[3] A reproach too well deserved, for He had used every means to instruct them. When our Lord, who is the "Life Eternal" and the "Light of the world," appears in all His glory on the Day of Judgment He will have to make to many a similar reproach, for "The Light shone in darkness, and the darkness did not comprehend it."[4]

We see from this what contemplation is meant to do in the

---

[1] Si diligitis me, mandata mea servate (Joann., xiv, 15).

[2] Jam non dicam vos servos, quia servus nescit quid faciat dominus ejus (Joann., xv, 15).

[3] Tanto tempore vobiscum sum, et non cognovistis me? (Ibid., xiv, 9).

[4] Lux in tenebris lucet, et tenebræ eam non comprehenderunt (Joann., I, 5).

spiritual life; it raises us to the knowledge of God. Every Christian while yet in this life is called to the contemplation of God. We find Adam gifted with a very high and sublime contemplation when he came forth from the hands of his Creator, and had he not sinned, this gift would have remained with him as the clear dawn of the light of glory. Even after the fall all the saints of the Old Testament come before us as great contemplatives; and lest we should be tempted to think that the time devoted to this exercise is wasted and useless, our Lord taught positively that those who choose a life of contemplation choose the better part.

St. Paul was evidently referring to contemplative souls when he said to the Corinthians: "But we all, beholding the glory of the Lord with open face, are transformed into the same image from glory to glory, as by the Spirit of the Lord."[5] He thus assigned to contemplation its proper place in the work of our soul's perfection. The Fathers echo the teaching of the Apostles; to quote but one, St. Athanasius goes so far as to attribute the first sin to an interruption in the exercise of contemplation: "While the first man applied himself to God," he says, "and contemplated the Divinity, he turned his eyes away, and kept aloof from all corporeal things; but as soon as, yielding to the persuasion of the serpent, he ceased to think of God and to contemplate Him and began to apply himself to the consideration of himself, from that moment he let himself be carried away by the desire of earthly things, and he knew that he was naked, not so much by the want of garments as because he was deprived of the contemplation of divine things. Then he directed his mind to things opposed to the things of God, for he had no sooner abandoned the contemplation of his Creator than he fell down headlong into the inordinate desire of earthly

---

[5] Nos vero omnes revelata facie gloriam Domini speculantes, in eamdem imaginem transformamur a claritate in claritatem, tamquam a Domini Spiritu (2 Cor., iii, 18).

things."[6]

According to this teaching the life of our Lady, in order to be a most perfect life, such as it really was, could not have been other than a contemplative life, and this the Gospel narrative indicates in these words: "But Mary kept all these words, pondering them in her heart."[7] The Abbot of Cluny, St. Odilo, speaking of the Blessed Virgin Mary, said: "She gave herself up wholly to divine contemplation."[8] The Apostles established a separate order of deacons, that they might be able to give themselves to prayer as well as to the ministry of the word: "But we will give ourselves continually to prayer, and to the ministry of the word."[9] This of course did not exclude the deacons from contemplation, as the death of the glorious St. Stephen proves, preceded as it was by the admirable vision which he himself describes: "Behold, I see the heavens opened, and the Son of Man standing on the right hand of God."[10] As to the Apostles they never allowed their heavy cares and solicitudes to withdraw them from their communings with God. St. Peter's vision at the hour of Sext, at the very time of the vocation of the centurion Cornelius, and the avowal which St. Paul makes concerning the great revelations he received in his intimate communication with God, clearly show that these men of colossal holiness lived in the highest contemplation. St. Augustine, speaking of St. John, says: "He gazed fixedly upon the eternal Beauty."[11] And when, by reason of his advanced age,

---

[6] St. Athana., cont. Gent. init.

[7] Maria autem conservabat omnia verba hæc, conferens in corde suo (Luc. ii, 19).

[8] Se totam contulit divinæ contemplationi (Ser. x, Assumpt. B.M.V.).

[9] Nos vero orationi et ministerio verbi instantes erimus (Act., vi, 4).

[10] Video cœlos apertos, et Filium hominis stantem a dextris Dei (Ibid., vii, 56).

[11] Lucis æternæ fixis oculis contemplator (In Joann., Tract., xxx).

he could no longer spread the kingdom of his Master by the ministry of apostolic preaching, the fruit of his contemplation became the treasure of the universal Church.

After the Apostles and the martyrs, contemplatives have always proved to be the strength and even the fecundity of the Church, the Bride of Christ. The admirable bloom of Christianity in the fourth century coincides with the period of the Fathers of the Desert. Cassian gives a full description of them, and shows how at that time contemplation had a privileged place in Christian society. They never lost sight of the end for which man was created; the principal interest of a baptized soul, said they, is to take the surest and most direct road for reaching God: "For what doth it profit a man if he gain the whole world and suffer the loss of his own soul?"[12] Deeply penetrated with this teaching, souls sacrificed everything that they might not be distracted from what appeared to them the one thing necessary. "Those," says the venerable Abbot of Saint Victor, "who place all their joy and happiness in the contemplation of divine things, punish themselves as for a kind of sacrilege, if they are withdrawn from it for an instant by involuntary thoughts and distractions. They weep for having turned their eyes away from their Creator and fixed them upon vile creatures, reproaching themselves as for an act of impiety. And although the eye of their heart turns with extreme eagerness to the splendour of divine light, they cannot tolerate these thoughts of earth which, like passing clouds, obscure the true light their soul is enjoying."[13]

Might we not take this as a description of those Cherubim, who "round about and within are full of eyes," whose sight, strong as the eagle's, can bear unceasingly and undazzled the splendour of the Divine Sun? Elsewhere Cassian is still more

---

[12] Quid enim prodest homini, si mundum universum lucretur, animæ vero suæ detrimentum patiatur? (Matth., xvi, 26).

[13] Cassian, Coll., xxiii, cap. viii.

explicit, and, speaking of the one thing necessary, he says: "This one thing is the contemplation of God. We must esteem it above all the merits and virtues of the just; above all things, good and useful, yea, even great and admirable, that we have seen in St. Paul. Tin is a useful thing, but when compared to silver it appears vile; silver itself loses its brilliancy when compared with gold. . . . So, in like manner, the virtues of the saints are good and useful for this life and for the next, but when compared with divine contemplation they seem of little worth."[14]

We admit that the words of Cassian seem strong and perhaps exaggerated; but it is well to quote them in order to show that the ancient solitaries at least esteemed no sacrifice too hard that should enable them to attain the blessing of high contemplation, which is the preparation for, and advance towards the beatific vision.

It is important therefore to define clearly what contemplation is in the Christian sense of the word. Summing up what tradition says, we would call it a simple and amorous gazing upon God and His mysteries, aided by grace or the gifts of the Holy Ghost. St. Gregory the Great gives almost the same definition: "Contemplation," says this doctor, "is a pleasing and gentle act, which raises the soul above herself, makes her desire things divine, despise things earthly, and discover things the most hidden."[15]

Contemplation, in truth, does not always attain the height here described by St. Gregory, but none the less it is very different from simple thought or even meditation; for thought wanders here and there, has no fixed end, and consequently possesses little efficacy; it seems to us well represented by the rapid glance spoken of by St. James: "For he beheld himself, and

---

[14] Cassian, Coll., xxiii, cap. iii.

[15] S. Greg., lib. II, Homil. 2 in Ezech.

presently forgot what manner of man he was."[16] As for
meditation, it applies only with pain and effort to supernatural
things; but contemplation ascends to them with ease, and
steadily abides in them. An ancient author of the seventh
century calls contemplation "a spiritual converse in which the
senses have no part."[17]

But in order to make these explanations better understood
it will be well to introduce here an important distinction.
Contemplation may be either ACQUIRED or INFUSED. It is
acquired when the understanding, though helped by grace
nevertheless acts in its own proper way, naturally and
conformably to the ordinary rules of its working. Then God's
action and man's action are combined; they act simultaneously.
It is easy to understand that this kind of contemplation, since
it is called acquired, is not above the reach of man when aided
by ordinary grace.

But if the soul is raised above her habitual way of acting, if
she is, as it were, passive in God's hands and He makes her
work according to His good pleasure, this contemplation is the
work of God rather than of man: it is called INFUSED, given by
God to the soul, and she has simply to receive it. All reasoning,
all the ordinary discursive acts are then suppressed; God stirs
the soul, and leaves her to maintain a steady attention, but this
is so simple and tranquil that she seems to be receiving the
action of God rather than to be herself acting. Benedict XIV, in
his book "On the Canonization of Saints," gives a very clear
definition of infused contemplation. "Contemplation," he says,
"is a simple intellectual sight, accompanied by a sweet love of
divine and revealed things proceeding from God, who applies
the understanding to know and the will to love these divine
things by filling the intellect with vivid light and the will with

[16] Consideravit enim se, et statim oblitus est qualis fuerit (Jac. i, 24).

[17] Conversatio spiritualis est actio sine sensibus (S. Isaac, lib. de
Cont. Mund., cap. xxix).

the flames of His love."[18]

Contemplation, in its widest sense, has been excellently described by St. Denis, under the figure of a triple movement, circular, direct and oblique, by which he designates three operations of the human mind, all belonging to contemplation. After speaking of the angelic spirits he says: "The soul has also this triple movement: its circular movement consists in leaving all external things, in entering within itself, in gathering up its spiritual faculties and bringing them back to unity in such a manner that, enclosed as it were within a circle, its movements may no longer wander. Freed from external things, recollected within itself, brought back to perfect simplicity, closely united with the angelic spirits, so simple and so pure, guided by them as it were by the hand, together with them it loses itself in the Sovereign Beauty, in the good which is all perfect, incorruptible, without beginning and without end. The oblique movement of the soul consists in its reception according to the proportions of its being, of divine illustrations, not in a way purely intelligible and in unity, but under the form of reasonings and discourses and by many and various processes. Finally, the movement of the soul is direct, when instead of falling back upon itself, of entering into its inmost depth and its only centre—this we have said is the circular movement—it approaches external things, then using them as varied and complex symbols it raises itself by their means to a contemplation which is perfect in unity and purity."[19]

The final end and only aim of these three movements is always to get back to the Eternal Truth, bringing all to God both within and without. Hence contemplation consists in living before the face of God, considered either in Himself or in what He has accomplished for the sake of man. It consists,

---

[18] De SS. Beatif. et Canon. liii, cap. xxvi, a. 7.

[19] *Of the Divine Names*, chap., iv, n. 9.

moreover, in seeing and relishing these things in preference to
all others, as the royal Psalmist invites us: "Come ye to Him,
and be enlightened, and your faces shall not be confounded. . .
. Taste, and see that the Lord is sweet."[20]

Contemplation, therefore, is not a science that affects the
understanding only; it is a turning of the whole soul, intellect
and will together to behold the Divine Light; in its first degree
it seems in a special manner to waken within us the gift of
piety, under the form of tenderness of devotion more or less
habitual, which would make us willingly say with St. Peter:
"Lord, it is good for us to be here: if Thou wilt, let us make here
three tabernacles."[21] The soul has no more long reasoning;
something tells her that her Lord is with her; she relishes Him,
she enjoys Him; in a word, she experiences what is felt with
one dearly loved. Without doubt this consolation that gladdens
the soul is neither entirely sensible nor perfectly spiritual in
acquired contemplation, but it is the first link of a mysterious
chain which ends in heaven. The soul begins to find a special
charm in the most well-known truths; they come before her in
new lights which she wonders how she could have never seen
before; and although she is not conscious of any extraordinary
illumination, she finds in these same truths, which are at once
ancient and new, a splendour hitherto unseen, and a sweetness
that ravishes her.

Contemplation, like faith, has not abundant considerations.
In proportion, as it becomes more elevated and perfect, its
simplicity suppresses all reasoning; the soul becomes daily
more supple under the influence of the Divine Spirit; she adapts
herself to a mode of action altogether new, and she ends by

---

[20] Accedite ad eum, et illuminamini; et facies vestræ non
confundentur. . . . Gustate et videte quoniam suavis est Dominus
(Ps., xxxiii, 6, 9).

[21] Bonum est nos hic esse; si vis, faciamus hic tria tabernacula
(Matth., xvii, 4).

seeing all things in God, that is in one; and she sees this one in all.

Nevertheless, man's contemplation is affected by his nature, and does not absolutely resemble that of the angels, who have not to free themselves from the servitude of the body and of the imagination and whose intelligence is gifted with admirable stability. Generally speaking man attains to contemplation only by long efforts and the use of many means; and it is on this account that we have spoken of the proximate and remote preparations, of the practice of virtue, of prayer and of meditation, because the degree of contemplation depends upon the purity of the soul. The darkness of our understanding, the malice of our will, the unruliness of our passions and senses, the images of sensible things that fill our mind, all form a very thick cloud which prevents us from seeing God by contemplation and from uniting ourselves to Him. The more we succeed in triumphing over these obstacles, in healing the wounds which original sin has opened in us and which our actual sins have still more enlarged and ulcerated, the more also will the path to contemplation be made straight before us; we mean that kind of contemplation which depends upon us: "Blessed are the clean of heart, for they shall see God."[22] As to INFUSED contemplation it is evident that it comes directly from God, and that no effort of ours can produce it; but as God is just, He does not leave our labours without reward. When, therefore, the way is cleared of all obstacles our Lord does not disappoint the creature whom He was the first to love; He invariably surpasses all her hopes.

St. Teresa shows the close link there is between the reform of self and the advance in contemplation: "A pretty way indeed to seek the love of God!" she says. "Some souls desire it in all its perfection and all at once, and yet they retain their affection for other things; they make no effort to excite within themselves

---

[22] Beati mundo corde, quoniam ipsi Deum videbunt (Matth. v, 3).

holy desires, nor to rise above the things of earth, and yet with all that they presume to lay claim to spiritual consolations! Such a thing cannot possibly be, for reserves of this kind are incompatible with perfect love. Thus it is because we do not give ourselves totally and entirely as a gift to God that He does not give us all at once the treasure of perfect love."[23]

For charity is the beginning and the end of contemplation; this latter draws all its perfection from charity, and increases in proportion to the soul's progress in that virtue: "The desire of contemplation proceeds from love of the object which is to be contemplated; for where the love is, there is the eye," says the angelic Doctor.[24] St. Denis also traces the path which the soul must traverse in order to attain the highest contemplation: "It behoveth us to be led to God, as to the Principle of all good, by prayer, and then, approaching nearer and nearer to Him, to be initiated into the knowledge of those best gifts which are contained in Him. For he indeed is present to all things, but all things are not present to Him. But when we supplicate Him with holy prayers, that is, chaste and free from illusions, and with a tranquil mind prepared for divine union, then we become present to Him."[25]

St. Thomas thus comments on this passage: "To approach God three things are necessary. The first is that the heart be purified from all carnal and worldly affections which would captivate and chain it down to earth; this is chaste prayer. In the second place the mind must be divested of all low and darksome ideas which would hinder it from relishing spiritual things and from rising to God; this is having a tranquil mind and free from illusions. Finally, it is necessary that our will be

[23] *Life of St. Teresa*, vol. I, chap. xi.

[24] Contemplationis desiderium procedit ex amore objecti: quia ubi amor, ibi oculus (In III. Sent. Dist. xxxv, art. 2).

[25] *Of the Divine Names*, chap, iii, n. 1.

constantly turned to God by ardent charity and devotion; this is having a heart prepared for divine union."[26]

From all this teaching it evidently results that contemplation, especially that kind which is above the reach of our efforts, is a grace much to be desired, and one that we must ask of God with perseverance and in all humility and reverence. The doing so can in no way be contradictory to what has been said already on the subject of aspiring after extraordinary ways. For it is always important, and we love to repeat it, to make a distinction in the diverse desires which we are allowed to foster for infused contemplation.

This kind of contemplation comprises graces of a double order: GRACES GRATUITOUSLY GIVEN, that is, extraordinary gifts accompanied with external manifestations; and SANCTIFYING GRACES which are the infused virtues and the gifts of the Holy Spirit, brought into activity by a special favour. The first mentioned are in no way to be desired; the second, on the contrary, are the object of a lawful desire: "Be emulous for the better gifts";[27] provided that this desire is humble, duly moderated and accompanied by the practice of solid and of even heroic virtues. We ought to desire things for the sake of their perfection. Now contemplation is the act which best befits our intelligent nature and our character as children of God. To exercise our faculties in the knowledge and the love of Eternal Truth, to receive a special and exceptional communication of the gifts of the Holy Ghost, finally, to be united to God with our whole soul, is not this the bliss most of all to be desired here below? "Her conversation hath no bitterness, nor her company any tediousness."[28] That most prudent virgin St. Teresa

---

[26] S. Thom, in lib. *De Div. Nom.*, I, iii.

[27] Æmulamini charismata Meliora (1 Cor., xii, 31).

[28] Non habet amaritudinem conversatio illius, nec tædium convictus illius (Sap., viii, 16).

encouraged this ambition in her daughters; and, conformably with tradition and the practice of all holy persons, she exhorted them to persevere in those exercises and prayers which might draw down upon them the divine favours. Moreover, it is but following the counsel of the Holy Spirit Himself who inspired these words: "Let nothing hinder thee from praying always, and be not afraid to be justified even to death: for the reward of God continueth for ever."[29] Finally, our Lord Jesus Christ has sanctioned the desire of attaining habitual and perfect contemplation, which is the noble end of all the exercises of the contemplative life, by calling it "the better part," and declaring that it shall not be taken away from those who make it the object of their choice.

---

[29] Non impediaris orare semper, et ne verearis usque ad mortem justificari: quoniam merces Dei manet in æternum (Eccli xviii, 22).

CHAPTER XVI
Of the Unitive Life

CHARITY is the perfection of Christianity, the end to which all God's Commandments, all the Gospel counsels, all spiritual exercises and all favours in contemplation tend: "For the end of the Commandments is charity from a pure heart and a good conscience and an unfeigned faith."[1] Now the last work of perfect charity, is to unite us so closely to God, that we become but one spirit with Him: "He who is joined to the Lord, is one spirit."[2] For though the three theological virtues unite us to God, nevertheless, to charity, the most excellent of the three, belongs the honour of perfecting the union prepared by faith and hope, according to that beautiful sentence of St. Augustine: "The house of God is founded by faith, built up by hope and perfected by charity."[3]

If, however, it is true to say that all who have charity enjoy in a certain way union with God, and that hence their actions are meritorious; still we must acknowledge that charity has divers degrees and that it is not perfect in all the just. The first effect of charity is to withdraw man from sin; the second degree consists in a certain strengthening against sin, in consequence of sustained efforts in seeking after good and in the practice of virtue; finally, perfect charity is that which reigns in the soul

---

[1] Finis autem præcepti est caritas de corde puro, et conscientia bona, et fide non ficta (1 Tim., 1, 5).

[2] Quid adhæret Domino unus spiritus est (1 Cor., vi, 17).

[3] Domus Dei credendo fundatur, sperando erigitur, amando perficitur (St. Aug. Serm. xxii, in Verb. Dom.).

when all trace of sin is effaced, both as to the guilt and the penalty, when consequently there is no longer any clinging even to venial sin, and when virtue if occasion so require, is resolutely practised to even an heroic degree. This perfect charity is that which establishes the soul in the Unitive Life: then there remains no obstacle between God and the soul which loves: "He that abideth in charity, abideth in God, and God in him."[4] Or as the sacred Canticle renders it: "My Beloved to me, and I to Him."[5]

Our ancient Fathers were well acquainted with this state; with tears they begged of God to bestow that grace upon them, and made every effort not to put any obstacle in the way. Cassian's testimony on this subject is very telling. "As long as we are doing penance," he says, "and are tormented with the recollection of our sins, the fire which burns our conscience must be extinguished by the torrent of our tears. But when, having persevered a long time in humility and contrition of heart, the thought of sin has been effaced; when the thorn which was wounding the soul has been removed by the grace and mercy of God, then we must hope that pardon has been granted to us, and that we are entirely purified from our sins. We cannot, however, obtain of God this freedom otherwise than by destroying all our old passions and becoming truly clean of heart, for this grace is not granted to the cowardly and negligent who make no efforts over themselves."[6]

St. Paul in his Epistle to the Ephesians, in which he paints so complete a picture of the soul's onward course to God, prays that all those whom he has brought forth in Christ may be rooted and founded in charity.[7] By using the two words—rooted

---

[4] Qui manet in caritate, in Deo manet, et Deus in eo (1 Joann., iv, 16).

[5] Dilectus meus mihi, et ego illi (Can., ii, 16).

[6] Cassian, Coll, xx, cap. vii.

[7] In caritate radicati et fundati (Eph. iii, 12).

and founded—the Apostle clearly shows that he thirsts to see in these souls not merely the weak and fluctuating charity of beginners, but that of the perfect, and the sequel of his discourse proves this most evidently.

In truth, the triumph of grace is complete in this degree only, because in it union is achieved. It is scarcely necessary to point out here that, in this stage, when we speak of union of the soul with God, we are no longer considering that substantial union, whereby God is present to every creature, and without which all that is would cease to exist; but rather, a union with God and a transformation into God by love: a union so real, a transformation so true, that in the impossible hypothesis that God were not in the soul by His essence, presence and power, He would nevertheless be there in virtue of this new title. Then the soul possesses Him by knowledge and by love. This latter union can be effected only when there is a likeness of love between the Creator and the creature; and it is consummated when the two wills, that of the soul and that of God, become uniform, that is to say, when there is in the one nothing that is displeasing to the other. Now, as we said in the beginning, it is not sufficient to eliminate from our acts what is repugnant to God, but we must also eliminate from the impulses of the soul whatever is displeasing to Him; we must avoid not only voluntary imperfect acts, but get rid of even bad tendencies, so as to have command over the first movements. And when everything in the soul has become conformed to the will of God, no further obstacle remains to its perfect transformation.

Isaias in these beautiful and triumphant words well expressed the intimacy of divine union: "Thou shalt no more be called Forsaken; and thy land shall no more be called Desolate; but thou shalt be called My pleasure in her, and thy land inhabited. Because the Lord hath been well pleased with thee;

and thy land shall be inhabited."[8] The Lord who dwells in the soul makes all things germinate therein, both flowers and fruits; and the creature then feels in herself what a living earth would feel on some glad spring day when all vegetation is thrilling with life, and the flowers in bloom are yielding their sweet fragrance.

Moreover the soul sees accomplished in herself that which our Lord commanded us unceasingly to pray for, namely, that His will may be done on earth as it is in heaven. This is a petition astounding indeed if we seriously reflect upon it; a petition which reveals to us how fully the treasures of God are within our reach, even in this valley of tears, when we on our part consent to carry to their farthest limits the practical consequences of our regeneration. Then indeed new relations are formed between God and the soul, relations which He Himself thus describes: "Whosoever shall do the will of My Father that is in heaven, he is my brother and sister and mother."[9]

Our Lord enumerates here, and no doubt designedly, only the bonds formed by blood, not by alliance, as though He would prove that the spirit of adoption does a real work in us and not something that is fictitious. This union is not only real, but even more true than that of the flesh. It is for this very reason, so full of divine delicacy that in the Canticle of Canticles the bride is always named "Sister";[10] God having wished to show thereby that, even before the union, the soul is raised by the Holy Spirit to a kind of equality, and that her Baptism has made

---

[8] Non vocaberis ultra derelicta, et terra tua non vocabitur amplius desolata; sed vocaberis voluntas mea in ea, et terra tua inhabitata; quia complacuit Domino in te, et terra tua inhabitabitur (Isa., lxii, 4).

[9] Quicumque fecerit voluntatem Patris mei, qui in coelis est, ipse meus frater, et soror, et mater est (Matth., xii, 50; Marc., iii, 35).

[10] Cant, v, 1.

her "a partaker of the divine nature."[11] There are of course divers degrees in this relationship, for the soul is more or less closely united to God according to the measure of her conformity to the divine will: the sister and the brother are certainly less close than the mother. This truth was recognised by the ancient Fathers, and we find St. Gregory the Great saying: "He who by believing is the brother or sister of Christ, becomes by preaching, His mother if, by his word, the love of God is generated in the hearts of others."[12]

Union with God, the fruit and term of charity, is then not only a most excellent good, but also an end to which all Christians should strive to tend. But does this imply that all can reach it by the same means? This is a point that is of the greatest importance for us to examine.

In the Church there are two ways whereby the Christian may attain perfection, which consists in union, transformation and likeness to God by perfect charity. These two ways differ in their means, but the union resulting from them is identical; perfection gained by either of these two ways produces in us the same reality of devotion, the same effects. On the one side and on the other these are a great interior calm, a kind of stability in good, an angelic purity of mind and heart, a generous contempt of earthly things, a universal stilling of the passions, the practice of eminent virtue, an uninterrupted desire of pleasing God and of imitating our Lord Jesus Christ, an entire submission to the divine Will, and the exercise of works of mercy to our neighbour. Finally, by the one way and the other, when charity is the same, man is established in an equal degree of merit and of holiness.

After saying these few words about the sameness of the end

---

[11] 2 Peter i, 4.

[12] Qui Christi frater et soror est credendo, mater efficitur prædicando, si per ejus vocem amor Domini in proximi mente generatur (S. Gre. Homil. III in Evangl.)

to which these two ways of the Unitive Life lead, we must of
necessity determine what are the characteristics proper to each,
in what they are different from each other, and w'hat is their
respective value.

The first of these ways is the way of action, the common
and ordinary way. With only the ordinary helps of grace it can
lead all men to perfection. Our Lord is exhorting to this kind of
perfection when He says: "Be you therefore perfect, as also
your heavenly Father is perfect."[13] And St. Peter in his Epistles
says: "But according to Him that hath called you, who is holy,
be you also in all manner of conversation holy, because it is
written: You shall be holy, for I am holy."[14] In many other
passages of the sacred Scripture we find mention of this call to
the perfection of Christianity and to holiness as set forth in the
Gospel, and this it is that opens to us the Unitive Life.

The saints also have proved that the active or ordinary way
suffices to bring the soul to perfect charity. We will quote St.
Teresa who on this subject has some important remarks: "Every
Christian may, with the help of grace, reach divine union,
provided he strive with all his power to renounce his own will
and to cleave to the will of God. Oh, how many say and believe
that they are in these dispositions! and for my part, all that I
can say is, if they really are, they have obtained from God all
they could desire. They need no longer trouble themselves
about the delicious union of which I spoke before, for what is
best in it is that it proceeds from the one of which I am now
speaking, and it is even impossible to attain the former, if the
latter is not already possessed, I mean to say, this entire
submission of our will to the will of God. . . . In this union of

---

[13] Estote ergo perfecti, sicut et Pater vester coelestis perfectus est
(Matt., v, 48).

[14] Sed secundum eum, qui vocavit vos, sanctum, et ipsi in omni
conversatione sancti sitis, quoniam scriptum est: Sancti eritis,
quoniam ego sanctus sum (1 Peter i, 15, 16).

pure conformity to the will of God, it is not necessary that the powers be suspended. God is all-powerful, and He has a thousand ways of enriching souls and of leading them into these mansions without taking them by that short way of which I have spoken, I mean to say, without raising them to that intimate union with Him, whence after a few moments, they come forth quite transformed. But take notice, my daughters, that in every case the mystic worm must die, and that in this union of pure conformity to the divine Will it will have a harder death. . . .

"This is the union which I have desired all my life long, and which I have always asked of our Lord. It is the one easiest to distinguish, and it is the most secure. But alas! how few attain to it, and how souls deceive themselves in thinking that they have done everything when they avoid offending God, and live in the religious state! . . . God asks only two things: one, that we love Him, and the other, that we love our neighbour. We must then work at this; by faithfully accomplishing these two things, we shall do the will of God and shall be united to Him. . . . The most certain sign whereby we can know whether we are faithfully practising them, is in my opinion, to have a sincere and true love of our neighbour. For we cannot know for certain how far our love of God goes, although there may be great indications by which we might judge of it: but we see much more clearly in what regards the love of our neighbour. . . . It behoves us then very much to consider well what is the disposition of our soul, and what is our exterior conduct in regard of our neighbour. If all is perfect in one and in the other, then we may be in all security; for, considering the depravity of our nature, we could never perfectly love our neighbour if there were not in us a great love of God."[15]

Nothing could be added to teaching so excellent, so just and so practical. However, we will observe in passing that union

---

[15] *The Interior Castle*, 5th Mansion, iii.

with God by the infused way derives all its excellence from that
same end which is reached by the ordinary way, "since," says
St. Teresa, "what is best in this union is that it proceeds from
the one of which I am now speaking." 'And indeed union with
God cannot be real unless there is conformity to the Divine
Will. St. Bernard also admirably discriminates between these
two ways: "Active charity is commanded unto merit: affective
charity is given in reward."[16] The excellence of the ordinary
way of reaching union with God consists in its being sure, free
from illusions and always within our reach; and also in the fact
that by it we may, without ambition, desire to attain perfect
charity; without danger strive to acquire it; and without
rashness or presumption unceasingly ask it of God.

Nevertheless, we have here but one side of the truth. It is of
great importance that we should see both sides in order to form
a correct judgment of the unitive life. There can be no doubt
that in many passages of the Scriptures we are encouraged and
even commanded to seek after perfect charity, and that
nowhere is heaven promised in any exclusive way to the
contemplative life as St. Gregory has already said: "Without the
contemplative life they who neglect not to do the works that lie
in their power can enter into the heavenly country; but without
the active they cannot enter, if they neglect to do the good
which they can do."[17] However, though the second way is not
in its essential point better than the other, which is the
perfection of charity, yet our Lord Jesus Christ having
pronounced sentence in its favour, it must have its prerogative.
Plainly, in that Gospel text which confers upon it a real claim

---

[16] Caritas in opere mandatur ad meritum: caritas in affectu datur in
præmium (S. Bern. Serm. L in Cant.)

[17] Sine contemplativa vita possunt intrare ad coelestem patriam, qui
bona qua; possunt operari non neqliqunt: sine activa autem intrare
non possunt, si negligunt bona operari quæ possunt (S. Greg. Homil.
iii in Ezech.)

to nobility, our divine Lord attributes its excellence not only to the end which is the unitive life, but also to the means, since He speaks clearly of Mary's choice. This choice can refer only to the exercises of the contemplative life, which alone are within our human reach; then our Lord seems to encourage this choice when He says: "It shall not be taken from her." Might we not enlarge upon these words by saying that those who shall have voluntarily and generously embraced the exercises of the contemplative life, and who shall at the same time have neglected nothing which secures conformity to God's will in us, will obtain from His gratuitous goodness all the good things which they might have lawfully desired in choosing Mary's part? It is, therefore, conformable to the Gospel teaching to assert that in two souls in which the perfection of charity is equal, the one that attains union by the mystic way has some advantages.

The first of these is that the soul, in a more elevated way, knows and possesses God. The understanding and the will produce their more noble acts in a manner that is not the ordinary one, by a special action of the gifts of the Holy Spirit, so that the soul seems freed not only from earthly things but even from earthly images. The union is more intimate, more sweet, more full of joy, although it is not more meritorious. The second advantage is that God gives therein to the human soul a foretaste, as it were, of beatitude, and a kind of experience of the good things to come.

But if, in order to clear our ideas, it is necessary thus to discriminate between the two ways leading to union with God, we own that it is very rare and, in practice, even impossible to admit, that souls whose fidelity to God has reached even to perfect conformity with the divine Will should be deprived of all the graces of the other (mystic) way. We believe that such a supposition cannot possibly be realized. As a fact, the two ways mingle; and if the way of conformity to the Divine Will seems to be the special way of a soul rather than the mystic way, it is as equally inadmissible to suppose that souls can arrive at divine union by action only, as it is to think that they can reach it solely by contemplation, without joining to contemplation the practice of virtue. As soon as charity has reached certain proportions in the soul, it obtains for her special and infused graces.

Error frequently arises from the fact that, in the contemplative life, every infused grace is taken for a grace of union, an assumption which is a grave illusion, too often causing souls to be accredited with perfection who have not yet reached it; to avoid this illusion great care must be taken to have proof that the effects of perfect charity are in the soul, before concluding in favour of her entrance into the unitive life. In the Gospel our Lord says clearly: "Not every one that saith to Me, Lord, Lord, shall enter into the kingdom of heaven. Many will say to Me in that day: Lord, Lord, have we not prophesied in Thy name, and cast out devils in Thy name, and done many miracles in Thy name? And then will I profess unto them: I never knew you: depart from Me, you that work iniquity."[18]

So then these "many" had received most real favours, graces gratuitously given; but they had not yet attained union with God, since perfect conformity to the Will of the heavenly Father, which is always indicated by the generous practice of virtue, was wanting. Among the fruits of contemplation the grace of union is something so elevated, and it so profoundly changes the human soul that this favour is to be recognised principally by its effects. St. Denis, in two passages which we

---

[18] Non omnis qui dicit mihi: Domine, Domine, intrabit in regnum cœlorum; sed qui facit voluntatem Patris mei qui in cœlis est, ipse intrabit in regnum cœlorum. Multi dicent mihi in illa die: Domine, Domine, nonne in nomine tuo prophetavimus, et in nomine tuo dæmonia ejecimus, et in nomine tuo virtutes multas fecimus? Et tunc confitebor illis: quia numquam novi vos, discedite a me, qui operamini iniquitatem (Matth., vii, 21-23).

will give in succession, seems to have described a grace of this kind. "For," he says, "as ignorance and error create division, in like manner spiritual light, when it appears, brings back and unites into one compact whole the things that it reaches; it perfects them, turns them towards the Being who truly is, corrects their vain opinions, recalls their manifold views, or rather their capricious imaginations, into a knowledge which is one, true, pure and simple, and fills them with a light which is unity, and which produces unity."[19] Here there is question of God's action upon the understanding, but afterwards he speaks of the same divine action upon the will.

"Divine love ravishes out of themselves those who are possessed by it, to such a degree that they belong no more to themselves, but rather to the object loved. This is seen in superiors who devote themselves to the government of inferiors; in equals who live in mutual regard one for another; in inferiors who abandon themselves to the direction of those above them. Hence the great Paul, inebriated with holy love, cried out in an ecstatic transport: 'I live, now not I, but Christ liveth in me.'"[20]

Evidently there is here question of a divine operation which does not merely touch the human soul, like many very real and very supernatural favours of contemplation, but rather of a grace which deeply penetrates it, renews it, rectifies it, corrects it, and may go so far as entirely to transform it.

Error on this point is often met with in those who have the guidance of others, and it is a great danger. For if a grace of union be supposed to exist where it really does not, too much will be required from the soul that is thought to have received it, and she will fall into discouragement, for she can take steps proportionate only to her stature. Or perhaps the very nature of the graces which she has received will be called into doubt,

---

[19] *Of the Divine Names*, iv, n. 6.

[20] *Of the Divine Names*, iv, n. 13.

under pretext that the soul has not at once obtained holiness and perfection. We must always bear in mind that there is a gradation in the favours bestowed in contemplation, and that each produces effects corresponding to its degree and elevation. Now graces of union are of the highest kind, and ordinarily suppose a long succession of graces and a faithful cooperation with these graces.

When the soul is admitted into the Unitive Life by the contemplative way, it is generally easier to verify that fact than if she reached it by the ordinary way of the insensible growth of charity. First, because the divine working changes the soul at once, and so she is more easily made aware of the renovation—of the renewing of her youth—which is the first effect of the divine contact. Just as a person coming suddenly out of darkness into full daylight perceives the contrast better than another, who reaches midday by the imperceptible advance of the sun. Secondly, because the union which is brought about by the contemplative way has in it something that comes nigh to eternal things, not only as to its essence, which is perfect charity, but as to its mode—a special light engendering a sweetness and a beatitude which in no way increase the merit but which render the union more perceptible and more easy to recognise.

Still the Unitive Life is but a stage in our pilgrimage, in via, consequently it is not a final end for the human soul, and can always be more and more developed. Even perfect charity has innumerable degrees, and the apostle ardently desires that it should unceasingly grow in us even unto the day of eternity: "But doing the truth in charity we may in all things grow up in Him who is the head, even Christ."[21] In this world the perfection of charity is not a fixed and absolutely permanent state; it is a continuous desire of attaining, and not a tranquil

---

[21] Veritatem autem facientes in caritate, crescamus in illo per omnia, qui est caput, Christus (Eph. iv, 15).

rest in the good already attained, as we learn from many passages of St. Paul's Epistles. "Brethren," he says, "I do not count myself to have apprehended. But one thing I do; forgetting the things that are behind, and stretching forth myself to those things that are before, I press towards the mark, to the prize of the supernatural vocation of God in Christ Jesus. Let us therefore, as many as are perfect, be thus minded."[22] To be able thus ever to advance constitutes at once both the privilege and the inferiority of the present life.

Experience has shown that union with God has three degrees, which are sufficiently distinct in their effects to be easily recognised; simple union, ecstatic or affective union, and transforming or perfect union. These three kinds of union belong to the last three "Mansions" of the "Interior Castle"; they have been so well described by St. Teresa that nothing further remains to be said about them. To close our subject here we will merely add a word upon simple union and its characteristics. This order of graces is distinguished from lower ones by several marked differences.

The soul then feels and tastes God within her own self, whereas before she felt Him near her. The ordinary exercise of her faculties is suspended for a time more or less long, but without any suspension of the external senses. The true and deep sense which she has of God's presence is so vivid that it is not only under the shadows of faith that she knows that God is present within her, but by a most sweet experience. Often this sentiment is accompanied by an impression of renovation, such as would be the actual feeling of the effect of a plenary indulgence. A distance henceforth lies between this new life

---

[22] Fratres, ego me non arbitror comprehendisse. Unum autem, quæ quidem retro sunt obliviscens, ad ea vero quæ sunt priora extendens meipsum, ad destinatum persequor, ad bravium supernæ vocationis Dei in Christo Jesu. Quicumque ergo perfecti sumus, hoc sentiamus (Phil, iii, 13-15).

and the old life; God has bestowed upon the soul a general and entire pardon, and has even given her habits conformable to her state.

Nature has received a deathblow, from which it will not recover; for although these favours are delicate, they cannot be lost without grave infidelities, and they are by their very nature so deep and powerful that it is not easy to destroy their effect.

Nevertheless, though this simple union with God is very intimate, it is not stable but transitory, as to the sentiment which it produces. St. Teresa is of opinion that it never lasts much longer than half an hour, and we must on the subject believe her experience. This short space suffices to give the soul a pliancy unknown to her before, which pliancy the sacred Canticle thus expresses: "My soul melted, when my Beloved spoke."[23] Sometimes the feeling of devotion awakened in the soul is of such a nature that tears flow from the eyes without her being conscious of it. St. Catharine of Sienna speaks of this kind of tears in her Dialogue: "If the soul, while advancing in the knowledge of self, perfectly despises and hates herself; if she thus gains a true knowledge and an ardent love of my goodness, she begins to unite and conform her will to mine, and to feel interiorly the joy of love and compassion for her neighbour. Immediately the eye, wishing to satisfy the heart, pours out tears excited by charity towards me and love of her neighbour."[24]

Finally, little by little the virtues shine forth in all her acts. The soul is full of courage, is patient and persevering, zealous for God's interests, having a great desire at her own cost to assist her neighbour.

These effects are not found in all in the same degree, but they must always exist in some measure before the union can be verified. It happens sometimes that the soul, having received

---

[23] Cant. v, 6.

[24] Dialogue ix, 6.

this grace, perceives all at once within herself a return, as it were, of her old struggles; but this movement is of short duration, and does not occasion much danger. The evil nature has received the deathblow; it will infallibly succumb, and these violent crises are but the convulsions of an agony which leads to the new life.

The soul thus prevented by grace should be particularly vigilant in maintaining in the least detail great conformity to the will of God. She has for this a special strength; she ought never, even in desire, wittingly to incline to any imperfection whatsoever; for as God can admit of none, there would arise from this inclination a deep divergency from Him, a kind of rupture between the soul and Him. We say designedly that the soul should not wittingly consent to any imperfection, for she will often by surprise fall into imperfections and venial sins without being able entirely to escape them, such is the condition of our poor nature. Therefore, though the soul which has resolutely entered the Unitive Life, has passed through the greatest dangers of the spiritual life, she ought not to relax her vigilance, but ever to bear in mind those words of the wise man: "He that contemneth small things shall fall by little and little."[25] What would be unnoticed in others, what would in former times have been unnoticed in herself, would now imperil the treasure which she possesses and which she might lose by any voluntary infidelity: "But we have this treasure in earthen vessels, that the excellency may be of the power of God, and not of us."[26] The more closely certain gifts resemble angelic gifts the greater risk there is of all at once losing them. In this respect the example of Moses[27] is very startling; for having a second time struck the rock, instead of following step by step

---

[25] Qui spernit modica paulatim decidet (Eccli xix, 1).

[26] Habemus autem thesaurum istum in vasis fictilibus, ut sublimitas sit virtutis Dei et non ex nobis (2 Cor., iv, 7).

[27] Num., xx, 12.

the order of God, he was not allowed to enter the Promised Land. Nevertheless, this disobedience was not of such a nature as to deprive him of God's friendship. In like manner the soul that fails in watchful delicacy may, without losing entirely her intimacy with God, at least risk her entrance into the Promised Land, that is to say, her admission to that happy state of transforming union, in which, according to the words of St. Paul, she is replenished with the very fulness of God.

This vigilance, however, does not make the soul restless, nor pusillanimous, nor timid, which fact is an evident sign that she is guided by the Holy Spirit. Her way is love, she acts by love only, according to that sentence of the beloved disciple: "He that feareth is not perfected in charity."[28]

A soul that has attained the Unitive Life possesses a very special power of intercession, the whole secret of which power lies in her perfect conformity to the will of God: "Now we know that God does not hear sinners; but if a man be a server of God and doth His will, him He heareth."[29] The very remarkable example related by St. Gregory the Great with regard to St. Scholastica, shows this very clearly: "By a most just judgment," says the holy Doctor, "she could do more who loved more."[30]

At that moment the will of the graceful dove of Cassino was more conformed to the will of God than was that of the illustrious Patriarch Benedict; and thus she gained the victory over him. Even in the highest and most strongly marked Unitive Life, the union is not always equally intense and actual; and without ceasing to be solidly established in it, the soul may then receive from God graces of a lower order. Her state as to its essence and merit continues to be that of union; she receives,

---

[28] Qui timet non est perfectus in caritate (1 Joann., iv, 18).

[29] Scimus autem quia peccatores Deus non audit, sed si quis Dei cultor est et voluntatem ejus facit, hunc exaudit (Joann., ix, 31).

[30] Justo valde judicio, illa plus potuit, quæ amplius amavit (2 Dialog., xxx).

nevertheless, favours which seem to belong to an inferior order. The glorious dove Scholastica hastened her flight, having already caught a glimpse of the ark opening to receive her, and of the hand of the divine Noah stretched forth to bring her in without delay. St. Benedict, as to his state, was at that time equally great, but his actual union with God was less intense than that of his sister.

CHAPTER XVII
Of Prophecy, as understood in Ancient Times

E have easily recognised in infused contemplation the existence of two orders of graces which it is extremely important not to confound; graces gratuitously given, and gifts which truly elevate and sanctify the soul that receives them. The first are compatible with imperfection, they may be found in even a state of sin; the others always suppose the absence of sin, and ordinarily they are granted only to souls sufficiently prepared by long purifications and very perfect dispositions. Graces gratuitously given are more external, and frequently have no other object than the profit of our neighbour; sanctifying graces transform the human soul by reaching into its very depths. But the Apostle St. Paul has on this subject given such complete and extensive teaching that it will suffice for our purpose to comment upon his words.

"Now concerning spiritual things, my brethren, I would not have you ignorant,"[1] said he to the Corinthians. At the very outset he shows by these words that it is useful and profitable for the faithful to know the course of the divine workings in the human soul. He then enumerates the many splendid gifts given by the Holy Spirit to the Church, gifts permanently bestowed upon her which subsist and which will subsist in her to the end: "Now there are diversities of graces, but the same Spirit; and there are diversities of ministries, but the same Lord; and there are diversities of operations, but the same God, who worketh all in all. And the manifestation of the Spirit is given to every man

---

[1] De spiritualibus autem nolo vos ignorare, fratres (1 Cor., xii, 1).

unto profit."[2]

These gifts, which are visible to every one, and which are distributed by God to His creatures with sovereign liberty, are therefore favours altogether gratuitous and exceptional. In them God has directly in view the profit of His Church, and sometimes also the advantage of individuals. Moreover, our Lord promises them to His apostles as signs of their mission: "And these signs shall follow them that believe: in My name they shall cast out devils; they shall speak with new tongues; they shall take up serpents; and if they shall drink any deadly thing it shall not hurt them; they shall lay their hands upon the sick, and they shall recover."[3] So regularly are these signs intended for the profit of those who witness them, that even in the canonized saints they appear to be the result not of their sanctity, but of the sphere in which they lived. The apostles, for instance, having to found numerous centres of Christianity, were especially enriched with them; God frequently condescends to manifest great prodigies to simple souls, while He hides Himself from the curious and the proud. Hence our Lord multiplied His miracles in Galilee, but refused to satisfy the vain curiosity of Herod. St. Paul speaks eloquently before the Areopagus, but He does not there work any of the signs which our Lord had put in his power.

For in point of fact these gifts are under the control of him who has received them; he can at will use them or not use them, so long as God has not recalled them.

---

[2] Divisiones vero gratiarum sunt, idem autem Spiritus. Et divisiones ministrationum sunt, idem autem Dominus. Et divisiones operationum sunt, idem vero Deus qui operatur omnia in omnibus. Unicuique autem datur manifestatio Spiritus ad utilitatem (1 Cor., xii, 4-7).

[3] Signa autem eos qui crediderint, hæc sequentur: In nomine meo dæmonia ejicient, linguis loquentur novis: serpentes tollent, et si mortiferum quid biberint non eis nocebit; super ægros manus imponent, et bene habebunt (Mar., xvi, 17, 18).

St. John of the Cross goes even so far as to say that those who possess them should be sober in the use of them, under pain of being momentarily turned aside from the one thing necessary. This explains that sentence of St. Paul: "And the spirits of the prophets are subject to the prophets."[4] He is undoubtedly here speaking, as the context shows, of graces gratuitously given, for it is in them that the gifts of the Spirit are subject to those who have received them, and, as St. Gregory remarks, these miraculous facts or prodigies are accomplished in two ways: "Those that are intimately united with God, in two ways work miracles when circumstances require; sometimes they do them in virtue of prayer, sometimes in virtue of their power."[5]

These gifts, as we have already remarked, are not an infallible sign of the degree of charity existing in the soul; examples in proof of this abound in the holy Scriptures. Balaam spoke under divine inspiration; Caiphas prophesied at the time of our Lord's Passion, but simply because he was high priest that year. In the order of miracles we know that pagans using the sign of the Cross have cast out devils and healed the sick; these facts are so well known that it is unnecessary for us to dwell longer upon them. But what shows that these gifts come from God, even when the agent is not in grace with Him, is the end they are intended to bring about, which end is invariably the salvation, the conversion and the sanctification of souls. But in such a case we must observe that the grace gratuitously given is for only a determined and transitory act. It could not be otherwise, for being a divine power it cannot permanently reside where the Holy Spirit is not. Without this reserve God would run the risk of lending Himself to what might deceive man.

However, in the just these supernatural gifts have a certain

---

[4] Spiritus prophetarum prophetis subjecti sunt (1 Cor., xiv, 32).

[5] 2 Dialog, xxx.

permanency. But in this kind of regular concession nothing can become for man a subject of pride any more for example than the perpetuity of the priesthood in the priest; even when these gifts are man's possession, they do not cease to be always the property of God. This domain belongs absolutely to the divine good pleasure. God gives His gratuitous graces to whom He pleases, when He pleases and in the measure He pleases. And in the same way He takes them back again to Himself. At one time permanent and, as it were, continuous, at another transitory and suffering interruptions, there is always in them a certain weak point which betrays the precarious and dependent title on which man has received them.

In the Book of Kings the example of Eliseus shows clearly that even the fullest gift of prophecy does not embrace all knowledge, for he says to his disciple: "Let her alone, for her soul is in anguish, and the Lord hath hid it from me and hath not told me."[6] In truth the gift of discerning spirits and of discovering the secrets of hearts does not apply to all times, nor to all spirits, nor to all the secrets of hearts, but only to the times and in the measure that God wills for the profit of souls.

Moreover, all this order of things should hold a much lower place in our estimation than the admirable security in which the Sacraments place us. Therefore, these gifts, though they may be useful, are never indispensable for salvation; persons would expose themselves to even deplorable illusions by desiring them for themselves, and it would be positively irreverent to make them subjects of experiment and of curiosity, or, as we have already said, to lessen in favour of them the sovereign esteem which we ought to have for the Sacraments.

Among these graces gratuitously given we must admit also that they are far from being all of equal value, and we cannot

---

[6] Dimitte illam; anima enim ejus in amaritudine est, et Dominus celavit a me, et non indicavit mihi (4 Reg., iv, 27).

esteem them everywhere equally. The great Apostle proceeds to show this when he says: "But be zealous for the better gifts. And I show unto you yet a more excellent way."[7] This way is that of charity; not of charity in its first degree, but of charity truly perfect and consummate. Such are the Apostle's instructions to his children in Jesus Christ.

While cautioning them against an exaggerated and exclusive esteem for what is extraordinary, he thus shows that the whole perfection of the Christian life consists in charity. Charity gives these mystic gifts their real value; for he says: "Charity never falleth away, whether prophecies shall be made void, or tongues shall cease, or knowledge shall be destroyed. For we know in part, and we prophesy in part. But when that which is perfect is come, that which is in part shall be done away."[8] "Follow after charity, be zealous for spiritual gifts; but rather that you may prophesy."[9] And to the Thessalonians the Apostle gives the same counsel: "Extinguish not the Spirit. Despise not prophecies. But prove all things; hold fast that which is good."[10] Just as he tempers enthusiasm regarding spiritual gifts, so he blames the contempt which some might have of them, and strives to inspire them with a reasonable, well-ordered and somewhat restrained esteem for them.

St. Paul no doubt foresaw that under pretext of advanced science naturalism would try to restrict the action of God, to stifle the Holy Spirit, to set a limit to supernatural workings and

---

[7] Æmulamini autem charismata meliora. Et adhuc excellentiorem viam vobis demonstro (1 Cor. xii, 31).

[8] Caritas numquam excidit, sive prophetiæ evacuabuntur, sive linguæ cessabunt, sive scientia destruetur. Ex parte enim cognoscimus, et ex parte prophetamus. Cum autem venerit quod perfectum est, evacuabitur quod ex parte est (1 Cor., xiii, 8-10).

[9] Sectamini caritatem; æmulamini spiritalia, magis autem ut prophetis (Ibid., xiv, 1).

[10] Spiritum nolite extinguere: prophetias nolite spernere. Omnia autem probate; quod bonum est tenete (1 Thess., v, 19-21).

to say that nothing is real but that which is perceived by the senses. Doubtless illuminism is a danger, but it is not more contrary to faith than naturalism. St. John admonished the first Christians to be on their guard: "Dearly beloved, believe not every spirit, but try the spirits if they be of God; because many false prophets are gone out into the world."[11] Is there anything surprising in this? False coin proves only that there is true coin, and true coin is esteemed in proportion as the false is despised; whereas many men fall into the most ridiculous and puerile credulity in consequence of their having refused to submit themselves heart and soul to faith, as we see in our own days. Do we not know very well that "Satan himself transformeth himself into an angel of light."[12] But we have the means by which to tear off his mask when we remain submissive, respectful and faithful children of the holy. Catholic, Apostolic and Roman Church, the sovereign and infallible mistress of truth: "Understanding this first, that no prophecy of Scripture is made by private interpretation."[13]

In what then does that favour consist which St. Paul wished us to desire above all others? "But rather that you may prophesy."[14] Evidently it is not prophecy as understood nowadays, in quite a modern sense, namely, as the revelation of things to come. In the mind of St. Paul, as in holy Scripture and the teaching of the ancients, prophecy means a special outpouring of the Holy Spirit, who triumphantly takes possession of the superior faculties of man and subjects them to the action of God. Prophecy is the sum total of all those

---

[11] Carissimi, nolite omni spiritui credere, sed probate spiritus si ex Deo sint: quoniam multi pseudo-prophetæ exierunt in mundum (1 Joann., iv, 1).

[12] Ipse Satanas transfigurat se in angelum lucis (2 Cor. xi, 14).

[13] Hoc primum intelligentes, quod omnis prophetia Scripturæ propria interpretatione non fit (2 Pet., i, 20).

[14] Magis autem ut prophetetis (1 Cor., xiv, 1).

gratuitous graces which have knowledge as their object; it does not comprise future things only, but extends in a comprehensive manner to all divine things.

Prophecy embraces all supernatural visions, corporeal, imaginary and intellectual. It sometimes also means a special light granted either for understanding or for judging what others have seen. The divine reality of these visions is recognised in the fact that God, while using the faculties of man as a natural basis, applies them in a way that is absolutely beyond their power.

Thus the corporeal vision is the extraordinary manifestation under a physical and sensible form, of an object which, without such manifestation, the external senses could not perceive, and which, without supernatural help, the intellect could not understand. By its very nature it is easy to see that this order of vision is less elevated and more subject to delusion. In general, God makes use of it only for those who are still much attached to earthly things, in order by these sensible means to draw them. Far from being the sign of great virtue, it is rather a mark of weakness and infirmity. These graces can be judged only by the effects they produce, and these alone determine their value. They ought never to be desired and rarely to be accepted on account of the extreme danger of illusion.

In the imaginary vision the imagination falls under the action of God, for man could not by the ordinary way of its working cause it to produce forms so noble and so beautiful, which suggest intellectual truths hitherto quite unknown. And even when God merely brings back in the imaginary vision things that the senses have already perceived they become invested with a dignity and a comprehensiveness which they had not by nature. God does not act against nature, but in a manner superior to nature. To the imaginary vision belong divine and supernatural dreams.

In this order of favours illusion is to be feared, for the imagination, being a faculty upon which creatures can act, may

easily be deceived by the demon. Here again the effects help us
to determine what has been their cause. If this vision can
neither be produced nor hindered at one's own pleasure, if it
leave very great peace in the soul, finally, if the virtues, and
especially the spirit of humility and submission, increase, there
can be no doubt that God is the author of it. This kind of favour
should not be desired, nor long dwelt upon any more than the
corporeal vision. St. John of the Cross gives an excellent reason
for this. "In acting thus," he says, "we are delivered from the
risk and labour of discriminating between good and bad visions.
The attempt to do so is not profitable at all, but rather waste of
time and an occasion of many imperfections and
disquietudes."[15]

Intellectual vision, by the very reason of its more elevated
nature, is much less subject to illusions than imaginary vision
or corporeal vision. It seems to be the most perfect act of
infused contemplation, especially if that vision not only shows
divine things to the soul, but moreover discovers to her their
signification. Then it is called revelation; for to reveal is to tear
away the veil.

Intellectual vision is the certain and evident manifestation
of a truth or of an object made to the understanding without
the actual help of sensible images. This vision may be more or
less perfect; sometimes notions already acquired are in a
supernatural way set forth in the intellect, sometimes
intellectual species or forms are directly communicated to it.
Intellectual vision thus seems to stand midway between the
obscure knowledge of faith and the clear vision of God. The
light that illumines the object of the vision is not yet the light
of glory, but it is even now a magnificent development of the
gifts of understanding and wisdom united with the light of
prophecy.

St. Basil, commenting upon the Prophet Isaias, gives us a

---

[15] *The Ascent of Mount Carmel* II, xvii.

very high idea of intellectual vision, which he calls a gift of
God, a light super-added to our intellect, to enable us to
contemplate and to conceive divine things. There is this
difference between God and man: man cannot make known his
thoughts nor manifest them to another without using some
medium or corporeal means; whereas God, elevating the
understanding, directly impresses upon it the knowledge that
He wishes to reveal concerning His mysteries. According to St.
Augustine it was to this higher kind of vision that St. Paul was
raised in the rapture spoken of in the Second Epistle to the
Corinthians.[16]

Unlike other mystic phenomena, intellectual vision may
sometimes be of long duration. St. Teresa speaks of an
intellectual vision of our Lord which lasted more than two
years. We have in the lives of the saints other examples of this
kind.

We may conclude from what has been said that this kind of
vision is scarcely possible without perfect charity, and that it is
produced in part by prophetic light; hence we can better
understand those words of the Apostle when he says: "Be
zealous for spiritual gifts; but rather that you may prophesy."[17]
Thus understood, prophecy is no longer merely a grace
gratuitously given; it belongs to the order of sanctifying grace.

Ecstasy also, as a special phenomenon, may be called a
grace gratuitously given, and as such it may sometimes be
granted to imperfect souls, even to sinners, as for example, to
St. Paul on the road to Damascus. But more commonly it is a
degree of union with God; and in this light ecstasy is linked
with charity and helps to sanctify the soul. We must speak of
it in this latter point of view.

Ecstatic union, taken in general, is a supernatural elevation
of the soul to heavenly things, an elevation which is brought

---

[16] Chap. xii.

[17] Æmulamini spiritalia, magis autem ut propheticis (1 Cor., xiv, 1).

about by the Holy Spirit, and which suspends the ordinary action of the senses. The word ecstasy signifies that the soul, whose natural way is to arrive at the knowledge of truth by means of the external senses, is raised by abstraction from the senses into the region of the supernatural. If this elevation takes place with violence the ecstasy is called rapture. God is the cause of this supernatural attraction; He acts upon the understanding and upon the will. In the one it is truth that captivates, in the other it is love; and this happy captivity momentarily withdraws the soul from the use of her senses.

The holy Abbot John, with great simplicity and without scientific phraseology, spoke of this to Cassian: "I remember that the Divine Goodness favoured me and ravished me to such a degree that I forgot the burden of the body. My soul isolated itself all of a sudden from the external senses, and separated itself so much from the things of this world that my eyes and ears became insensible; my mind was so absorbed in the meditation of divine truths that frequently in the evening I could not say if I had eaten anything all day or if I had fasted the previous day. To avoid this uncertainty a basket is given to each of the solitaries containing his provisions for the week; there are two loaves a day, and he can see on Saturday whether he has forgotten to take his food."[18]

So then these men of angelic lives were well acquainted with ecstatic union. They concerned themselves much less than people do in these days about the external effects of ecstasy, the importance of which is very secondary, since they are found in natural and in even diabolic ecstasy; but what they esteemed was that God should so take hold of the understanding and the will as to bring about the suspension of the senses. This possession by God cannot be of long duration, and only by miracle is it extended to many hours. Although God is the author of ecstasy, and though ecstatic union is more elevated

---

[18] Cassian, Coll, xix, 3.

than simple union, it may be said that ecstasy comes from the weakness of the creature unable as yet to bear the divine action, rather than from the excellence of this divine communication. Our Lady certainly never had an ecstasy; and when the soul is raised to the highest reach of contemplation and to the consummation of charity, she very habitually escapes it, though God communicates Himself to her so fully that the Beatific Vision alone lies beyond these, His manifestations.

Ecstatic union produces in the soul admirable effects: an ardent desire of serving God, an extreme contempt of the world and of earthly things, a greater knowledge of God and of self, an ardent thirst after God, accompanied by a lively desire of seeing Him, a wound of love at once delicious and painful, a great interior jubilation which manifests itself sometimes under a most charming form. Certain psalms were written in ecstatic union, and they can easily be recognised by their rapturous tone. One real ecstasy is sufficient to produce in a most complete manner all these effects.

But the predominant effect of all is a valiant and truly heroic virtue. St. Francis of Sales expresses this very piquantly. "When," says he, "we see a soul that has raptures in prayer, by which she goes out from, and mounts above herself in God, and yet has no ecstasy in her life, that is, leads not a life elevated and united to God by abnegation of worldly concupiscences, by mortification of natural wills and inclinations, by an interior sweetness, simplicity, humility and, above all, by a continual charity; believe, Theotimus, that all these raptures are exceedingly doubtful and dangerous .... for what can it profit the soul to be ravished unto God by prayer, while in her life and conversation she is ravished by earthly, base and natural affections; to be above herself in prayer and below herself in life and operation, to be angelic in meditation and brutish in conversation. . . . It is a true mark that such raptures and ecstasies are but operations and deceits of the evil spirit."[19]

The holy doctor makes one important remark. We have said that in simple union the soul has the sense of God's presence within herself; whereas in ecstatic union, especially in rapture, she has almost always the sense of an attraction above herself. If this attraction is not promptly victorious, and does not at once unite the soul with its divine object, there results an anxiety, the more painful as no one can at pleasure cause it to cease. If the ecstasy goes so far as flight of the spirit, which is the quickest form of rapture, the soul is torn away from herself so suddenly that she does not suffer the same anguish.

There are similar differences in the way in which the soul returns to her natural state. Sometimes God allows her to come back suddenly, but it seems then that she has neither been so far nor so high, otherwise she could not bear the violent transition; sometimes He seems to lay her down gently upon the earth and with precaution to leave her to herself, lest her nature should be shattered. If she is not yet very spiritualized, she remains a long time as it were stupified, inebriated, and she takes up the life of the senses again only little by little.

No small courage is needed to support so powerful a divine action. When it is first felt the instinct of animal life wakes up with a strange force and inspires the whole inferior part with a terror like to that which the approach of natural death might cause. In truth the soul knows not whither she is going, and as long as she is not joined to God she feels a strange struggle between the superior part, which, like a bird, is striving to escape, and the inferior part, which is opposing a desperate resistance. If the soul is courageous, she resolutely faces death. It seems indeed that the natural life would be in real danger, if it were not that He who has made us knows well, whilst working in us, how to bring about a separation from self without destroying us.

---

[19] Treatise on the Love of God, VII, vii.

To resist with all our might the divine action then becomes a duty, and it is also a means of knowing whether the working is truly God's, because in that case the resistance will be useless, and will save the poor creature from the responsibility of seeming to seek favours so far above her, which seeking would be presumptuous.

St. Peter, when witnessing the prodigies worked by his divine Master, cried out: "Depart from me, for I am a sinful man, O Lord."[20] This should always be our first movement, and the justice which we render to ourselves. After that, God is the Master, and nowhere does He more fully make this felt than in the union of which we are now treating, wherein the creature is like a feather which the wind raises and wafts about at pleasure. It is also like the working of a sieve in the cleansing of wheat: the human spirit, we believe, is purified and spiritualized while undergoing the ecstatic movement; it learns to live above and beyond the senses in a liberty which no human industry could ever have obtained for it. Only God can bring about such freedom and render the human soul, that is to say, a spirit created to be adapted to organs so simple.

We must know also that the cause of ecstatic union is not always admiration and joy; knowledge and love may indeed be exercised upon dolorous subjects also, and compassion, in its turn, may occasion ecstasy. Only God knows the depth and the extent of these sufferings.

One last remark: a perfect imaginary vision, when a person is awake, and also an intellectual vision in its less perfect degrees, most frequently bring with them suspension of the senses and ecstasy. We might, however, quote some examples to the contrary. Beyond that, the soul, being divinely strengthened, no longer fails in that manner, because God's action entirely excludes the imagination. We believe also that this is the reason why, by an extraordinary grace of God, it is

[20] Exi a me quia homo peccator sum, Domine. (Luc., v, 8).

possible that contemplation is not interrupted even during sleep. Such was our Lord's contemplation and that of the Blessed Virgin; but this culminating point, which belongs to transforming union, deserves to be treated apart.

Thus then, in the wide sense given to it by St. Paul, prophecy comprises elevated and excellent gifts which amount, at least indirectly, to sanctity. In this light we can explain that sentence of Proverbs: "When prophecy shall fail, the people shall be scattered abroad."[21] Whereas the Prophet Joel shows on the contrary that bountiful mercy will take the form of an outpouring of supernatural gifts: "And it shall come to pass after this that I will pour out My Spirit upon all flesh: and your sons and your daughters shall prophesy."[22]

God does not always give spiritual gifts to the most perfect; the souls that possess them retain their several degrees of advancement, and prophecy, as we see, has almost indefinite degrees; when, however, charity creates intimacy between God and the soul, He seems to long to communicate Himself to her.

When Abraham in his generous fidelity had left without hesitation his country and his kindred, the Lord lets fall this marvellous word: "Can I hide from Abraham what I am about to do?"[23] One would think that God can have no secrets from a soul that is so closely united to Him. And in fact Abraham treats with God of the fate of the guilty cities with a liberty which reveals the closest intimacy. And thus does it come to pass with a soul that has no pretensions to extraordinary things, who would even be led to fly from them were it not that the force of her love and the divine condescension raise her up while she is free from self-consciousness.

---

[21] Cum prophetia defecerit, dissipabitur populus (Prov. xxix, 18).

[22] Erit in novissimis diebus, effundam de Spiritu meo super omnem carnem, et prophetabunt filii vestri et filial vestræ (Joel ii, 32; et Act. ii, 17).

[23] Num celare potero Abraham quæ gesturus sum? (Gen., xviii, 17).

Neither does she reflect upon what may be taking place in other souls, she knows only that God is treating her as He treated Moses: "And the Lord spoke to Moses face to face, as a man is wont to speak to his friend."[24]

Such are the mysterious intimacies of the sacred Canticle, which the humble and simple soul does not desire, does not ask for, from which she turns away as much as she is able; but if God takes from her the power to do so, if He leans towards her, she bows down with the ingenuous simplicity of a child, and repeats after her august queen and Mother: "My spirit hath rejoiced in God my Saviour. Because He hath looked down on the lowliness of His handmaiden. . . . Because He that is mighty hath done great things to me; and holy is His name."[25]

---

[24] Loquebatur autem Dominus ad Moysen facie ad faciem, sicut solet loqui homo ad amicum suum (Exod., xxxiii, 11).

[25] Exsultavit spiritus meus in Deo salutari meo, quia respexit humiltatem ancillæ suæ . . . quia fecit mihi magna qui potens est, et sanctum nomen ejus (Luc., I, 47-49).

CHAPTER XVIII
A New Series of Trials which belong to the Unitive Way

NO soul can make progress in union with God without becoming daily more and more purified. We have already seen, in speaking of ecstatic union, that the higher the soul rises the less does God spare her. Divine love is in very truth a strong and generous wine, sustaining the soul in heights above herself, but that love ever enforces the law of total self-abnegation. If persons coveting extraordinary favours had for one single day to bear the burden of those who live in closest union with God, they would be speedily divested of their presumption.

In point of fact, at the beginning of the spiritual life God accommodates Himself to the stature of the soul as heretofore both Elias and Eliseus did to the dead children in order to raise them to life; but when she lives the true life, God adapts her to Himself, and then everything in her that is unfit for union must irremissibly disappear.

Simple union has given the soul a first interview, as it were, with God; ecstatic union has enabled her to celebrate very high spiritual betrothal with Him; but she cannot attain transforming union without having by a species of voluntary death immolated her whole being to God. This death is not a physical and natural death, but a moral and mystic death of which we find frequent mention in the writings of the ancient Fathers. In the seventh century St. Maximus says: "When the body dies, it is separated from all the things of earth. In like manner the soul dies when it reaches perfect contemplation and withdraws its thoughts from all the things of this world."[1] Before him St. Gregory had said: "For what is meant by the grave, save a life of contemplation, which as it were buries those dead to this world inasmuch as it hides them in the interior world away from all earthly desires?"[2] St. Denis and also Clement of Alexandria speak of this death, and our Lord Himself in the holy Gospel exactly describes it when He says: "Unless the grain of wheat falling into the ground die, itself remaineth alone. . . . He that loveth his life shall lose it; and he that hateth his life in this world keepeth it unto life eternal."[3]

In the Scriptures and the writings of the Fathers no state is more clearly pointed out to us than is this one. In particular, Job and Jeremias describe in accents of marvellous depth what the soul experiences at the moment of this death which prepares the way for a true resurrection. Now, this death is not accomplished all at once as our natural death is; it is consummated only by a succession of trials which St. Bernard longed to see completed when he cried out: "Would that I might frequently die by this death!"[4]

In the early trials already spoken of, God afflicted the senses in order to purify and elevate them: His object was by the help of grace to bring the sensitive appetite under the dominion of the reason; but here the reason itself has to be brought into subjection to God. Now, there is a far greater distance between

---

[1] S. Max., 2 de Carit. 62.

[2] Quid enim sepulchri nomine nisi contemplativa vita signatur, quæ nos quasi ab hoc mundo mortuos sepelit? (St. Greg. Moral., lib. VI, xvii.)

[3] Nisi granum frumenti cadens in terram mortuum fuerit, ipsum solum manet. . . . Qui amat animam suam, perdet eam; et qui odit animam suam in hoc mundo, in vitam æternam custodit eam (Joann., xii, 24, 25).

[4] Utinam hac morte ego frequenter cadam! (S. Bernard, SerM. 52 in Cant.)

God and the creature than between the superior part of the soul and its inferior part; hence it results that, if in the first trials the natural faculties undergo severe purification, in these final trials the supernatural faculties are in their turn struck that they may receive a more excellent life after having endured a purification so much the more painful as it is more interior.

In vivid language St. Paul describes the terrible probing which precedes the soul's entrance into God's rest: "For the word of God is living and effectual and more piercing than any two-edged sword: and reaching unto the division of the soul and the spirit, of the joints also and the marrow, and is a discerner of the thoughts and intents of the heart. Neither is there any creature invisible in his sight; but all things are naked and open to His eyes, to whom our speech is."[5] Here we have exactly portrayed the manner in which the death we are speaking of is brought about. God alone acts therein without intermediary. He reaches those secret depths, that centre of the soul where He alone can make His dwelling, and this in order to work therein a purification which is indeed marvellous. Everything in the human mind and heart is there searched with rigorous exactitude.

This death or purification could not be accomplished without suffering, and, as all those who have gone through it confess, no suffering can be compared to it, though it in no way pertains to sensible pain. The cause of this state may be thus explained: a most pure light penetrates the soul to her very depths in order to show her on the one hand her own miseries and on the other the greatness of God; every other reality

---

[5] Vivus est sermo Dei, et efficax, et penetrabilior omni gladio ancipiti; ac pertingens usque ad divisionem animæ et spiritus, compagum quoque ac medullarum, et discretor cogitationum et intentionum cordis. Et non est ulla creatura invisibilis in conspectu ejus; omnia autem nuda et aperta sunt oculis ejus ad quem nobis sermo (Heb., iv, 12, 13).

seems to be in darkest night. For the more clear and evident
divine things are in themselves, the more obscure and hidden
are they to the soul. Therefore the divine light, bursting upon
a soul which is not yet able to bear it, envelops it in appalling
spiritual darkness.

That same wisdom, "the Word living and effectual,"[6] who in
glory unceasingly purifies and enlightens the blessed spirits
purifies and enlightens in this state the soul also. But that
which constitutes the beatitude of spirits already purified is an
intolerable suffering for those who are still filled with
innumerable miseries. Thus weak eyes suffer extremely from a
light which rejoices healthy eyes. "The uncreated beauty," says
the great Areopagite, "because it is simple, good and the
principle of perfection, is also pure from all vile alloy;
nevertheless it communicates its light to men according to the
personal dispositions of each and by a divine mystery remakes
them according to the model of its sovereign and immutable
perfection." This is a very profound remark and one that
exactly expresses the nature of the passive purification of the
spirit.

The source, then, of the suffering does not come from God,
although the light comes from Him, but it is the soul's natural
and spiritual infirmity that causes it. The spirit is entirely
plunged in the knowledge of her own miseries and evils; the
divine light distinctly discovers them to her and persuades her
that of herself she is incapable of anything else. She sees herself
so impure and so miserable that she thinks that God is rising up
against her and she against God: so much so that in order to
exercise the virtue of hope she has to make an heroic
submission of her judgment. What remains of past lights and
joys is now but a torment; for concerning them the memory
retains only what God allows it to retain. In some mysterious
way the light speaks thus to her: "Under the apple tree I raised

---

[6] Hier., Cœl., Cap. iii.

thee up: there thy mother was corrupted, there she was defloured that bore thee."[7] She then feels all the weight of her sad heritage and no longer knows whether she is worthy of love or of hatred.

Nevertheless, let notice be taken of this fact, which is a certain indication of the passive purification of the spirit: the soul has the certainty that no new fault has by her been committed; in herself she cannot find any evil act, any evil tendency that is not at once disavowed; she knows that God has many times shown her immense love and has given her the assurance of even the fullest pardon; but the new light which oppresses her infirmity so evidently reveals to her her misery, that from these remembrances she is incapable of drawing the least consolation or the least help. It seems to her that she has done nothing well and nothing good; that she is, as it were, full of imperfections and of evil. Yet at the least sign from our Lord she is ready to sacrifice everything, even the very marrow of her being. Nay, it sometimes happens that the soul, seeing herself reduced to so strange a spiritual poverty and given up to so incomprehensible a loneliness in regard of God, experiences a terror full of anguish, for she knows well enough that no created being can come to her aid.

It was by anguish of this kind that, for the space of fifteen years, God purified St. Rose of Lima. In her case, however, there was this special feature, that during all that period, she passed only half the day in profound darkness, whereas during the other half, being in the prayer of ecstasy, she was comforted by the divine light. On the other hand, St. Mary Magdalene of Pazzi, during five successive years was subjected to these interior torments. With St. Teresa, these trials were neither so long nor so pronounced, or rather she does not fay so much stress upon them, and perhaps also the experienced theologians

---

[7] Sub arbore malo suscitavi te; ibi corrupta est mater tua; ibi violata est genitrix tua (Cant, viii, 5).

who directed her enabled her more rapidly to surmount them
by marking out for her a very safe line of conduct.

In short, God tempers these trials; He intersperses them at
His good pleasure with the other states, according to the end
He has in view, and the position in which He has placed the
soul that He is thus trying. We believe that His design is, in a
very special way, to strengthen in her the theological virtues
and at the same time to purify her spirit. As a matter of fact,
faith is exercised with incredible energy, a faith simple, naked,
cleansed from all alloy, from all visible help, and firm as a rock.
Hope above all is put to the test, for, as we said before, all that
the soul so evidently sees, all that her faith shows her, seems to
force a conclusion very different from that which the virtue of
hope would inspire. But she hopes in some sort, against all
hope, because she rests solely upon the promises of our Lord
Jesus Christ. She sacrifices her own judgment, she despises the
claims and the protestations of even reason itself, in order to
cling exclusively to the certainty of the divine promises
guaranteed as they are by the omnipotence and the mercy of
God.

As for charity, who shall say how pure and how disengaged
from self-love this virtue becomes in an atmosphere such as
this? With what purity does the soul now desire God's glory,
and rejoice in His divine perfections, even when they seem to
be armed against her! Love of her neighbour increases
singularly and becomes capable of a devotedness like to that of
Moses when he besought the Lord to strike him out of the Book
of Life rather than reject His people; and to that of St. Paul who
wished to be anathema for his brethren.

For this again is another characteristic feature of these
trials. The suffering is too deep to embitter the soul, and she
remains gentle, humble and pliant; and although she is an
object of horror to herself, she is patient with herself and
resigned. We must, however, add that these trials unlike the
earlier ones, are not a source of danger to the soul, because she

is now strong and full of abnegation.

The sacred Canticle in one word describes the trials which even in the very midst of the "enclosed garden," seize upon the Bride. While she contemplates with joy and holy pride the beautiful productions which have sprung up under the divine breathing of the north and of the south wind, under the life-giving rays of the Sun of Justice: "I knew not," she says in all simplicity, "my soul troubled me for the chariots of Aminadab."[8] These chariots, with their terrible noise, are the temptations and obsessions by which the devil tries to persuade the soul that he has power to snatch her away from her divine Spouse. Indeed when the light of which we have spoken plunges her into darkness and anguish, God permits her to be assailed by divers temptations which sometimes go very far: temptations against faith, fear of damnation, privation of the most legitimate consolations, a most intense and profound feeling of being forsaken by God and of His anger, murmurings, revolts and insurmountable disgust for everything.

St. Paul seems to have had in view this state of trial when he wrote to the Corinthians: "In all things we suffer tribulations, but are not distressed: we are straitened, but are not destitute: we suffer persecution, but are not forsaken: we are cast down but we perish not: always bearing about in our body the mortification of Jesus, that the life also of Jesus may be made manifest in our bodies. For we who live are always delivered unto death for Jesus' sake: that the life also of Jesus may be made manifest in our mortal flesh. So then death worketh in us, but life in you."[9]

---

[8] Nescivi: anima mea conturbavit me, propter quadrigas Aminadab (Cant., vi, 11).

[9] In omnibus tribulationem patimur, sed non angustiamur; aporiamur, sed non destituimur; persecutionem patimur, sed non derelinquimur; dejicimur, sed non perimus; semper mortificationem Jesu in corpore nostro circumferentes, ut et vita Jesu manifestetur

This admirable teaching reveals the effects of the passive purification of the spirit, or the mystic death, effects which are of two kinds: some removing the obstacles standing in the way of divine transforming union, and others bearing witness to the union with God which already exists. The Apostle shows clearly that sufferings such as he endures arise from no other cause than a greater intimacy with Jesus crucified. Everywhere he bears about with him the death of Christ; it is this death that works unceasingly in him, and infuses life into all those whose souls have been given to him. Therefore by this mystic death he is associated with our Saviour in the work of redemption.

What is this but the teaching of the great Apostle in that programme of the spiritual life, quoted by us at the very outset: "That being rooted and founded in charity, you may be able to comprehend with all the saints, what is the breadth and length, and height, and depth, to know also the charity of Christ which surpasseth all knowledge."[10] All the saints comprehended this vast mystery of the redemption; not only they understood it in theory, but they experimentally grasped it, and in some sort, as far at least as they were able they compassed it all round. They are, as it were, a chosen set of subordinate redeemers, in whom God, if we may so speak, again crucifies His Son for the salvation of the world, and in them and by them carries on His work.

All this anguish, all these trials and temptations have one end: "For we know that to them that love God, all things work together unto good, to such as according to His purpose are

---

in corporibus nostris. Semper enim nos, qui vivimus, in mortem tradimur propter Jesum, ut et vita Jesu manifestetur in carne nostra mortali. Ergo mors in nobis operatur, vita autem in vobis (2 Cor., iv, 8-12).

[10] In caritate radicati et fundati, ut possitis comprehendere cum omnibus sanctis, quæ sit latitudo, et longitudo, et sublimitas, et profundum: scire etiam supereminentem scientiæ caritatem Christi (Eph., iii, 18, 19).

called to be saints. For whom He foreknew, He also predestinated to be made conformable to the image of His Son: that He might be the first born among many brethren."[11] Who will care to say that this is not a grand destiny? But at the same time we can quite understand that it must be bought at the cost of a close participation in the sufferings of the Man-God, by a real experience of them, which even makes the soul cry out: "My God, my God, why hast Thou forsaken me?"[12] The Son of God Himself was not satisfied with merely using His divine and His infused science to become acquainted with all that the work of expiation should require from Him, and with the extent of the debt contracted towards the Father in consequence of having taken upon Himself our sins, but "whereas indeed He was the Son of God," says St. Paul, "He learnt obedience by the things which He suffered."[13] His submission to the will of His heavenly Father was heroic. How then could our submission to it be otherwise? "For unto this are you called: because Christ also suffered for us, leaving you an example that you should follow His steps."[14]

Our Lord wishes to draw us into His footsteps, to glory in being able to point exultingly to the holy soul as to a stalwart warrior: "What shalt thou see in the Sulamitess but the companies of camps?"[15] In truth these trials obtain for the soul a complete victory, and for this reason which St. John of the

---

[11] Scimus autem quoniam diligentibus Deum omnia cooperantur in bonum, iis qui secundum propositum vocati sunt sancti. Nam quos præscivit, et prædestinavit conformes fieri imaginis Filii sui, ut sit ipse primogenitus in multis fratribus (Rom. viii, 28, 29).

[12] Deus, Deus meus, quare me dereliquisti? (Ps. xxi.)

[13] Et quidem cum esset Filius Dei, didicit ex iis quæ passus est obedientiam (Heb. v, 8).

[14] In hoc enim vocati estis: quia et Christus passus est pro nobis, vobis relinquens exemplum ut sequamini vestigia ejus (1 Pet. ii, 21).

[15] Quid videbis in Sulamite, nisi choros castrorum? (Cant., vii, 1.)

Cross develops in an admirable manner: "Usually the soul never errs, except under the influence of its desires, or tastes, or reflections, or understanding, or affections, wherein it is generally overabundant or defective, changeable or inconsistent; hence its inclination to that which is not becoming it. Therefore it is evident that in these respects the soul is secure against error, when all these operations and movements have ceased. It is then delivered, not only from itself, but from its other enemies, the world and the devil, who, when the affections and operations of the soul have ceased, cannot assault it by any other way, or by any other means. . . . O spiritual soul, when thou seest thy desire obscured, thy will arid and constrained and thy faculties incapable of any interior act, be not grieved at this, but look upon it rather as a great good, for God is delivering thee from thyself, taking the matter out of thy hands; for however strenuously thou mayest exert thyself, thou wilt never, because of the impurity and torpor of thy faculties, do anything so faultlessly, perfectly and securely as now, when God takes thee by the hand, guides thee safely in thy blindness along a road and to an end thou knowest not, and whither thou couldst never travel guided by thine own eyes and supported by thine own feet."[16] "The Holy Spirit," says Thauler, "does two things in us; He empties us, and then fills the void which He has made. The emptying is the first and principal operation; for the more empty we, are the greater is our capacity for receiving. . . . . The water must run out before the fire can enter .... in order that God may enter, the creature must go forth .... the animal soul must disappear that the reasonable soul may develop. When the first preparation is accomplished, the Holy Spirit at once carries out His second operation. He fills the capaciousness of the heart which He has emptied."[17]

We might add that when the reasonable soul herself has

<hr/>

[16] *The obscure Night*, II, xvi, Translat. David Lewis.

[17] Thauler, *Second Sermon for Pentecost.*

been touched, when the mystic death is accomplished in her, God gives back to her a higher life which is her real transformation, her last stage before reaching heaven, the true triumph of grace and the consummation of charity, for she then practises the virtues which St. Thomas puts in a category apart: "But certain virtues belong to those who have already become like unto God; they are those which are called virtues of the soul now purified. . . . These virtues are the appanage of the blessed in heaven, or of those who have attained perfection in this life."[18] The Lord then comes, and marvellously enriches the soul, leading her to a real experience of heavenly good things.

We think it right, however, to say one word more concerning a species of trial that may be experienced in affective union, but which, being a means of purification, may also find its place here. This divine operation always precedes the third degree of the Unitive Life. It consists in a very deep and very spiritual wound which divine love inflicts upon the heart, accompanied with so vehement a desire of seeing and possessing God, that, according to St. Teresa, he who has received it suffers a real martyrdom. In fact, a wound inflicted by the sharpest arrow can give but a faint idea of the pain experienced by the soul at the slightest thought of the delays which may still hinder her speedy flight to her Lord.

This wound evidently carries fire and sword into the innermost depths of the soul, and burns out whatever remnant of earth is still left therein. It causes pain so intense, so unspeakable that, if the soul did not restrain herself, she would utter loud cries; the whole system seems to be dislocated, and the burning heat of the soul is so vehement that it seems as if she must needs be consumed by it. The desire of death then

---

[18] Quædam vero sunt virtutes jam assequentium divinam similitudinem; quæ vocantur virtutes jam purgati animi . . . virtutes dicimus esse beatorum, vel aliquorum in hac vita perfectissimorum (S. Thom., I, 2 quæst. LXI, art. 5).

becomes so violent that no consideration whatever can
moderate it; the soul is as it were deaf to the arguments which
might help her to support life, for her will, violently drawn
towards the sovereign beauty, seems no longer in a condition
to resist this attraction. If all the blessings of earth and of
heaven were offered to her she would remain insensible to
them, and in the absence of her Lord she experiences so great
a sense of loneliness that all created things serve only to render
her grief more bitter. She cannot place her rest in any joy; she
longs with all her might to see her chains broken at last; and
there can be no doubt that in these brief moments her life is in
great peril.

The ancient Fathers were well acquainted with this wound
of divine love. St. Basil thus explains the desires, the effects and
the wonderful impressions to which it gives rise in the soul.
"What more admirable," he says, "than the divine beauty? What
thought more agreeable or more sweet than that of God's
splendour? What desire of the spirit can equal the violence and
vehemence of that which God gives to the soul now purified
from all vice, and in all truth able to say, 'I am wounded with
love.'[19] The eyes of the flesh cannot contemplate this beauty—it
is perceived only by the soul and by the spirit. When this
beauty touches some holy souls, it at once leaves in them the
sting of an intolerable desire, so that wearied with the present
life they cry out: 'Woe is me that my sojourning is prolonged!'[20]
'When shall I come and appear before the face of God?'[21] And
again: 'To be dissolved and to be with Christ, a thing by far the
better.'[22] And again: 'My soul hath thirsted after the strong

---

[19] Vulnerata caritate ego sum (Cant, ii, 5, lxx).

[20] Heu mihi quia incolatus meus prolongatus est (Ps., cxix, 5).

[21] Quando veniam et apparebo ante faciem Dei? (Ps. Xli, 3).

[22] Dissolvi et esse cum Christo multo magis melius (Phil., i, 23).

living God.'[23] And again: 'Now dost Thou dismiss Thy servant, O Lord.'[24] This life becomes to them a burden as though it were a prison; in fact, those saints whose souls had been wounded by the desire of God were able only with difficulty to restrain the impetuosity of their transports. Then, wholly given up to this insatiable desire of seeing the divine Beauty, they prayed that they might continue for all eternity in the contemplation of their Lord's loveliness."[25] St. Ambrose also, in his "Exhortation to Virginity," mentions this wound of love. St. Augustine, in one of his transports, says of himself: "Thou hast wounded my heart with the arrows of Thy charity; and I carried Thy words as so many darts fixed in my entrails."[26] Finally, the austere St. John Climacus, in the 33rd degree of his "Holy Ladder," uses this beautiful language: "When one is wounded with the dart of love," he says, "I sleep because nature obliges me thereto; but my heart watches on account of the fulness of its love. Note, O faithful soul, how after the ferocious beasts—that is, bad desires—have disappeared, the soul like the hart, wounded by the arrow of love, above all other things, desires God and faints away in Him. The intensity and the cause of hunger are not always apparent; but thirst is visible to every eye—it reveals the ardour of love. Therefore one who was on fire with desire of God cried out: 'My soul hath thirsted after the strong, living God.'[27] One of the ordinary effects of holy charity is to absorb certain souls, according to this sentence:[28] 'Thou hast wounded my heart.'"[29]

---

[23] Sitivit anima mea ad Deum fortem vivum (Ps., xli, 3).

[24] Nunc dimittis servum tuum Domine (Luc., ii, 29).

[25] S. Basil., in lib. Regul., fusius tract. inter II.

[26] Confess. IX, cap. ii.

[27] Sitivit anima mea ad Deum fortem vivum (Ps., xli, 3).

[28] Vulnerasti cor meum . . . vulnerasti (Cant., iv, 9).

[29] Scala Parad., grad. xxx.

We might without any difficulty multiply quotations from these mighty men to whom God revealed all the secrets of holiness. They all disclose the mysterious operations of love, its purifying and sweetly painful action, until its fire has entirely destroyed all that it can consume. God visits the soul; but it is not to heal, it is to wound, to make a void rather than to satisfy. Hence the vigour of divine love seems intolerable, and leaves in the soul inexplicable languishing: "Stay me up with flowers, compass me about with apples: because I languish with love,"[30] says the Canticle. The soul cannot find any comfort except in the practice of the most solid and heroic virtues and in the service of her neighbour, if it should please her Lord in the midst of these trials to maintain in her any physical strength. But it is not to leave her thus that God has made this soul pass through the purgatory of love; the end of all these diverse operations is the fulfilling of that desire of the Apostle: "That you may be filled unto all the fulness of God."[31]

---

[30] Fulcite me floribus, stipate me malis, qui amore langueo (Cant, ii, 5).

[31] Ut implcamini in omnem plenitudincm Dei (Eph. iii, 19).

CHAPTER XIX
Of those who are Filled unto all the Fulness of God

HEN the human soul has been faithful to the impulses of grace, and when, being resolved to unite herself more closely to God, she has put herself entirely into the hands of His divine Majesty, God continues the course of His mercies, and however magnificent His gifts may have been up to this time, they could not for a moment be put side by side with the wonderful favours reserved for the soul in the supreme or transforming union, called sometimes mystic theology, which is an experimental and immediate perception of God.

We can easily conceive that to be apt for such a favour the soul must have been purified to her very depths, elevated and remade. St. Paul's words to the Romans must have been accomplished in her: "For if we have been planted together in the likeness of His death, we shall be also in the likeness of His resurrection. Knowing this, that our old man is crucified with Him, that the body of sin may be destroyed, to the end that we may serve sin no longer. For he that is dead is justified from sin."[1]

The soul has even beforehand been deprived of all that is sensible in her devotion and has trodden that way of which our Lord spoke to His apostles when He said: "But I tell you the

---

[1] Si enim complantati facti sum us similitudini mortis ejus, simul et resurrectionis erirnus. Hoc scientes, quia vetus homo noster simul crucifixus est, ut destruatur corpus peccati, et ultra non serviamus peccato. Qui enim mortuus est, justificatus est a peccato (Rom. vi, 57).

truth: it is expedient to you that I go; for if I go not the
Paraclete will not come to you, but if I go, I will send Him to
you."[2] St. Mary Magdalene, who was accustomed to such tender
intimacy with our blessed Lord, had, after the resurrection, to
go by another path of divine love. As the recompense of her
fidelity He says to her: "Do not touch Me, for I am not yet
ascended to My Father, but go to My brethren, and say to them:
I ascend to My Father and to your Father, to My God and to
your God."[3] Thus at the very moment when the Master seems
to repulse her, He gives her the mission of proclaiming the
close bonds formed between God and man, for the hour is come
when that manifestation so ardently prayed for by our Saviour
is at last perfected: "And I have made known Thy name to
them, and will make it known: that the love wherewith Thou
hast loved Me may be in them and I in them."[4]

Indeed, according to the teaching of St. Thomas, the
invisible mission of the divine Persons takes place on three
occasions. The first is in Baptism and in the justification of the
sinner; the second is made to the blessed as soon as they enter
heaven: "To the blessed there is made an invisible mission in
that very beginning of their beatitude";[5] the third is
accomplished when man, being already purified, acquires a new
degree of grace and of virtue: "Likewise an invisible mission is

---

[2] Ego veritatem dico vobis: Expedit vobis ut ego vadam: si enim non
abiero, Paraclitus non veniet ad vos; si autem abiero, mittam eum ad
vos (Joann, xvi, 7).

[3] Noli me tangere; nondum enim ascendi ad Patrem meum. Vade
autem ad fratres meos, et die eis: Ascendo ad Patrem meum, et
Patrem vestrum, Deum meum, et Deum vestrum (Joann, xx, 17).

[4] Notum feci eis nomen tuum, et notum faciam: ut dilectio qua
dilexisti me, in ipsis sit et ego in ipsis (Joann. xvii, 26).

[5] Ad beatos facta est missio invisibilis in ipso principio beatitudinis
(St. Thom., I, quæst. xliii, art. 6).

given for the advance of virtue or the increase of grace."[6] From this principle we may conclude that the Holy Spirit, who is eternal love, by this higher union, comes to enrich the human soul in a way altogether new, which for her is like a true Pentecost. It is thus that St. Augustine explains the nature of the descent of the Holy Ghost upon the Apostles: "On that day He was present to His faithful, not merely by the grace of justification, but by the very presence of His Majesty Himself; and there was in the vessel not merely the odour of the balsam, but the very substance of the ointment itself."[7]

God is present in the soul of the just man by His immensity and by the sanctifying grace which He produces in it; but the soul cannot perceive this union unless God, who is, so to say, hidden within her, communicates and makes Himself known to her powers, and unites Himself to them so that these powers can act upon Him as their object. Then God, by a singular grace, manifests Himself in such sort that He Himself, who created and who preserves the soul, becomes for the understanding an object of experimental knowledge, and for the will an object of truly admirable possession.

St. Bernard has some remarkable words on this subject, when in his commentary on the Canticle of Canticles he gathers up all the ardent sighs and transports of ecstatic union, and points out that the soul is not yet satisfied with all these favours unless she more immediately still possesses her heavenly Spouse: "Unless also by a special prerogative she receives Him coming down from on high into her intimate affections and into the very marrow of her heart, and hath Him

---

[6] Etiam secundum profectum virtutis, aut augmentum gratiæ fit missio invisibilis (Ibid.)

[7] Adfuit ergo in hac die fidelibus suis non jam per gratiam justificationis, sed per ipsam præsentiam majestatis: atque in vasa non jam odor balsami, sed ips substantia sacri defluxit unguenti (Serm., 185, de temp.)

whom she desires not in figure, but poured into her very self."[8]
St. Thomas, in his precise and vigorous language, describes real
union when he says: "For inasmuch as love transforms, it brings
about that the lover even enters into the one beloved, and
contrariwise; so that nothing of the loved object remains
ununited to the lover."[9]

In the fourteenth century blessed Angela of Foligno
describes this state: "My soul is made certain that God is within
her, when she feeleth Him in a way different from what she is
wont, with a notable and redoubled feeling, and with such great
love and divine fire that all love of soul and body is taken from
her; and she speaketh and knoweth and understandeth things
which she hath never heard from any mortal; and she
understandeth them with great light, and it is an exceeding
punishment for her to be silent about them; and if she be silent,
she is silent out of zeal not to displease her love, nor to give
scandal, and out of humility, because she desireth not to speak
of such exceeding high things. ". . . Likewise in this feeling, by
which the soul is made certain that God Almighty is within her,
there is given unto the soul so perfect a will that the whole soul
is truly in harmony therewith, and all the members of the body,
in all things and in every kind of way, are in harmony with the
soul, and are made truly one with her, nor do they in any way
resist her will. And she willeth perfectly the things that are
God's, which formerly of a truth she was not in the habit of
willing with her whole will. And this will is given by grace, and
in it the soul knoweth that God Almighty is in her and giveth
her security. For it is given unto the soul to desire God, and the

---

[8] Nisi et speciali prærogativa intimis illum affectibus atque ipsis
medullis cordis cœlitus illapsum suscipiat, habeatque præsto quem
desiderat, non figuratum, sed infusum (S. Bern. In Cant.

[9] Ex hoc enim quod amor transformet, facit amantem intrare ad
interiora amati, et contra; ut nihil amati amanti remaneat non
unitum (In III sent. Dist. xxiv, quæst. 1, art ad 4).

things which are God's, after the likeness of the true love with which God hath loved us; and the soul feeleth that God, who cannot be measured, is mingled with her, and hath given her His company."[10]

However incredible such a grace may seem, it is, nevertheless, attested and described by St. Denis himself with a precision and a fulness which have never been surpassed: "There are among us," he says, "spirits called to a like grace, as far as it is possible for man to resemble the angel; they are those who, by the cessation of all intellectual operation, enter into the ineffable light. Now they speak of God only with negation, and this is highly fitting; for in these sweet communications with Him they are supernaturally enlightened concerning this truth, namely, that God is the cause of everything that is, but is nothing of all that is, so greatly does His Being surpass every being."[11]

And elsewhere he says: "There is a still more perfect knowledge of God which results from a sublime ignorance, and is accomplished in virtue of an incomprehensible union, it is when the soul, leaving all things and forgetting herself, is plunged into the floods of divine glory, and gains light amid the splendid abysses of unfathomable wisdom."[12]

The admirable St. Augustine, in his "Confessions," owns that the Lord in His merciful goodness raised him to these high regions: "Sometimes, O Lord, Thou admittedst me to an affection very unusual in my inmost soul, rising to a strange sweetness, which if it were perfected in me I know not what in it would not belong to the life to come. But through my miserable encumbrances I sink down again into these lower

---

[10] *Visions and Instructions of Blessed Angela of Foligno,* liii.

[11] *Of the Divine Names,* i.

[12] *Ibid.,* vii.

things."[13]

St. Gregory is not less sublime than the Bishop of Hippo when he says: "God, in some sort, makes Himself seen by a soul that breathes only for Him, without, however, being known as He is. He makes Himself heard in the depths of the heart, without being heard by the ear. He pours Himself into the bosom, without going forth out of Himself. He lets Himself be touched, though He is without a body. He abides with the soul and in her without occupying any place. But if a soul keeps far from her mind all thought of earthly things, in order to love God only, she feels some spark of that divine fire, and perceives some ray of that divine splendour; or if she does not comprehend His excellence and what God is in Himself, she knows at least what He is not. For she perceives that He is above every essence. A soul that in this state contemplates the Divinity, is ravished in admiration, and so many wonderful things are shown to her that they infinitely surpass all that the mind of man can understand."[14]

No state then seems to have been more fully recognised by the Fathers than that of the perfect union which is achieved in the highest contemplation; and in reading their writings we cannot help remarking the simplicity with which they treat of it. They acknowledge its sublimity, describe its marks, encourage the tending to it, seem to think it frequent, and simply look upon it as the full development of the Christian life. By their vast faith and depth of doctrine they seem to have kept the people of their day free from those personal pretensions and that ignorant presumption which have since engendered so many errors and obliged spiritual writers, when treating of these matters, to speak with great reserve. While we are in our present condition as wayfarers, there are certainly snares on all sides, and the spiritual life has its perils; but by dint of showing

---

[13] Lib. X, xl.

[14] Moral., lib. III, cap. xxiii.

only the snares, the ambushes and the pitfalls, souls are kept at a distance who would have risen very high, and would have rendered great glory to God, while perhaps the opposite reflection is lost sight of, namely, that pusillanimity has its dangers as well as presumption.

This little digression must not make us overlook an apparent contradiction in the language of all authors who have spoken of supreme union. While some, like St. Denis, call contemplation infused knowledge, *radium tenebrarum, divina caligo,* "a ray of night, a divine darkness," or again, sublime ignorance and negative contemplation; others speak of the wonderful lights which the soul receives therein, of an intellectual vision of the august mystery of the Trinity which is given to her, a vision which in some sense is almost permanent. But between these two ways of speaking there is no real difference; they simply show the poverty of human language. In point of fact, all these expressions which speak of darkness or ignorance simply indicate that as God communicates Himself to the created intelligence without any symbol or image, but by a special light which is not yet the Light of Glory, the understanding at least sees that He is invisible and incomprehensible, a condition which is very far removed from that of seeing nothing of God. St. Bonaventure lays down precisely this ascending: "The first degree is to forsake every sensible thing; the second, to forsake every intelligible thing; the third, to enter into the cloud where God dwells.[15]

St. Denis, ever inexhaustible on this subject, uses the same language. "We may observe," he says, "that Moses was enjoined first of all to purify himself, and thus to separate himself from the profane; that the purification being completed, he heard the varied sound of trumpets and saw divers fires that opened out

---

[15] Primus est derelinquere omnia sensibilia: secundus omnia intelligibilia, tertius, ingredi caliginem, ubi apparet Deus (Itiner., V, Dist. 6).

into innumerable pure rays; and that finally, leaving the multitude, he ascended to the summit of the mountain accompanied by some chosen priests. Nevertheless he does not yet there enjoy God's familiarity; he contemplates not the Divinity which is invisible, but the place where the Divinity appears. This in my opinion gives us to understand that the most divine and elevated things which we are permitted to see and to know are, in some sort, the symbolic expression of what is contained in the sovereign nature of God; an expression which reveals to us the presence of Him who eludes all thought and who has His throne beyond the heights of heaven. Then, delivered from the world of sense and the world of the intellect, the soul enters into the mysterious obscurity of a holy ignorance, and renouncing all scientific ideas, she loses herself in Him who can neither be seen nor taken hold of, she is given up wholly and entirely to this sovereign object without belonging either to herself or to others; she is united to the Unknown by the most noble portion of herself and by reason of her renunciation of all science; finally, she gains in this sublime ignorance a knowledge which the understanding could never master.[16]

This sublime ignorance, of which the incomparable Areopagite speaks, is as it were the characteristic feature of transforming union, and it is frequently indicated in the holy Scriptures. It is symbolized by the veil which Rebecca carefully draws over her when she meets her spouse, and by the mantle with which Elias covers his face in the presence of the Lord. As for Moses, he reminds his people that God's approach on Mount Sinai was marked by mysterious darkness: "And you came to the foot of the mount, which burned even unto heaven; and there was darkness and a cloud and obscurity in it."[17]

---

[16] *Myst. Theol.* cap. i.

[17] Et accessistis ad radices montis, qui ardebat usque ad cœlum: erantque in eo tenebræ et caligo (Deut., iv, 11).

Again, it is the fulfilment of our Lord's promise in Osee: "I will espouse thee to Me in faith."[18] This is perfect union but in the shadows of faith.

Another figure of this lofty contemplation is given in those passages of the sacred Books in which mention is made of mysterious clouds. In Exodus we read as follows: "And the Lord went before them to show the way, by day in a pillar of a cloud, and by night in a pillar of fire, that He might be the guide of their journey at both times."[19] This divine manifestation producing such different effects represents the double way in which the highest reach of contemplation may be explained; the pillar of a cloud is that ignorance by means of which the very midday of eternal things may be faced; the pillar of light on the contrary shines in a dark place, *in caliginoso loco,* and gives to all the inferior world a divine splendour which enables us to perceive how it all harmonizes with the superior world.

St. Paul, having to speak of visions and revelations, avows that he had been raised to that point where God shows Himself to be ineffable: "I know a man in Christ .... such an one rapt even to the third heaven. And I know such a man, whether in the body or out of the body I cannot tell, God knoweth: that He was caught into paradise, and heard secret words which it is not granted to man to utter."[20] This paradise is no other than the heaven of the soul, where is produced the highest contemplation of which no human language can give any idea. It is very remarkable that having reached the third heaven,

---

[18] Sponsabo te milii in fide (Osee ii, 20).

[19] Dominus præcedebat eos ad ostendendam viam, per diem in columna nubis, et per noctem in columna ignis, ut dux esset itineris utroque tempore (Exod. xiii, 21).

[20] Scio hominem in Christo ... raptum hujusmodi usque at tertium cœlum. Et scio hujusmodi hominme (sive in corpore, sive extra corpus, nescio Deus scit); quoniam raptus est in Paradisum; et audivit arcana verba, quæ non licet homini loqui (2 Cor. xii, 2-4).

which, according to the Fathers, represents intellectual vision, the Apostle does not speak of having SEEN, but rather of having HEARD, as though he would tell us that this high region belongs to faith and not to vision. The following recommendation has reference to this order of ideas; "Whilst we look not at the things which are seen, but at the things which are not seen. For the things which are seen are temporal, but the things which are not seen are eternal."[21]

The contemplative, then, in the act of contemplation perceives things eternal, not by way of ordinary vision, but by a real experimental perception. God reveals Himself, and He reveals Himself as He is, that is to say, one and triune. In point of fact, the soul is introduced into perfect union by a most high knowledge of the august and adorable Trinity. Our Lord's word at the Last Supper is fulfilled in all its power and fulness: "We will come to Him, and will make our abode with Him."[22] Not only do the three divine Persons manifest their presence in the soul, but they abide there in such sort, though not always with equal brightness, that for the most part the soul feels that she is in this divine company. This is so characteristic a feature of the third degree of the Unitive Life that St. Denis begins his treatise on mystical theology with an invocation to the Holy Trinity, which must be read in the text itself.

Then is realized the deep longing of the Church, when she puts these words into God's mouth as He bends down to the soul: "Come, O my chosen one, and I will place my throne in thee; for the King hath greatly desired thy beauty."[23] God has really established His throne in her, as in a little heaven, for the

---

[21] Non contemplantibus nobis quæ videntur. Quæ enim videntur, temporalia sunt; quæ autem non videntur, æterna sunt (2 Cor., iv, 18).

[22] Ad eum veniemus, et mansionem apud faciemus (Joann. xiv, 23).

[23] Veni, electa mea, et ponam in te thronum meum; quia concupivit Rex speciem tuam (In Offic. Virg.)

Master Himself has said: "Now this is Eternal Life: that they may know Thee, the only true God, and Jesus Christ whom Thou hast sent."[24] The soul lives in a close and conscious intimacy with the three divine Persons; for if she is united in a special manner to the Son, who alone is Spouse, the hour has come for her to know the eternal Father also in a deep and mysterious intimacy according to the text: "The hour cometh when I will no more speak to you in proverbs, but will show plainly of the Father. In that day you shall ask in My name: and I say not to you, that I will ask the Father for you: for the Father Himself loveth you."[25] The Father and the Son communicate their substantial love to this soul; the Word glories in being the Spouse of the human nature which He has created; the Father who created all things by His Son, makes it His joy to treat the bride of His Son with the tenderness of real paternity; and the Spirit who consummates this sacred union in the soul, causes her to produce fruits worthy of the everlasting Paternity and of union with the Son.

The great Patriarch Abraham, whom the sacred Scripture brings before us as raised to close familiarity with God, had this revelation of the august Trinity, when he received the Lord under the form of three Angels, whom he worshipped as only one; and this example is not a solitary one in the Old Testament, though truths, and especially the mystery of the adorable and ever peaceful Trinity, were then still enveloped in shadows. This is not to be wondered at: God condescending from those times to raise some chosen souls into higher regions, and unveiling Himself to these souls, taught them to

---

[24] Hæc est vita æterna: ut cognoscant te solum Deum verum et quem misisti, Jesum Christum (Joann., xvii, 3).

[25] Venit hora cum jam non in proverbiis loquar vobis, sed palam de Patre annuntiabo vobis. In illo die in nomine meo petetis: et non dico vobis quia ego rogabo Patrem de vobis; ipse enim Pater amat vos (*Ibid.*, xvi, 25-27).

know Him such as He is, one in essence and three in Person.

The New Testament, which according to the divine plan was to make this sublime knowledge; of God universal, contains the recital of manifestations still more explicit. At our Lord's Baptism, for instance, this manifestation is made in a sensible manner. But in our present state, that is as wayfarers, in via, the highest stage of contemplation is nowhere more visibly portrayed than in the mystery of the Transfiguration. We might say that in this mystery our divine Saviour had wished to give us a complete picture of the state we are endeavouring to describe. First, the apostles see our Lord in bodily vision as they ascend the mountain; then the glory of the Word shines forth upon His Humanity as in a most noble imaginary vision. Moses and Elias represent the two elements which have upheld the soul so far in the way—the law of the divine precepts, and the direct illuminations of prophecy. Peter then thinks that no farther advance can be made, and that they must stay there; but God determines to introduce His chosen ones into a still deeper manifestation of Himself: "And as he was yet speaking, behold a bright cloud overshadowed them. And lo! a voice out of the cloud saying: This is My beloved Son, in whom I am well pleased; hear ye Him."[26] The cloud by its luminous brightness leads them into the divine darkness which hides the sensible vision and even the splendour of the Humanity of the Lord Jesus; then it is that the awful mystery of the Holy Trinity unveils itself to them and each of the three divine Persons, giving to the apostles a magnificent testimony, they lose their clear sight of all the rest.

The same luminous cloud again hides the Lord Jesus at the moment of His triumphant Ascension: "And when He had said these things, while they looked on, He was raised up: and a

---

[26] Adhuc eo loquente, ecce nubes lucida obumbravit eos. Et ecce vox de nube, dicens: Hic est Filius meus dilectus in quo mihi bene complacui; ipsum audite (Matth., xvii, 5).

cloud received Him out of their sight."[27] The apostles being thus invited henceforth to seek God in that cloud, which ten days later was to put them in possession of all the splendid gifts which their divine Master had promised and obtained for them. The perfect bride, which is the Church as well as the soul, can say then: "I sat down under His shadow, whom I desired."[28] The shadow of Eternal Truth is the Holy Spirit who, in an ineffable manner, unites the soul to her well-Beloved; and as the shadow always reproduces the reality from which it proceeds, so the divine Spirit can impress, on the soul of the bride, only the likeness of Him who is "the image of God and the figure of His substance."[29] Sometimes the work of this divine Spirit has gone so far as to engrave a physical resemblance with the divine type as in the case of St. Francis of Assisi, St. Catharine of Siena and others.

It is in the light of this sublime teaching that we must gather the Church's meaning in certain of her liturgical rites, such as the giving of the ring to consecrated virgins: "*Desponso te*—I espouse thee to Jesus Christ the Son of the eternal Father. . . . Receive, therefore, the ring of faithful love, the seal of the Holy Spirit, that thou mayest be called the Spouse of God."[30] In like manner among the rites of monastic profession, the most ancient and general one is solemn prayer in the triple invocation of the divine Persons. The Acts of the Martyrs give ample testimony to the fact that in souls closely united to God the characteristics of transforming union have always been the same. The glorious virgin Cecilia, having finished her course

---

[27] Et cum hæc dixisset, videntibus illis, elevatus est, et nubes suscepit eum ab oculis eorum (Act., i, 9).

[28] Sub umbra illius quem desideraveram sedi (Cant., ii, 3).

[29] Imago Dei et figura substantiæ ejus (Heb., i, 3).

[30] Desponso te Jesu Christo, Filio summi Patris . . . accipe ergo annulum fidei, signaculum Spiritus sancti, ut sponsa Dei voceris (Ex Rit., Consecrat. Virg. In Pontifical. Rom.)

and ended her mysterious three days delay, stepped forth upon the shores of eternity, but in that last act she left as a seal upon her mortal remains the sign of her faith in the august Trinity, and that sign now remains after the lapse of so many years, ever bearing witness to the secrets hidden in the heart of that virgin, martyr and apostle, whose privilege it was, by her ardent words, to bring so many souls to the saving waters of Baptism in the name of the Father and of the Son and of the Holy Ghost.

The great Doctor St. Hilary, commenting on Psalm cxviii, verse 32, says: "I have run the way of Thy commandments, when Thou didst enlarge my heart:" that heart is dilated which through faith is thrown open and made capable of receiving the teaching of God. This also is said of those who believe: "And I will dwell in them and walk in them." Therefore that heart is dilated in which the mystery of the Father and of the Son abides; in which the Holy Spirit takes delight by reason of the spaciousness of the dwelling."[31]

In the fourteenth century Denis the Carthusian uses the same language: "Then genuinely, sweetly and with the keenness of a purified mind wilt thou contemplate the things of faith and the grounds whereon they claim to be believed; moreover, thou wilt in a godlike manner calmly and continuously behold the more than glorious glory of the Trinity, the divine emanation and communication within God, the mutual insight, the love, the fruition, the eternal expression of God's being in three Persons supereminently lovely, supereminently happy and supereminently holy. Then, in comparison with the infinite and illimitable God, every creature

---

[31] Viam mandatorum tuorum cucurri dilatasti cor meum. Dilatatum est cor, quod per fidem capax doctrinæ Dei panditur. Et hoc de credentibus dictum est: Et inhabitabo et inambulabo in eis. Cor igitur dilatatur, in quo sacramentum Patris et Filii residet; in quo capaci habitatione Spiritus sanctus delectatur (S. Hilar., tract. in Ps., cxviii).

will be to thee mean and narrow; and then too wilt thou find
only in thy own God thy one consolation and one affection."[32]
The same author likewise says that God now keeps nothing
hidden from the soul, she becomes the confidant of all His
divine secrets. Since she has generously renounced all things,
even all intellectual enjoyment, God makes it up to her by
communicating Himself in all His fulness: "Because I have not
known learning, I will enter into the powers of the Lord."[33]

Cassian also gives several interesting evidences of the form
which prayer takes in the state of transforming union: "The
fourth kind of prayer befits those who have eradicated from
their hearts whatsoever can wound the conscience, and who
contemplate in the peace and purity of their soul the mercies
which God has bestowed upon them in times past, and which
he is still bestowing upon them at the present moment, or the
good things which He is preparing for them in the future, and
then, with flaming hearts they pour forth that ardent prayer
which neither thought can conceive, nor tongue express. The
soul which has attained this degree of purity and is deeply
rooted in it does not, however, neglect the other kinds of
prayer; she frequently goes from one to the other like a rapid
flame; she offers to God ineffable prayers which the Holy Spirit
secretly vivifies with ineffable groanings, and she conceives so

---

[32] Tunc ea quæ fidei sunt, cum rationibus credendorum et purificatæ
mentis intelligentia contemplaberis dulciter et sincere, ac
supergloriosissimam Trinitatis gloriam, emanationem et
communicationem ad intra, mutuam intuitionem, dilectionem,
fruitionem, consistentiam æternalem, superdeliciosum,
superfelicissimam et supersanctissimam intueberis deiformiter,
assidue et serene. Tunc respectu infiniti et incircumscriptibilis Dei
erit tibi angusta et modica omnis creatura, in solo quoque Deo tuo
erit consolatio omnis et affectio tua (Dionys. Carthus., Flam. Div.
Amoris).

[33] Quoniam non cognovi litteraturam, introibo in potentias Domini
(Ps. lxx, 16).

many things at one and the same time that she could not at any other moment express them nor even rehearse them in her memory."[34]

Elsewhere the venerable author gives some other features not less characteristic: "He who reaches this state, possesses together with simplicity and innocence, the virtue of discretion; he can exterminate the most venomous serpents and trample Satan under his feet. Like unto a spiritual heart by the fervour of his soul, he feeds upon the high mountains of the prophets and the apostles, and satiates himself with their highest mysteries. Strengthened by this heavenly food he becomes so penetrated with the sentiments expressed in the Psalms that he seems no longer to recite them from memory, but rather to compose them himself, as a prayer flowing from the depth of his own heart; or at least it will seem that they were made especially for himself."[35]

It was of this high prayer that Saint Antony spoke, as Cassian again declares: "This holy man," he relates, "said this superhuman and heavenly word concerning prayer, namely, that there is no perfect prayer if a religious whilst at prayer knows and perceives himself to be praying."[36] This means that the soul, being altogether taken up with her divine object, makes no reflection whatever upon herself, as St. Francis of Sales so delicately expresses it: "For if God deigns to give the sacred repose of His presence, they voluntarily forsake it to note their own behaviour therein and to examine whether they are really in content, disquieting themselves to discern whether their tranquillity is really tranquil and their quietude really quiet so that, instead of sweetly occupying their will in tasting the sweets of the divine presence, they employ their

---

[34] Cassian, Coll. ix, cap. xv.

[35] Cassian, Coll., x, cap. Xi.

[36] *Ibid.*, xxxi.

understanding in reasoning upon the feelings they have; as a bride who should keep her attention on her weddingring without looking at the bridegroom who gave it to her."[37] Such weaknesses as these belong not to this high region, and Bossuet was correct when his great genius made him say: "It seems that this prayer, by its great simplicity, is less perceived in itself than in its effects."[38]

St. Gregory of Nyssa says that in consummated union, the soul passes into God—*migrat in Deum*—is mingled with God—per mixta et contemperata.

St. Gregory Nazianzen uses the same expression, *purissimæ luci commisceri.* St. Odo of Cluny calls this union "the sweet murmur of the word said in secret." Cassian considers that in this union the soul becomes so refined and spiritualized that henceforth he calls her simply *attenuata mens,* so little of self now remains in her.

The great prophetess St. Hildegarde, in her inimitable style, has traced the portrait of her own soul, and she thus throws strong light upon the marvellous things which God can accomplish in a human being who is perfectly docile to His grace. In this portrait it is easy to recognise the gift of infused contemplation, both as to what in it may be stable and what is necessarily transient. The glorious daughter of St. Benedict thus speaks: "Since my infancy, before my bones and my nerves and my veins were strengthened, until this present time, when I am more than seventy years of age, I see this vision constantly in my soul. According to the good pleasure of God, my soul at one time ascends into the heights of heaven and into the divers regions of the air; at another she walks amidst different peoples though they dwell in distant regions and unknown places. And because in my soul I see things after this manner, I also contemplate them according to the various changes of the

---

[37] *Treatise on the Love of God,* Book VI, chap. x.

[38] *Inst. sur les Etats d'O raison,* liv. II, 16.

clouds and of other creatures. These things I do not hear with my ears, nor perceive by the thoughts of my heart, nor by the combined action of my live senses; I see them only in my soul, and the eyes of my body remain open, for I have never suffered the fainting away of ecstasy; I see them when awake by day and by night. Frequently I am motionless through infirmities, very frequently I have been pressed down with such grievous maladies that my death seemed imminent; but God has sustained me to this day.

"The light which I see is not local, but it is infinitely more brilliant than the cloud which envelops the sun. In this light I cannot contemplate height nor length nor depth; I see that this light is called the shadow of the living light. Just as the sun, moon and stars are reflected in the waters, so in this light, writings, discourses, virtues and certain human acts clothed in forms, shine before me.

"I preserve for a long time the remembrance of all that I have either seen or learnt in this vision; and I remember at what time I either heard or saw. Simultaneously I see, I hear, I know, and in an instant I learn what I know, what I see not in this light, that I know not, for I am not learned. I have only just learned how to read. What I write in vision, I see and hear; I repeat no other words than those that I hear; I express in Latin words devoid of elegance, what I have perceived in the vision. To write as the philosophers write I am not taught in this vision; the words of the vision are not like those spoken by the lips of men; they are like a bright flame, like a light cloud balancing itself in pure air.

"It is no more possible for me to know the form of this light than to penetrate perfectly the sphere of the sun. In this light from time to time, and not often, I see another light, which I understand as the living light. I cannot say when and how I see it; but while I contemplate it, all sadness, all anguish is taken away from me, so much so, that putting off the ways of the old woman I then assume those of a simple young maiden.

"But on account of the continual infirmities I suffer, it is very fatiguing for me to express the words and visions that are shown to me. When however my soul sees them, I am in the enjoyment of them, so changed that, as I have just said, I forget all suffering and tribulation. What I see and hear in this vision my soul draws, as it were, from a fountain which always remains full and is never exhausted.

"Thus my soul never fails to have this light which I have described above as the shadow of the living light, and I see it as I behold a starless sky through a light cloud. It is in this light that I frequently see what I must say, and what I must answer to those who interrogate me concerning the splendour of the said living light."

Then the great contemplative sums up what happens to her from so continual and sublime a state: "I completely forget myself, both as to soul and as to body; I count myself for nothing; I turn myself to the living God, I leave all these things to Him, that He who has neither beginning nor end may deign in all things to keep me from evil. And thou who dost seek my words, together with all those who in faith desire to hear them, pray for me that I may persevere in the service of God."[39]

While making allowance for the special gifts wherewith the soul of St. Hildegarde was adorned, and for the marvellous fulness that was bestowed upon her, we find in these pages a perfect description of the state of supreme union, both as to what in it is stable and as to what is transient. Moreover in another passage of the same letter, the holy prophetess clearly indicates the way whereby these heights are attained: "Those who in the ascent of their soul," she says, "have drawn their wisdom from God and have counted themselves as nothing, those have become pillars of the heavens."

We should leave our work very imperfect were we not to add that the complete development of the gift of wisdom

---

[39] *Analecta Sacra*, tom. VIII, Epist. ii.

corresponds absolutely with all that can be said on perfect union, just as the gift of understanding seems to be more manifest in ecstatic union. Our sacred Books contain most exact descriptions of this; among others, we will choose the prayer of thanksgiving cf Jesus the son of Sirach: "I will give glory to Thee, O Lord, O King, and I will praise Thee, O God my Saviour. . . . When I was yet young, before I wandered about, I sought for wisdom openly in my prayer. I prayed for her before the temple, and unto the very end I will seek after her; and she flourished [in me] as a grape soon ripe, [that is to say, before the day of eternity]; my heart delighted in her. ... To Him that giveth me wisdom I will give glory. . . . My entrails were troubled in seeking her [i.e., in the trials of which we have spoken], therefore shall I possess a good possession."[40]

Thus spoke a prophet who had reached the apogee of the spiritual life, and who was experiencing within himself in full splendour all that the gift of wisdom establishes in the heart of man. This it is that gives complete satiety to the creature thus favoured; so that most often things that trouble other souls can in no wise move her. The whole life is transformed, it belongs to God, it is spent for God; the soul assumes "angelic manners," to quote the beautiful expression of the Church in many legends of the saints: this is a very comprehensive expression which we must take heed not to interpret in the limited sense of one particular virtue. It is with this wide meaning that we must understand it in the eulogy of the glorious Patriarch of monks: "The man of God, Benedict, was placid in countenance and adorned with angelic manners; and so great brightness shone round about him, that while still on earth he dwelt in

---

[40] Confitebor tibi, Domine rex, et collaudabo te Deum Salvatorem meum . . . Cum adhuc junior essem, priusquam oberrarem, quæsivi sapientiam palam in oratione mea. Ante eam; et effloruit tamquam præcox uva; lætatum est cor meum in ea. . . Danti mihi sapientiam dabo gloriam. . . Venter meus conturbatus est quærendo illam; propterea bonam posidebo possessionem (Eccli li).

heaven."[41]

All this beautiful ordering of life comes from the gift of wisdom which creates in the soul the tranquillity of order. St. Augustine did not fail to observe this mutual relation, and he thus speaks of it: "Wisdom befits the peaceable in whom all things are well-ordered, and in whom moreover no movement arises contrary to reason, but everything is subject to the spirit of man, and man himself is subject to God. It is of these that our Lord is speaking when He says: "Blessed are the peacemakers, for they shall be called the children of God."[42] Not without reason does the holy Doctor apply to supreme union the beatitude of the peacemakers, for in point of fact it is not only patience in adverse things that is then practised, but peace; it is not only virtue that reigns in these souls, but beatitude.

The property of this state then is to establish the soul in peace. Our Lord seems to have accomplished His promise in her: "Behold I will bring upon her as it were a river of peace,"[43] and to have realized that aspiration of the soul: "Lord, Thou wilt give us peace, for Thou hast wrought all our works for us."[44] Then is fully verified that saying of the bride in the Canticles: "I am become in His presence as one finding peace."[45]

The bride of the peaceful king has, by her union with Him, herself become *pacifica*, for she has treasured up and put into action that word of her divine Spouse: "Peace I leave with you, My peace I give unto you,"[46] which is thus commented upon by

[41] Erat vir Domini, Benedictus, vultu placido, moribus decoratus angelicis; tantaque circa cum claritas excreverat ut in terris positus in cœlestibus habitaret (In Offic. S. Bencdicti).

[42] Serm. Dom. In monte, lib. I, cap. iv.

[43] Ego declinabo super eam quasi fluvium pacis (Isa., lxvi, 12).

[44] Domine, dabis pacem nobis, omnia enim opera nostra operatus es nobis (Ibid., xxvi, 12).

[45] Facta sum coram eo quasi pacem reperiens (Can., viii, 10).

[46] Pacem relinquo vobis; pacem meam do vobis (Joann., xiv, 27).

St. Denis: "But what might not be said of that peace which was given to us in the charity of Jesus Christ? For by it we have learnt no longer to be at war with ourselves, with our brethren, with the holy angels; but, on the contrary, in their society and according to the measure of our strength, to produce divine works under the impulse of Jesus who operates all in all, creates in us an ineffable peace predestined from all eternity, and reconciles us with Himself in the Spirit and in Himself and by Himself with the Father."[47]

Yes, this ineffable peace, which thus takes possession of the human soul, at the same time establishes therein a solemn silence and a marvellous and tranquil activity; it is what St. Paul wished to the Philippians when he said: "And the peace of God, which surpasseth all understanding, keep your hearts and minds in Christ Jesus."[48] It evidently goes beyond the sensitive part of the soul, though it restrains and rules it, in order to take possession of the higher faculties, the intellect and will, which it maintains in order and equilibrium. "Thou touchedst me," says St. Augustine, "and I burned for Thy peace."[49] This peace is the fruit of a certain solidity in good which the soul obtains only in the state of transformation into God. It is the well-ordered form of perfect charity, and supposes in the soul possessing it an admirable and habitual subordination, which places her among the truly obedient. This is the course of St. Benedict when leading his disciples to holiness: "That by the labour of obedience thou mayest return to Him from whom, by the sloth of disobedience, thou hadst departed."[50] But the holy patriarch himself is only imitating the most glorious models, for

---

[47] Of the Divine Names, xi, n. 5.

[48] Et pax Deie quæ exsuperat omnem sensum, custodiat corda vestra, et intelligentias vestras in Christo Jesu (Philip, iv, 7).

[49] Tetigiisti me, et exarsi in pacem tuam (Conf., lib. X, 27).

[50] Ut ad eum per obedientiæ laborem redeas, a quo per in obedientiæ desidiam recesseras (In Prol. S. Reg;.)

our Lord Jesus Christ coming into the world, "taking the form of a servant, being made in the likeness of men,"[51] did not content Himself with this form of a servant, but made Himself "obedient unto death, even to the death of the cross."[52] As to the Queen of angels and of men, she called herself the "handmaiden," so fully had she established herself in the plenitude of subjection towards God, and disengaged her liberty from all that could be an obstacle to the perfection of our Lord's reign in her. After this why should we be astonished that noble souls, such as St. Agatha, disdained all greatness and all titles in order to lay claim only to this one: "I am the handmaiden of Christ, therefore I act as a servant."[53] Such is the true liberty which the Holy Spirit produces; for "where the Spirit of the Lord is there is liberty."[54]

It is certain that in perfect union, the soul has a very great facility in doing what is right, and that, by reason of a supernatural light and strength, she habitually in an heroic degree practises the virtues. This form of union with God corresponds to the perfect age of Christ, and to the fulness of His years as far as it is possible to attain such perfection here on earth; the soul is then in a state to yield supernaturally what in the fulness of his strength, life and fruitfulness, might be expected from man here below. When she has arrived at this point, there is established in the soul a just discernment of what is most perfect; it is what our Fathers called discretion, the mother of all virtues. Then, and then only, the soul knows both what is most perfect in itself, and what is most perfect for her; in this consists true discernment. Then she can offer herself to

---

[51] Formam servi accipiens, in similitudinem hominum factus (Philip, ii, 7).

[52] Obediens usque ad mortem, mortem autem crucis (Ibid, ii, 8).

[53] Ancilla Christi sum; ideo me ostendo servilem habere personam (Ant. 4, I. Noct. in Offic. S. Agathæ, V.M.)

[54] Ubi autem Spiritus Domini, ibi libertas (2 Cor., iii, 17).

God in the way that the Church in her legends relates of St. Teresa and of several other saints: "She made that most difficult of vows—to do always what she understood to be the most perfect."[55] Such a vow cannot be prudently made except in a state in which it can be accomplished with a kind of facility, and on condition that it rests on a well-tried basis, for which mere good will cannot be a substitute; for neither a spiritual edifice nor a material one is built by beginning at the top.

On this subject the teaching of Dom Gueranger, which we several times heard from his lips, was as follows: "It is rare that the soul consents generously to the total death of nature, and as a refusal on one single point is enough to make God withdraw, this, in part, explains why so few attain perfection. And yet it is only when perfection is attained that souls can think of vowing to do always what is the most perfect. Hence, in the canonization of saints, the Church makes a special examination of those vows which may give evidence of presumption and imprudence in the persons who have made them. On the contrary, when made by souls who are in a fit state to offer them to God, they add new lustre to their holiness."

In these high regions the most heroic virtue has nothing forced or strained; it bears out the portrait of charity as traced to the Corinthians by St. Paul: "Charity is patient, is kind, charity envieth not, dealeth not perversely, is not puffed up, is not ambitious, seeketh not her own, is not provoked to anger, thinketh no evil, rejoiceth not in iniquity, but rejoiceth with the truth; beareth all things, believeth all things, hopeth all things,

---

[55] Maxime arduum votum emisit, efficiendi semper quidquid perfectius esse inteligeret.

endureth all things. Charity never falleth away."[56] Arrived at this perfect fulness, it resembles the beautiful gilded garment of the bride, "surrounded with variety"; since far from absorbing everything into itself, as false mystics say, charity upholds, enhances, brings out, ennobles the other virtues like a rich and brilliant groundwork.

Nevertheless, although consummate union is always accompanied by this perfect charity, it is well to say that the soul cannot completely escape venial sin. This privilege is reserved for the union of heaven, and we give the reason of this in the distinction which it is important to establish between the state resulting from contemplation, and the act itself of perfect contemplation.

"Here on earth," says St. Thomas, "the last perfection of men, as far as they are capable of it, is the operation which unites them to God. But this operation cannot be continual; the weakness of our human nature obliges it to be frequently interrupted, and we are as far from perfect beatitude as we are from the unity and continuity of this act. Only in heaven will the operation which will make us blessed be simple, continuous and eternal, like that of the angels. The participation that man here on earth can have in this beatitude is by so much the greater, as it is more simple and more continuous, and as it is found in the most simple and most continuous operation of the contemplative life, which is contemplation."[57]

Thus then contemplation is an act and not a habit. There can be no doubt that so long as the soul perseveres in the act of perfect contemplation she cannot offend her divine Spouse; but

---

[56] Caritas patiens est, benigna est. Caritas non æmulatur, non agit perperam, non inflatur, non est ambitiosa, non quærit quæ sua sunt, non irritatur, non cogitat malum; non gaudet super iniquitate, congaudet autem veritati; omnia suffert, omnia credit omnia sperat, omnia sustinet. Caritas numquam excidit (1 Cor., xiii, 4-8).

[57] I, 2 quæst., 3 art. Ad 4.

outside that she cannot be so united to God and so vigilant over herself that some imperfections will not manifest themselves in her. Nevertheless, in spite of this frailty, it is certain that from the perfect, though not continuous act of contemplation, there follows a certain stable and permanent union. The soul saturated with light and love is unceasingly drawn towards the infinite Good, and, according to the teaching of St. Thomas, the soul which has once received the light of prophecy preserves a kind of aptitude for again being enlightened by it.

From all that has been said we may conclude that the whole perfection of the soul that is admitted to the transforming union consists in returning, as far as she is free to do so, and as far as she can do so, to the refined and spiritual simplicity of perfect contemplation. Generally speaking it seems she is able to do so, as if the door of the centre of the soul having been once opened, it were never again to be closed. Nevertheless, God always remains free to bestow lesser favours, a freedom which can be explained only by the non-continuity of perfect contemplation. Thus, although ecstasy does not exist in the state of which we are speaking, because there is neither a going forth of the soul nor a suspension of the senses, God can always, by the splendour of a new light, suspend the understanding, and by the ardour of a greater love, suspend the will, and thus bring back the soul either to the kind of excess of ecstatic union, or to even less elevated favours. The change is not made in habitual union, but in the act of perfect contemplation which God interrupts to give the soul some other favour. We find in the holy Scriptures very striking examples of the non-continuity of the act of perfect contemplation, and at the same time of the ineffaceable graces of stable union which it leaves in man.

Moses one day said to the Lord: "Show me Thy glory." He answered: "I will show thee all good, and I will proclaim in the name of the Lord before thee: and I will have mercy on whom I will, and I will be merciful to whom it shall please Me." And

again He said: "Thou canst not see My face; for man shall not
see Me and live." And again He said: "Behold, there is a place
with Me, and thou shalt stand upon the rock. And when My
glory shall pass, I will set thee in a hole of the rock, and protect
thee with My right hand, till I pass; and I will take away My
hand, and thou shalt see My back parts, but My face thou canst
not see."[58]

Every point is touched upon in this sublime passage: the
liberty of God in the matter of extraordinary favours, the
successive manifestation of divine things, the principle of all
supernatural knowledge here in this world, namely, the light of
faith; finally, the obscurity of the meeting with God caused by
the divine Hand, that is to say, by the Spirit overshadowing and
hovering above.

While we here see contemplation as intermittent, the lasting
union of Moses with God is symbolized by the rays which
surrounded the prophet's head: "And when Moses came down
from the Mount Sinai, he held the two tables of the testimony,
and he knew not that his face was horned from the
conversation of the Lord."[59] This indelible mark, the brightness
of which St. Paul reproached the Jews with not being able to
endure, was most certainly the splendour radiating from God
residing in the soul of this sublime contemplative.

---

[58] Ostende mihi gloriam tuam. Respondit: Ego ostendam omne
bonum tibi, et vocabo in nomine Domini coram te; et miserebor cui
volvero; et clemens ero in quem mihi placuerit. Rursumque ait: non
poteris videre faciem meam; non enim videbit me homo, et vivet. Et
iterum: Ecce, inquit, est locus apud me, et stabis supra petram;
cumque transibit gloria mea, ponam te in foramine petræ, et
protegam dextera mea, donec transeam; tollamque manum meam,
et videtis posteriora mea: faciem autem meam videre non poteris
(Exod., xxxiii, 18-23).

[59] Cumque descenderet Myses de monte Sinai, tenebat duas tabulas
testimonii, et ignorabat quod cornuta esset facies sua ex consortio
sermonis Domini (Exod., xxxiv, 29).

All that we have said concerning what is permanent and what is intermittent in the state of perfect union will help us to determine the form which suffering takes in this state. As long as the act of contemplation lasts, suffering is scarcely possible, since contemplation is a participation of beatitude; but it claims its rights when the soul returns to herself, and when, without leaving the state of union, the act of contemplation is interrupted. There can be no doubt that, in spite of her love of suffering, which love has now become extremely keen, the soul thus united to God ought to strive nevertheless to tend ever to contemplation as to her most perfect act, in order to lend herself to those sufferings only which are expressly willed by God, sufferings which may be very acute, but which generally last only a short time and are of a special kind. Such were the sufferings of our Lord Jesus Christ and of our Lady. They are precious sufferings forming, as it were, a new ransom for the world, and they are of such a mysterious nature that it is difficult to make them understood by those who have had no experience of them.

It will perhaps be useful to say a few words here on the sufferings of a soul that has attained transforming union, were it only to convince those who have not yet reached that state, which is near to the beatitude of heaven, that in it suffering assumes proportions unknown in the other phases of the spiritual life. This is a truth which we must treasure, in order to convince ourselves that beatitude is never a falling back of the creature upon herself, but always a greater self-abnegation and a more complete contempt of her own personality. Divine love enters the soul in proportion as self-love disappears; when divine love has gained a complete victory, the soul can find in self none of that rest which carnal men think to be true happiness. Beatitude is the act whereby the soul of man is united to God; the more this operation becomes in us unified and continuous here on earth, the nearer do we approach the essence of beatitude.

From this teaching it follows that a soul solidly established in supreme union cannot suffer in the way that other souls suffer. Her suffering has no external cause; all comes directly from God, who permits her to be struck and wounded, as God the Father willed that the human nature of His Son should be tortured for the salvation of the world. The more perfect any being is, the more intense and keen does its suffering become, because all suffering springs from some disorder which is repugnant to this being in proportion to its perfection.

Another source of extreme torture is a certain contrast, of which we will now speak. It ordinarily happens that God maintains in the depths of the soul, even in the most intense physical or moral anguish, the sense of union, together with the silence and peace resulting from it. Nothing distracts her; she can taste the suffering in all its purity. The sword pierces the soul in its most sensitive part—the soul now perfectly purified and spiritualized, whose operations are of an exceedingly delicate nature. While piercing deeply, it reaches the centre where God resides and where no suffering can enter, and the effect is as if a sharp sword penetrating the heart were to meet in the midst with some powerfully active substance, which should dissolve the steel. In vain would the blade advance farther; its painful action would cease at that fixed point without being able to go beyond. Thus in the same soul there coexist the most piercing anguish and the serenity of heaven; extremes meet, and the contrast they present is an additional pain.

In this elevated region we notice another form of suffering. The truly spiritualized soul does not seem to be exposed there to temptation properly so called; but God permits that she should strive with the devil, spirit against spirit without the demon seeking to use any intermedium, although he profits by everything, even by physical infirmities, to subdue the soul.

This is indeed a singular combat "in the high places";[60] God takes pleasure in conquering and humbling the wicked angels by means of His servants.

The contact of the demon is then perceived as it were on the surface of the soul, under the form of a burning at once spiritual and sensible, caused by the proximity of a fiery spirit. If the soul is strong and perseveres in her union with God, the pain, although very acute, is bearable; but if she commits some slight imperfection, though purely interior, the demon advances accordingly and introduces his horrible burning farther into the soul, until by generous acts the soul is able to drive him back to the surface. We can easily imagine how repulsive to a holy soul is this contact with the unclean spirit, but happily that contact never endures for any length of time.

We think that to this kind of obsession, or "wrestling," belong certain struggles described in the lives of the great saints, who evidently had reached supreme union, and whose sufferings could not be attributed to the passive purifications which precede this state. Thus we see St. Mary Magdalene of Pazzi spending the last five years of her earthly pilgrimage in a fierce struggle, very different from the trials she had undergone before, and God heard in this manner the favourite prayer of His generous bride: "To suffer, not to die—*Pati, non mori.*"

That which these souls, so divested of themselves desire, as long as God wishes to leave them in this world, is to suffer, to labour and to combat for His glory. At times there strikes for them the hour of the "prince of darkness,"[61] who has been named "the prince of this world." They long to hurl him back

---

[60] Non est nobis collucatio adversus carnem et sanguinem, sed adversus principes et potestates, adversus mundi rectores tenebrarum harum, contra spiritualia nequitiæ in cœlestibus (Eph., vi, 12).

[61] Joann, xii, 31.

again into the abyss and to retard the victory of the beast, as St. John says, and the servile adoration of the infernal dragon, who is to reign by fear. For such combatants do indeed retard the terrible hour of which it is written: "And it was given unto him to make war with the saints, and to overcome them."[62]

But if this high state frequently entails combats such as these, the soul almost always enjoys in them, though in very different degrees, certain privileges such as intimacy with the holy angels. It is scarcely necessary to say that her prayer has very great power over the demons, especially over those which cannot be cast out, as our Lord says, except by prayer and fasting. In point of fact, the Gospel clearly teaches us that the general power of casting out devils, conferred upon the apostles, was insufficient against this order of infernal spirits.

It is true also that in this state the soul, by virtue of her union with God, has within herself great force of intercession, for she asks only for what is in accordance with God's will. She fully justifies that sentence of the Apostle: "Likewise the Spirit also helpeth our infirmity. For we know not what we should pray for as we ought; but the Spirit Himself asketh for us with unspeakable groanings. And He that searcheth the hearts knoweth what the Spirit desireth, because He asketh for the saints according to God."[63]

St. James the Less quotes as an example the admirable Prophet Elias, who had so evidently attained the summit of the spiritual life: "Elias was a man passible like unto us; and with prayer he prayed that it might not rain upon the earth, and it

---

[62] Et datum est illi bellum facere cum sanctis et vincere eos (Apoc. xiii, 7).

[63] Similiter autem et Spiritus adjuvat infirmitatem nostram: nam quid oremus, sicut oportet, nescimus; sed ipse Spiritus postulat pro nobis gemitibus inenarrabilibus. Qui autem scrutator corda, scit quid desideret Spiritus, quia secundum Deum postulat pro sanctis (Rom. viii, 26, 27).

rained not for three years and six months. And he prayed again, and the heavens gave rain."[64] In another circumstance the mere word of the prophet brings down upon the guilty fire from heaven, and his touch raises the dead.

This power of intercession is also due, no doubt, to the way it is exercised, a way very different from all the processes used in the less elevated regions of the spiritual life. Heretofore when the soul petitioned, she insisted with vehemence, and exhausted herself in this petition—a proceeding which in some sort uprooted her—whereas now she makes her intercession on her own ground, so to speak, because when she enters within her own soul, she no longer, as heretofore, finds herself, but the divine Majesty, she no longer sees herself, except as the temple of God. In the Divine Office, for instance, each prayer of the Church finds an echo in this sanctuary, not in a startling way like a passing flash of lightning, but in the great and calm light which abides, and which fills the soul almost without her perceiving that she enjoys it, just as in the physical order we perceive objects without thinking each time of the light which enables us to see them. It is no doubt this abiding within, and this freedom from violence that render the operation of the soul not only more powerful, but also more active and more continuous.

Sometimes there is produced a still more powerful kind of prayer; it is when the soul works without intercession and simply in virtue of her union with God—her words, her very acts are then invested with a special power. Thus the word of the Prince of the Apostles caused the death of Ananias and Saphira, and his mere shadow healed the sick. In like manner the glorious Patriarch Benedict by a simple look unloosed the fetters of the poor peasant who was unjustly bound—an act

---

[64] Elias homo erat similis nobis passibilis: et oratione oravit ut non plueret super terram, et non pluit annos tres et menses sex: et rursum oravit, et cœlum dedit pluviam (Jac. v, 17).

which caused St. Gregory to say: "This is that, Peter, which I told you, that those who in a familiar sort serve God, do sometimes, by a certain power and authority bestowed upon them, work miracles."[65]

The same holy Doctor observes, however, that this power is limited, as also is the knowledge of divine secrets, and with admirable delicacy he gives the reason of this: "For all such as do devoutly follow our Lord be also by devotion one with our Lord; and yet for all this, in that they are laden with the burden of their corruptible flesh, they be not with God; and so, in that they be joined with Him, they know the secret judgments of God; and in that they be separated from God, they know them not."[66]

We should never weary of drawing from this life of a contemplative written by a contemplative. We will further observe how God multiplies the action of His servants when they are closely united to Him, by permitting them to work at a distance: "If then Habacuc could in a moment, with his body, go so far and carry provision for another man's dinner; what marvel is it if the holy Father Bennet obtained grace to go in spirit, and to inform the souls of his sleeping brethren concerning such things as were necessary, and that as Habacuc about corporal meat went corporally, so Bennet should go

---

[65] Ecce est, Petre, quod dixi: quia hi qui omnipotenti Deo familiarius serviunt, aliquando mira facere etiam ex potestate possunt (Dialog;., lib. II, cap. xxxi).

[66] Omnes enim qui devote Dominum sequuntur, etiam devo tione cum Deo sunt: et adhuc carnis corruptibilis gravati pondere, cum Deo non sunt. Occulta itaque Dei judicia in quantum Deo conjuncti sunt, sciunt: in quantum disjuncti sunt, nesciunt (Dialog., lib. II, cap. xvi).

spiritually about the despatch of spiritual business?"[67]

God, seeing that this soul now breathes but for His glory and the service of her neighbour, increases her powers, her aptitudes and her means. It is difficult to say what is the depth of compassion, what the unbounded devotedness, what the ardent zeal of a soul thus united to God and transformed into Him. Clement of Alexandria seems to have known these its excellencies when he thus describes the gnostic or true contemplative.

"He is no longer subject to passions, except to those that have for their object the maintenance of the body, such as hunger and thirst. He has mastered all those that could trouble the soul, such as anger and fear, and through a steady condition of mind that changes not a whit, he does not admit even those that seem good, such as courage, zeal, joy and desire. He has no want as far as respects his soul, now that he associates through love with the Beloved One. . . . For, on the part of him who loves, love is not a desire taut a relation of affection of the soul with her sovereign Good, whom she embraces without distinction of time or of place; and being already in the midst of that in which she is destined to be, and having anticipated hope by knowledge, she does not desire anything, having as far as possible the very thing desired."

"The contemplative honours God not in the specified places nor on certain festivals nor on appointed days, but during his whole life and in every place. . . . His application to prayer and to divine things renders him meek, affable, patient. . . . He reads the holy Scriptures . . . he sings hymns and psalms . . . he prolongs his prayer during the night hours . . . he does not use

---

[67] Si igitur tam longe Habacuc potuit sub momento corporaliter ire, et prandium dferre; quid mirum si Benedictus Pater obtinuit, quatenus iret per spiritum, et fratrum quiescentium spiritbus necessaria narraret; ut sicut ille ad cibum corporis corporaliter perrexit, ita iste ad institutionem spiritalis vitæ spiritaliter pergeret? (Ibid., xxii.)

wordy prayers by the mouth. . . . In every place, but not ostensibly to the multitude, he will pray, but whilst engaged in walking, in conversation, while in silence, while occupied in reading and in works according to reason, he in every mood prays. . . . He continually praises God, and unceasingly glorifies Him like the Seraphim of Isaias. The dignity of the contemplative (gnostic) increases when he is charged with the government of others, and with procuring for them by instruction, the first and highest good, which is God."[68]

This fulness of union with God was the portion of all the patriarchs, of apostles and of all those who by their holiness have exercised a widespread influence on earth. Nevertheless, among the souls that attain to this high region, the degrees of sanctity are very varied as well as the gifts. In this vast world of perfect charity, God is prodigal of His favours to all, but according to the measure of His good-pleasure; and the soul, on her side, is capable of immense growth in holiness. That which seems the highest reach and term is often in reality but a new beginning.

For the interests of holy Church and the glory of God, it is more important than we are able to say that truly contemplative souls should be multiplied upon the earth. They are the hidden spring, the moving principle of everything that is for the glory of God, for the kingdom of His Son, and for the perfect fulfilment of His Divine Will.

Vain would it be to multiply active works and contrivances, yea, and even deeds of sacrifice; all will be fruitless if the Church Militant have not her saints to uphold her. Martha's works were all directed to our Lord Jesus Christ, but they did not suffice because they were not the "one thing necessary." Neither do the saints in heaven suffice to draw down the divine blessing upon this valley of tears; there must be some saints remaining still as wayfarers *(in via)*, which is the state in which

---

[68] Clem. Alexandriæ Stromat., lib. VI, cap. Ix; et lib. VIII, passim.

the Master chose to redeem the world. Our Lady herself would survive her beloved Son in order to sustain and pray for the Church. How could she have chosen that long martyrdom of fifteen years, unless she had seen in the divine light that the welfare of the bride of her Son depended upon it? Certain powers and a certain fruitfulness are then inherent to the present life; it has in itself so few charms that it will not have been useless to show, as we have done, that it has also some advantages.

In the latter days, when evils will be so extreme and salvation will be rendered more and more difficult by the fury of Antichrist and his agents, there will be more saints in heaven than in the most prosperous days of our Christian society; and yet the few faithful souls will thus complain: "Save me, O Lord, for there is no saint; truths are decayed from among the children of men."[69] In an inverse order the increase of holiness upon the earth is a pledge of safety more certain than any other appearance of prosperity.

It is then a duty to promote in ourselves and in others this movement of growth in union with God, animating ourselves with the words and the sentiments of St. Paul: "Now to Him who is able to do all things more abundantly than we desire or understand, according to the power that worketh in us, to Him be glory in the Church, and in Christ Jesus, unto all generations, world without end."[70]

---

[69] Salvum me fac, Domine, quoniam defecit sanctus; quoniam dimmutæ sunt veritates a filiis hominum (Ps., xi, 1).

[70] Et autem qui potens est omnia facere superabundanter quam petimus, aut intelligimus, secundum virtutem quæ operatur in nobis; ipsi gloria in Ecclesia et in Christe Jesu, in omnes generationes sæculi sæculorum. Amen. (Eph., iii, 20, 21).

CHAPTER XX
The True Adorers

E have just seen the soul arrive at the full expansion of the supernatural life, at a kind of success in realizing our heavenly Father's desire revealed in express terms by His Divine Son, at the state which ought to be the one object of our ambition.

Our Lord Jesus Christ, who, as the psalm says, is placed at the head of the book, that is to say who is the firstborn of every creature, took His mortal life with no other aim. Through His Incarnation itself, and in all the actions of His earthly career, His repeated self-abasement, His preachings, His miracles, His prayers, His sufferings, His death, His resurrection, Jesus Christ had no other purpose than to give to His Father all the glory that His holy humanity was capable of offering to Him. And He did not confine His zeal to this effort on His own part; He plainly wished to draw after Him all those of whom He was constituted the Head. He made known this rule by example and by word, revealing to us the hidden plans and secret desires of the ever-blessed Trinity.

One circumstance in particular of His earthly pilgrimage is of special importance in view of this, and deserves to be studied in its minutest details.[1] Our Lord, leaving Judea and going to Galilee, passes through Samaria, and stops, wearied by His journey, at Jacob's well. He was weary, and this weariness was real, while at the same time it was a condescension, for by it our Lord would show to all men the reality of His human

---

[1] Joann. iv.

nature, and that He would not use His power of working miracles on every occasion.

The well, being near at hand, was a suitable place at which our Lord might halt; for in the time of figures, wells were, for mysterious reasons, the places chosen in preference to all others for concluding alliances. The midday hour, that is to say the fulness of the light of day, was the time marked for the new revelation which Jesus was to make of the secret designs of His Father.

By the mouth of the Psalmist, Christ had sworn to take no rest until He had found a temple for God: "Until I find out a place for the Lord, a tabernacle for the God of Jacob."[2] But today the hour, the fulness of time having come, He sits in the road of wayfarers, and awaits the human race. Presently that human race, defiled and unconscious of its defilement, appears under the figure of the Samaritan woman, from whom Jesus deigns to ask a drink. Ah, poor sinful humanity, what could it offer to its Creator to slake His thirst?

Hence this request, full of deep mystery, disconcerts and astonishes the woman. However, through the mists of her ignorance, she catches a confused glimpse of the obstacles standing in the way of God's advances; and if the reasons which she gives are not the truest and best, they nevertheless express exactly the feeling of her powerlessness as well as of her astonishment. An abyss lies between the woman and the Lord, who asks a drink of her; but scarcely has she humbly acknowledged the obstacles than the Lord Himself offers to remove them. "*Si scires donum Dei!*—Didst thou but know the gift of God!"[3] Our Lord in His eagerness to open out new horizons before this poor blind humanity begins by striving to bring home to her her miseries: "Go, call thy husband, and

---

[2] Donec inveniam locum Domino, tabernaculum Deo Jacob (Ps., cxxxi, 5).

[3] Joann., iv, 10.

come hither."⁴

This "husband—*vir*" is interpreted by the Fathers, and in particular by St. Augustine, as being the intellect which ought to rule the rational creature. In the first place our Lord wishes to see the intellect reign in the Samaritan woman; He seeks to illuminate, to teach and to all these things happened to them in figures; and they are written for our correction, upon whom the ends of the world are come."⁵ The New Covenant, beginning with Christ our Mediator and Pontiff, brought, as our Lord Jesus informs the Samaritan woman, a new way of going to God: "Woman, believe Me, the hour cometh when you shall neither on this mountain nor in Jerusalem adore the Father."⁶ This mysterious hour which Christ announces is the time of His life on earth, in the course of which He teaches man the things that are real. It is the time when God will no longer be adored on Mount Garizim nor at Jerusalem, but interiorly in the secret temple of the heart and of the mind. As St. Augustine says: "If perchance thou seekest some high place—some holy place—make thee a temple for God within thyself. For the temple of God is holy, which thing are ye. In a temple wouldst thou pray? Pray within thyself. Only first be thou a temple of God, because He in His temple will hear him that prayeth."⁷

---

⁴ Vade, voca virum tuum, et veni huc (Joann., iv, 16).

⁵ Hæc autem omnia in figura contingebant illis; scripta sunt autem ad correptionem nostram, in quos tines sæculoruni devenerunt (i Cor. x, n).

⁶ Mulier, crede mihi, quia venit bora quando neque in monte hoc, neque in Jerosolymis adorabitis Patrem (Joann, iv, 21).

⁷ Si forte quæris aliquem locum altum, aliquem locum sanctum, in te exhibe te templum Deo. Templum Dei sanctum est, quod estis vos. In templo vis orare? In te ora. Sed prius esto templum Dei, quia ille in templo suo exaudiet orantem (August. in Joann., Tract, xv, cap. iv, 25)

Our Lord was not satisfied with revealing to mankind that the Old Covenant was to last but for a time; He would make known also the lasting glory of the new alliance.

"The hour cometh, and now is, when the true adorers shall adore the Father in spirit and in truth. For the Father also seeketh such to adore Him. God is a spirit, and they that adore Him must adore Him in spirit and in truth."[8] Such is the mysterious secret of the new relations of mankind with God its Creator. It is no longer a promise, "it now is—nunc est"; the time for the fulfilment has come, the fulness of supernatural life is about to be bestowed here below, and the sign by which the new race will be recognised is by its way of adoring God.

What is it to adore God in spirit and in truth? This question which presents itself at the outset is of vital importance for the human race, and calls for exact elucidation.

Like all things else that were to be consummated in the New Testament, this perfect adoration and these true adorers were prefigured in the Old Testament. As a skilful architect God foresaw His work, and laid the stepping stones. Moses was a true adorer; and the Lord Himself, having summoned Aaron and his sister to come before the Tabernacle, explained to them what this meant: "Hear My words: If there be among you a prophet of the Lord I will appear to him in a vision or I will speak to him in a dream. But it is not so with My servant Moses, who is most faithful in all My house; for I speak to him mouth to mouth; and plainly and not by riddles and figures doth he see the Lord."[9] The Lord here clearly marks out the line

---

[8] Venit hora et nunc est quando veri adoratores adorabunt Patrem in spiritu et veritate. Nam et Pater tales quærit qui adorent eum. Spiritus est Deus, et eos qui adorant eum, in spiritu et veritate oportet adorare. (Joann., iv, 23-24).

[9] Audite sermones meos: Si quis fuerit inter vos propheta Domini, in visione apparebo ei, vel per somnium loquar ad illum. At non talis servus meus Moyses, et in omni domo mea fidelissimus est; ore enim ad os loquor ei; et palam, et non per ænigmata et figuras Dominum

of demarcation between His ordinary servants, even those whom He prevents with His favours, and those who are in the state of true adorers in spirit and in truth.

Christian tradition has universally recognised and defined this state. The holy ambition of being numbered among these adorers by excellence, whom the Father so greatly longs for, has ever been proposed to souls as the object of their noblest desires. We will bring forward only two examples. St. Cyril of Alexandria, who has devoted a whole treatise to the subject of adoration in spirit and in truth, commenting upon this passage of the Gospel, says: "Rightly therefore does God accept the spiritual worshipper who does not in form and type carry in Jewish-wise the form of godliness, but in Gospel-manner, resplendent in the achievements of virtue and in rightness of the Divine doctrines, fulfilleth the real true worship."[10]

The learned Abbot Rupert goes farther still. "The true adorers," says he, "are not those who are ignorant of the object of their adoration, but those who have the true knowledge of it. They adore the Father not upon the mountain, not in Jerusalem, but in spirit and in truth. The adorers of the Father are they who receive from Him the spirit of adoption of sons and who become the members of His only Son. For to adore in spirit is to have received the spirit of adoption, whereby we cry: Father, Father! To adore the Father in truth is to abide in the Son, who said: 'I am the Truth.' Therefore the true adorers adore one only God, Father, Son and Holy Ghost, in the manifest and necessary distinction of persons."

"True adoration is the operation proper to the Holy Spirit; for it is first requisite that men should receive the Holy Spirit

---

videt (Num. xii, 6-8)

[10] Spiritualis adorator gratus est, qui non forma et figuris judaicis ad pietatem obumbratur, sed evangelica virtute fulgens, recta dogmatum disciplina, veram peragit adorationem (Cyril. Alex., Sup. Evang. Joann., lib. II, cap. xciii).

by means of a preventing grace, in order by Him to know and to confess that our Lord came in the flesh. This is the direct way of going to the Father. This is precisely why He says that they shall adore the Father in spirit and in truth, and not in truth and in spirit."[11]

From this teaching we may conclude that the true adorers whom the heavenly Father seeks are the children of God, the brethren of our Lord Jesus Christ, the temples of the Holy Spirit. The Father seeks them, because He knows that He will find them; and He will find them, because all things have been by eternal wisdom, strongly and sweetly disposed to bring about their existence. Seeing them so greatly desired by the Father, objects of such solicitude on the part of the Son, so tenderly loved by the Holy Ghost, we might be tempted to think that they form a species apart, a privileged caste, as it were, among mankind. They are however nothing of the kind. All men have been redeemed at the price of that most Precious Blood, the sovereign virtue of which more than suffices for the ransom of ten thousand worlds; all men are called to become those true adorers who worship God in spirit and in truth.

Nevertheless our Lord knew our innate powerlessness to attain those regions whose approach He pointed out to the Samaritan woman. No human effort can produce that union with God which is the essence of holiness. "Without Me you can do nothing,"[12] said our Lord. The Master Himself must advance towards His creature, He must uphold her, must raise her to Himself by anticipating and accompanying all her acts, that this poor creature may be able to give Him the return which He expects and which He seeks.

Plainly, though by true adorers we do not mean souls made blessed for ever by the vision of God, neither do we mean weak souls nor mere beginners in the service of God. The true

[11] Rup. Comment, in Joann., lib. IV, cap. iii.

[12] Sine me nihil potestis facere (Joann, xv, 5).

adorers are those who live in God, for God and with God, persevering in the only attitude which befits intelligent creatures, whose whole activity unceasingly tends towards God; they are those who are commonly called "saints."

Saints are men like the rest of us; only they seriously take to heart the conditions of their creation and the end which God had in view in creating them. Faithfully, and in the measure granted to them, they use all the graces that our Lord puts at their disposal. The very tenor of the Gospel narrative clearly shows that at the baptismal font the true adorers are born to the supernatural life by being made Christians. For it is at Jacob's well that our Lord makes known God's intentions to the Samaritan woman, and His first advance to her is the offer of a mysterious water, which is to be placed within the reach of all men and is to quench their thirst for ever. At our Baptism then we become true adorers, and in that Sacrament we are provided with all the forces requisite to make us those adorers, in spirit and in truth whom the Father seeks.

Moreover, the divine Food prepared for our nourishment contains within itself all that is calculated to stamp us with the character of true adorers. For our Lord Jesus Christ as Man, the Adorer by excellence, in strict obedience offered Himself, and unceasingly offers Himself to the glory of His Father. He never comes into us to inoculate us with His divine and human virtues until He has paid the debt of an adoration which surpasses the homage of all creatures. How then will He not form us to become true adorers who "being in the form of God thought it not robbery to be equal with God, but emptied Himself."[13] And He humbled Himself to the death of the cross in order to offer to His Father a tribute of adoration and of praise.

The true adorer follows his Master even unto the entire

---

[13] Cum in forma Dei esset, non rapinam arbitratus est esse se æqualem Deo; sed semetipsum exinanivit (Philip., ii, 6-7).

abnegation of himself, practising to the letter all that our Lord Jesus tells him, when He says: "If any man will come after Me, let him deny himself, and take up his cross and follow Me."[14] This way thus marked out is widely thrown open to all who are baptized; and if we persevere in thus following our Saviour, it will lead us to that perfection which will fulfil our heavenly Father's desire in our regard.

But above all things we must be convinced that no one can pretend to be an adorer in spirit and in truth if he has not resolutely broken with all idolatry. Now idolatry, if we are to believe the Apostle, is not confined to the worship of false gods. We can raise within ourselves many idols, and blindly offer sacrifice to them: "For know ye this and understand that no fornicator, or unclean or covetous person (which is a serving of idols) hath inheritance in the kingdom of Christ and of God."[15] To be true adorers we must have destroyed all these idols, we must have entirely purified our hearts of them, and have established within ourselves the dwelling place of God: "For you are temples of the living God, as God saith: I will dwell in them, and walk among them; and I will be their God, and they shall be My people."[16]

Hence in the true adorer the separation between darkness and light must be complete, for the special characteristic of such a one is solidity in good. All Christians adore God, and yet not all, strictly speaking, can claim the title of "adorers." In the Scriptures this appellation is so rare that, so far as we know, it

---

[14] Si quis vult post me venire, abneget semetipsum, et tollat crucem suam, et sequatur me (Luc. xvi, 24).

[15] Hoc enim scitote intelligentes, quod omnis fornicator, aut immundus, aut avarus quod est idolorum servitus, non habet hereditatem in regno Christi et Dei (Eph. v, 5).

[16] Qui autem consensus templo Dei cum idolis? Vos enim estis templum Dei vivi, sicut dicit Deus: Quoniam inhabitabo in illis, et inambulabo inter eos; et ero illorum Deus, et ipsi erunt mihi populus (2 Cor. vi, 16).

does not appear anywhere except in the fourth chapter of St. John's Gospel, in which is related the meeting of our Lord and the Samaritan woman. Adoration is the most noble act that an intelligent and free creature can perform. It is the form of divine love making a return to God in a created spirit; it is the homage of submission, of perfect subjection and obedience, offered by a contingent being to the necessary Being. Again, it is an act of solemn donation, and as it were an universal recognition by a most perfect holocaust, of the sovereign dominion of God.

But adoration in spirit and in truth is something more still; it is the only response of the intellect to the revelation which God makes of Himself in the unity of His essence and the Trinity of Persons. Such an act is only possible for a soul baptized in the name of the Father, of the Son and of the Holy Ghost. It was to such a one that St. Athanasius said: "We must adore God the Father in truth—that is to say, in the Son and in the Holy Ghost; that is, we must adore the triune God—we must adore the holy Trinity, God in three Persons."[17] This act of adoration in spirit and in truth, which Baptism enables the Christian to offer, does not however constitute him as an adorer properly so called, unless this adoration becomes in him not a passing and rare act, but a sort of permanent disposition, a kind of professional state and a constant attitude of soul.

The true adorer is he who, having abandoned all multiplicity, is brought back to perfect simplicity; the true adorer is he who, by a sustained effort, has been able to establish perfect harmony in his soul, there being now no discord arising from contradictory elements or rival claims, and thus he regains the primary unity of his being. The simple soul

---

[17] Oportet adorare Deum, scilicet Patrem, in veritate, id est, in Filio et in Spiritu sancto; hoc est, oportet adorare Deum trinum et unum, oportet adorare sanctam Trinitatem ac tres ejus personas (Ep. ad Serapionem).

has but one look, one love, one intention, one pretension, one end. One look, she sees but God; one love, she loves but God; one intention, she tends but to God; one pretension, to please God; one end, to possess God. She neither falls back upon the past, nor anxiously forecasts the future; she peacefully concentrates all her forces into the unity of the present hour, and in the present moment she sees but the unity of God's good pleasure. The simple soul lives in peaceful detachment and holy indifference—times, places, employments, successes, events of any kind never trouble the peace and security in which the total surrender of herself to God's good pleasure establishes her.

It is to express this kind of unity and simplicity, which implies the perfect restoration of man to that integrity in which God created him, that the holy Scriptures often speak of holy souls under the names of doves and virgins. When this restoration has been attained, the whole life becomes one continued homage of adoration to the most holy and ever-peaceful Trinity.

The true adorer therefore is he who, having cast forth out of his life all other cares, lives before God sheltered from human fears and passions: "Thou shalt hide them in the secret of Thy face."[18] Such a one now knows no darkness other than the darkness of faith; but faith is so pure that in speaking of it St. Laurence could boldly say: "There is no darkness in my night, but everything is resplendent with light."[19] The faith of the true adorer becomes his very life. God—Father, Son and Holy Ghost—becomes master of all his activity, directs and governs it so completely that, though applied by God to manifold duties and missions, the true adorer ever does but one work—the work of adoration.

To him may well be applied that beautiful sentence of St. Nilus in his book on prayer: "If thou be a theologian, thou wilt

[18] Abscondes eos in abscondito faciei tuæ (Ps., xxx, 21).

[19] Mea nox obscurum non habet; sed omnia in luce clarescunt.

pray truly; and if thou dost pray truly, thou art a theologian."[20]
And how is it possible that he should not be a theologian who
lives before the face of God, and whose interior activity is
ordained by God, is subject to God, and is entirely directed to
God? The state of such a one is again described by the same
holy Abbot when he says: "This state, this repose is a tranquil
habit of prayer which, in strong love, carries away the spiritual
soul into the heights of God." [21]

All the ancient Fathers look upon "true adorers" as those
who have attained the summit of the supernatural life; their
Baptism is, as it were, all in act: they work less by what they do
than by what they have become. Restored to perfect unity, they
go to God by a process less human than angelic: "Whither the
impulse of the spirit was to go thither they went; and they
turned not when they went."[22] It is what St. Nilus again says:
"Dost thou desire to pray? Flee away from earth, and
henceforth let thy conversation be in heaven, not by simply
conversing with God but by angelic acts and by a more elevated
knowledge of divine things."[23] Thus living in the immediate
application of their souls to God, these true adorers should, like
the blessed spirits who live in God's presence, ever strive to
urge and draw to Him those souls that still have need of
symbols, or that have not yet succeeded in freeing themselves
from the tyranny of the flesh, of the senses and of the passions,

---

[20] Si theologus es, vere orabis; et si vere oraveris, eris theologus.
(Tract., de Oratione, lx).

[21] Status orationis et habitus absque passione, amore summo ad
celestudinem intelligibilem rapiens mentem sapientem et spiritalem
(Tract. De Oratione, lii).

[22] Ubi erant impetus spiritus, iluc gradiebantur, nec revertebantur
cum ambularent (Ezech. i, 12).

[23] Cupis orare? Transferendo te hinc, conversationem jugiter in
cœlis habe, non nudo verbo simplicitur sed actu angelico et diviniore
cognitione (Tract. De Oratione, cxliii).

and that, being only beginners in the spiritual life, are still in the midst of multiplicity and division.

These are the adorers whom God the Father seeks. He is proud of having obtained them; for, being closely united to His only Son, they carry on and with superior force and vigour complete His work on earth. It is of them that St. Denis speaks when he says: "The perfection of the members of the hierarchy is by a courageous imitation to approach God, and what is still more sublime, to become His cooperators, as holy Scripture says: 'For we are God's coadjutors,'[24] and to show forth in themselves, according to the power that is in them, the marvellous effects of God's working."[25]

Again, it is to the true adorers in spirit and in truth that may be applied this passage of the same author, speaking of the angelic intelligences: "They are inundated with the light which surpasses all spiritual knowledge, and admitted, as far as their nature permits, to the vision of that supereminent Beauty, which is the cause and origin of all beauty which shines forth in the three adorable Persons; they enjoy the humanity of our Saviour otherwise than under the veil of certain figures in which His august perfections are portrayed; for by their free access to Him, they directly receive and comprehend His holy lights; finally, it is given to them in a higher way to imitate Jesus Christ, since they participate, according to their capacity, in the first outpouring of His divine and human virtue."[26]

And lest we should be reproached with falsely attributing to man that which is the privilege of angels only, we will again borrow these lines from the glorious Areopagite: "There are among us," says he, "some spirits called to a like grace, as far as it is possible for man to compare with an angel; they are those

---

[24] Dei sumus adjutores (1 Cor. iii, 9).

[25] De Cœl. Hier., cap. iii.

[26] De Cœlest., Hier., cap. Vii.

who, by the cessation of all intellectual operation, enter into intimate union with the ineffable light."[27] They are the true adorers in spirit and in truth; they literally carry out the order of the Apostle St. Paul: "Be ye followers of God, as most dear children; and walk in love, as Christ also hath loved us, and hath delivered Himself for us, an oblation and a sacrifice to God for an odour of sweetness."[28]

Such are the true adorers whom the heavenly Father seeks, after employing all His divine skill to form and fashion them. For if in the beginning the august Trinity seemed, as it were, to pause and reflect before the work of man's creation, this same God, one in substance and three in persons, in recreating man, does a still more admirable work, for by it He recovers and perfects His first work and the new creature receives a more faithful and noble impress of the divine Image and likeness.

---

[27] De Nom. Divin., cap. i.

[28] Estote imitatores Dei, sicut filii carissimi, et ambulate in dilectione, sicut et Christus dilexit nos, et tradidit semetipsum pro nobis oblationem et hostiam Deo in odorem suavitatis (Eph., v, 1-2).

THE CORONATION OF THE BLESSED VIRGIN
Peter Paul Rubens

CHAPTER XXI

Of the Place which our Blessed Lady holds in our Spiritual Life

BOOK on prayer would not be complete if it contained no mention of one of the principal agents in the work of our sanctification, if it failed to speak of that special help provided by our Saviour's goodness for enabling us to become true adorers; in a word, if it overlooked the important place held by the Blessed Virgin Mary in the spiritual life of each one of us.

After God, we owe our natural life to our father and mother, the salutary influence of the latter lasting sometimes through the whole of our life. The Decalogue makes no distinction between our parents, either in our love of them or in our duties towards them, and many are the lessons given in the holy Scriptures on this subject: "My son, hear the instruction of thy father, and forsake not the law of thy mother, that grace maybe added to thy head and a chain of gold to thy neck."[29] One of the causes of an impure life, according to the Holy Spirit, is to be found in a wrong attitude towards our parents: "There is a generation that curseth their father, and doth not bless their mother, a generation that are pure in their own eyes, and yet are not washed from their filthiness."[30] After our duties towards God there is in Christian morality nothing that is more strongly

---

[29] Audi, fili mi, disciplinam patris tui, et ne dimittas legem matris tuæ, ut addatur gratia capiti tuo, et torques collo tuo (Prov. i, 8,9)

[30] Generatio quæ patri suo maledicit, et quas matri suæ non benedicit. Generatio quæ sibi munda videtur, et tamen non est lota a sordibus suis (Prov. xxx, 11, 12).

insisted upon than our duties towards our parents.

Nevertheless the importance and sacredness of these natural ties is far surpassed by what, in the supernatural order, God has willed to establish for us. It is hardly correct, even in our language, to take as our exemplar the natural order; yea, rather it is the supernatural order that holds the priority; for though there is reality in the natural order, it is but the reflection, the copy of the things from above. Hence relationships and names in the natural order have less meaning and less strength than those of the supernatural order.

God's paternity over us is not a mere name and imputation, but a reality higher and more complete than human paternity, as St. Paul acknowledged when speaking of God the Father: "Of whom all paternity in heaven and in earth is named."[31] And although the divine paternity in our regard is not a paternity of nature, but of adoption, we must understand the words here in a particular sense. The adoption of which we are the object is not simply juridical and purely external, as among men; it contains a real filiation by the intrinsic change which takes place in us by elevating grace, which transforms us into new creatures, "partakers of the divine nature."

But our Lord Jesus Christ, who obtained for us that His Father should become our Father, has set no limits to His favours; and as man, having Himself a Mother, the true gem of her race, He would have her adopt us as her children, in virtue of an adoption very different also from juridical adoption. In point of fact, when in the sublime scene of the Annunciation our Lady gave her assent to the mystery of the Incarnation, and pronounced the words, "Behold the handmaid of the Lord; be it done to me according to Thy word,"[32] there can be no doubt that, divinely instructed, she assented to become the Mother,

---

[31] Ex quo omnis paternitas in cœlis ct in terra nominatur (Eph. iii, 15).

[32] Ecce ancilla Domini: fiat mihi secundum verbum tuum (Luc. i, 38).

not only of God, but also of man. For our Lord is not complete without us, since He is the Head and we are the members: "That He might be the firstborn amongst many brethren."[33] And Mary, Mother of the real body of her Son, was equally to be Mother of His mystical body. Just in the same way as we are the members of our Lord: "Because we are members of His body, of His flesh and of His bones,"[34] so also are we the true children of the Mother of God.

But this is not all: Mary is our Mother also by alliance. Most certainly the Blessed Virgin was not ignorant that her Son was the Saviour promised to mankind, and that out of mankind He should form His Church, His beloved bride: "Christ loved the Church, and delivered Himself up for it, that He might sanctify it, cleansing it by the laver of water in the word of life. That He might present it to Himself a glorious Church."[35] Mary knew the whole mystery of these divine nuptials, concerning which the Old Testament itself could not be silent, since their realization was the expectation and the desire of the whole world. She was acquainted with the language of the prophets, she knew that Jeremias in God's name had challenged sinful humanity, saying with tenderness: "Yea, I have loved thee with an everlasting love; therefore have I drawn thee, taking pity on thee."[36] And again: "Return, O ye revolting children, saith the Lord, for I am your husband."[37] Neither was she ignorant that

---

[33] Ut sit ipse primogenitus in multis fratribus (Rom. viii, 29).

[34] Quia membra sumus corporis ejus, de carne ejus et de ossibus ejus (Eph. v, 30).

[35] Christus dilexit Ecclesiam, et semetipsum tradidit pro ea, ut illam sanctificaret, mundans lavacro aquæ in verbo vitæ, ut exhiberet ipse sibi gloriosam Ecclesiam (Eph. v, 25-27).

[36] In caritate perpetua dilexi te: ideo attraxi te, miserans (Jer. xxxi, 3).

[37] Convertimini, filii revertentes, dicit Dominus, quia ego vir vester (Jer., iii, 14).

God had promised to contract a new alliance, even after the bride's infidelity to a first alliance, as He had declared by Ezechiel; "And I will remember My covenant with thee in the days of thy youth; and I will establish with thee an everlasting covenant"[38]—a covenant confirmed by the Prophet Osee, "And I will espouse thee to Me for ever; and I will espouse thee to Me in justice and judgment and in mercy and in commiserations."[39]

Our Lady, knowing all these and many other texts, could conclude from them that her Son would be the Bridegroom announced in the Canticle of Canticles. That being the case, her maternal heart would go forth towards that predestined bride, whose nuptial feast was to be prepared by her care: "Go forth, ye daughters of Sion, and see King Solomon in the diadem wherewith his mother crowned him in the day of his espousals and in the day of the joy of his heart."[40] In truth, our Mother, even from the days of Nazareth, looked upon us, in virtue of our alliance with the King her Son, as her children.

The declaration made to her on Calvary: "Woman, behold thy Son,"[41] was but the full revelation and public announcement of a truth which had long been familiar to her. At that solemn hour, when the Church was about to come forth from the open side of the new Adam, it was highly fitting that Mary's maternity should be proclaimed in all its fulness, as Isaias had sung of it in sublime prophetic language: "Before she was in labour, she brought forth; before her time came to be delivered, she brought forth a Man-child. Who hath ever heard such a

---

[38] Recordabor ego pacti mei tecum in diebus adolescentiæ tuæ, et suscitabo tibi pactum sempiternum (Ezech., xvi, 60).

[39] Sponsabo te mihi in sempiternum; et sponsabo te mihi in justitia, et judicio, et in misericordia, et in miserationibus (Osee ii, 19).

[40] Egredimini et videte, filiæ Sion, regem Salomonem in diademate quo coronavit illum mater sua in die desponsationis illius, et in die lætitiæ cordis ejus (Can., iii, 11).

[41] Mulier, ecce filius tuus (Joann, xix, 26).

thing? And who hath seen the like to this? Shall the earth bring forth in one day? Or shall a nation be brought forth at once, because Sion hath been in labour, and hath brought forth her children."[42] Here we have first a giving birth to an only Son, and that without labour; then to a whole nation in anguish and suffering; finally, that no error may be possible regarding the source of this double maternity, we have God declaring that He is without any human cooperation the author of this miraculous work. "Shall not I that make others to bring forth children myself bring forth? saith the Lord; Shall I that give generation to others be barren? saith the Lord thy God."[43]

Had not the august Virgin these prophetic words in her mind when the angel Gabriel assured her that the Holy Spirit should come upon her, that the power of the Most High should overshadow her, and that, without detriment to her virginity, she should become the Mother of God? Isaias, in prophetic light contemplating these marvels, congratulated the favoured object of them, and called upon all men to praise her: "Rejoice with Jerusalem, and be glad with her, all you that love her; rejoice for joy with her, all you that mourn for her."[44] All nature had responded to the appeal of this heroic Mother when she exclaimed: "O all ye that pass by the way, attend, and see if there be any sorrow like to my sorrow;"[45] and all nature had the

---

[42] Antequam parturiret, peperit; antequam veniret partus ejus, peperit masculum. Quis audivit unquam tale? et quis vidit huic simile? Numquid parturiet terra in die una, aut parietur gens simul, quia parturivit et peperit Sion filios suos (Isa. Ixvi, 7, 8).

[43] Numquid ego qui alios parere facio, ipse non pariam? Dicit Dominus; si ego qui generationem ceteris tribuo, sterilis ero? ait Dominus Deus tuus (Isa., lxvi, 9).

[44] Lætamini cum Jerusalem, et exsultate in ea, omnes qui diligitis eam; gaudete cum ea gaudio universi qui lugetis super eam (Isa., lxvi, 10).

[45] O vos omnes qui transitis per viam, attendite, et videte si est dolor sicut dolor meus (Thren., i, 12).

right to rejoice with her, but the children of her sorrow, ever bearing in mind that injunction of holy Tobias to his son: "Thou shalt honour thy mother all the days of her life, for thou must be mindful what and how great perils she suffered for thee,"[46] had a special right to rejoice with her.

Nevertheless our Lady's mission is no more ended when once the mysteries of the Incarnation and Redemption are accomplished than are these mysteries themselves which last through all generations and are only completed when the last of the elect has been formed. Mary is our Mother in the work of our sanctification; by her our Lord came to us, and by her He will always come—He who is ceaselessly coming till at the end of ages He will come for the last time to judge the living and the dead.

Mary untiringly cooperates in the formation of the mystical body of her Son, which is His fulness. Of this mystical body Christ is the Head, and Mary is the neck—*collum Ecclesiæ Mysticum*—while we are the members. Now, in a body the members are joined to the head, and communicate with it only by the neck, its throne and support.

Since our Lord comes to us through our Lady, she is our channel of supernatural life; it is through her that all non-sacramental graces come to us, and all the preparatory dispositions requisite for a fruitful reception of the Sacraments. And as each Sacrament is, strictly speaking, but an act of our Lord by and in His Church, it is again our Lady whom we meet in her Son. The Blood which empurples our chalice and our lips comes from her maternal heart, since it was from that immaculate source that the Word Himself drew it.

It is not without reason that the Church, applying to the Son of God and to His Virgin Mother certain texts of the Book

---

[46] Honorem habebis matri tuæ omnibus diebus vitæ ejus; memor enim esse debes quæ et quanta pericula passa sit propter te (Tob., iv, 3, 4).

of Wisdom, places on the lips of Mary these noble affirmations: "I am the Mother of fair love, and of fear, and of knowledge and of holy hope. In me is all grace of the way and of the truth, in me is all hope of life and of virtue."[47] She is the mother of these blessings; hence she can communicate them to her children, to whom she says: "He that shall find me shall find life, and shall have salvation from the Lord."[48] She is herself like a kind of sacrament, communicating to us life and supernatural blessings.

This is true with regard to all men, but it seems to be still more real in the case of souls who are advancing in the spiritual life. If we are to believe those words of the sacred Canticle: "I held him, and I will not let him go till I bring him into my mother's house, and into the chamber of her that bore me,"[49] a soul beginning to grow conscious of our Lord's presence within herself, feels more than any other the need of being sheltered and protected under the safe keeping of God's Mother; she feels the need of being upheld by that blessed Mother in those paths whereby she aspires not only to become the bride of the Son of God, but moreover to grow up to the revelation of their one common origin where she will be proclaimed His sister. Hence she once again repeats: "I will take hold of thee, and bring thee into my mother's house: there thou shalt teach me, and I will give thee a cup of spiced wine and a new wine of my pomegranates."[50] It is under Mary's eye that the bride

---

[47] Ego mater pulchræ dilectionis et timoris, et agnitionis et sanctæ spei. In me gratia omnis viæ et veritatis; in me omnis spes vitæ et virtutis (Eccli xxiv, 24, 25).

[48] Qui me invenerit inveniet vitam, et hauriet salutem a Domino (Prov., viii, 35).

[49] Tenui eum, nec dimittam, donec introducam illum in domum matris mea; et in cubiculum genitricis mea; (Cant, iii, 4).

[50] Apprehendam to et ducam in domum matris meæ; ibi me docebis, et dabo tibi poculum ex vino condito, et mustum malorum granatorum meorum (Cant, viii, 2).

triumphantly adopted by this blessed Mother will receive the most fruitful teaching; and divinely instructed, will learn to love her Lord with perfect charity. Is it not our Lady who possesses the secret of the mysteries of the Incarnation and of the Redemption? She it is who can reveal them to us, and while manifesting them, can witness to the greatness of the love wherewith we have been loved from all eternity, and thus make that fountain break forth which will enable us to give back to our God the tribute of our truest love.

Thus interested in the work of our sanctification, Mary is also our wall of defence against all the enterprises of the old serpent whose head ever lies low under her victorious foot. If the feeble and pusillanimous fear the dragon's terrible tail, let them take refuge under the protection of her who is "terrible as an army set in array."[51] She will inspire them with her own courage which is greater far than that of Judith, for her sons can chant with even more truth than did the Jewish people: "Thou art the glory of Jerusalem, thou art the joy of Israel, thou art the honour of our people, for thou hast done manfully .... therefore also the hand of the Lord hath strengthened thee, and therefore thou shalt be blessed for ever."[52] Those who feel themselves too weak for the battle need never hesitate to call for help to her, as Barac called for the help of Deborah: "If thou wilt come with me, I will go; if thou wilt not come with me, I will not go."[53]

In her prudence, graceful as Abigail, Mary is able to appease the true David, irritated by the low vulgarity of the countless Nabals who fill the world; she pleads their cause with success,

---

[51] Terribilis ut castrorum acies ordinata (Cant., vi, 9).

[52] Tu gloria Jerusalem, tu lætitia Israël, tu honorificentia populi nostri, quia fecisti viriliter. . . . Ideo et manus Domini confortavit te, et ideo eris benedicta in æternum (Judith xv, 10, 11).

[53] Si venis mecum, vadam; si nolueris venire mecum, non pergam (Jud., iv, 8).

and in her turn deserves to hear: "Go in peace into thy house, behold I have heard thy voice, and have honoured thy face."[54] And by her beauty captivating the king's heart far more than did Queen Esther, she appears in very truth, like a suppliant omnipotence—*Omnipotentia supplex.*

At the marriage feast of Cana what a Mother our Lady showed herself! In her condescension she is watchful over everything, and she, the guest, spontaneously would spare her hosts the humiliation of adverting to the failure of their wine. But that we might be the better instructed, instead of herself working a miracle, she had recourse to her divine Son, and said to Him: "They have no wine."[55] And our Lord, accustomed no doubt to His Mother's frequent and merciful interventions on behalf of men, replies to her in words which for those round about are an enigma, but which for the Mother who so well understood the mind of her Son are an answer to her request. Therefore she hastened to say to the waiters what she is unceasingly repeating to us: "Whatsoever He shall say to you do ye."[56] Then she withdraws, certain of the success of her all-powerful intercession in our regard.

In another circumstance, of which only tradition speaks, we again perceive the efficacy of our Lady's mediation—it is on Mount Calvary, where she stood silent. Scarcely had our Saviour's words proclaimed her maternity with respect to all men, than the thief, crucified at the right hand of her Son, at once ceases to blaspheme, and under the influence of a renovating grace which illumines, penetrates and transforms him, he humbly confesses his crimes, and concludes with this ardent prayer: "Lord, remember me when Thou shalt come into

---

[54] Vade pacifice in domum tuam; ecce audivi vocem tuam, et honoravi faciem tuam (1 Reg., xxv, 35).

[55] Vinum non habent (Joann., ii, 3).

[56] Quodcumque dixerit vobis, facite (Joann., ii 5).

Thy kingdom."[57] What has taken place in this soul, a moment before so hardened and so blinded? Mary has prayed that the Blood of her Son may be fruitful and do its work; and at once she has the joy of hearing the sentence of pardon falling from the lips of Him who, though in the midst of humiliations, is still Judge of the living and the dead, having all power to forgive sins.

Our Lord Jesus Christ, the just valuer of His Mother's love, knew how necessary this Mother was to us, and He would have considered that He had not wholly and entirely given Himself to us if He had kept her for Himself only. She is necessary to us not as the author of grace, but as the channel by which grace comes to us. Mary is not our end, because God has willed that nothing created should be our end; but she is the most delightful path which leads us to our end. Our weak eyes cannot bear long the splendour of the divine Sun; she gently and graciously screens and tempers its rays for us. This sweet Mother brings the eternal truth in some sort within our reach by giving us so exact an expression of it, that she becomes, after the Incarnate Word, the most perfect likeness of God's beauty. She compassionates our wants like the tenderest of mothers, and she watches over us like a visible providence, the image of that loving Providence which numbers the very hairs of our head.

And our consolation is that with respect to Mary, our Lady and our Mother, we are always children. The duties of our natural mother continue but for a time, and, though her love lasts, her office sooner or later ceases. But in the eyes of the ever-blessed Virgin we never grow old: "Ye shall be carried at the breasts, and upon the knees they shall caress you."[58] The

---

[57] Memento mei, Domine, cum veneris in regnum tuum (Luc., xxiii, 42).

[58] Ad ubera portabimini, et super genua blandientur vobis (Isa., lxvi, 12).

Apostle did not fear to say to the Galatians: "My little children, of whom I am in labour again, until Christ be formed in you."[59] But what can St. Paul's zeal be compared with that which our Lady displays in forming us to the likeness of her Son? However, the day will come when we shall have grown to maturity, when we shall have attained the fulness of the age of Christ; and yet we shall always continue to receive from Him, we shall always continue to receive from His Mother also; and, like God's reign, Mary's royal maternity will never have an end.

Having, therefore, proved that Mary is truly our Mother we must further understand that we have duties towards her: "He that honoureth his mother is as one that layeth up a treasure."[60] The more our blessed Mother's maternity surpasses natural maternity, the more ought our honour of her to exceed that which we pay to our natural parents.

More still, devotion of an ordinary kind such as we render to the saints will not suffice for our Lady; we worship her not with *dulia*, but with *hyperdulia*, superior homage, as theologians express it. In fact we can only rightly use the word devotion in respect to our Lady if we make it mean a worship that is not a matter of choice or of supererogation but of obligation, since the honouring of the Blessed Virgin Mary is part of our Catholic belief. And just as her motherhood in regard of us is based upon realities, and does not consist only in an incomparable mother's love and feeling towards us, so we on our side must be ever mindful that our childhood in regard of Mary is based upon a sum of doctrinal truth much deeper and stronger than tender sentiments of piety. We lower our worship of Mary by making it a mere devotion, and we lessen our love of her when it falls short of doctrine.

---

[59] Filioli mei, quos iterum parturio, donec formetur Christus in vobis (Gal., iv, 19).

[60] Sicut qui thesaurizat, ita et qui honorificat matrem suam (Eccli iii, 5).

To show in brief how perfectly just is this theological worship of our Lady, let us add that the dignity of the Mother of God makes her absolutely peerless and in fact a world apart. This divine maternity places her in a relation of singular intimacy with the Father, whose only Son is also her Son; with the Word, to whom she gave His human nature; with the Holy Spirit, for the Son of the Virgin as God, is the principle of this divine Spirit, and as a man, He is His holy and sanctifying fruit.

Moreover, the divine maternity is not for Mary a privilege only; it is also a source of eminent grace and incomparable sanctification. Therefore, not without reason did the angel proclaim her "full of grace."[61] To this starting point must be added the thirty years which she spent with Him who is the very source of grace and of supernatural beauty, her cooperation in the mysteries of the Passion, Resurrection and Ascension of our Lord, the Pentecostal grace, the fifteen years of solicitude and devotedness which she lavished upon the early Church, and in addition to all this, her constant increase of virtue, purity and charity. Hence we must acknowledge that after God no object can be found more worthy of our homage and love.

As the formal cause of our worship of the Blessed Virgin, we must also mention the signal prerogatives with which she has been endowed, and which she shares with no other creature, namely, her Immaculate Conception; her absolute immunity and freedom from all concupiscence, her exemption from all personal sin and from all imperfection, her exact correspondence to grace, her spotless virginity, her preservation from corruption in the tomb, and finally her triumphant Assumption. Her beginnings even are beyond the reach of man, as we sing in the psalm: "Her foundations are in the holy mountains. . . . Glorious things are said of thee, O city

---

[61] Gratia plena (Luc., I, 28).

of God."[62] Mary is altogether matchless as holy Church sings: *Nec primam similem visa est, nec habere sequentem.*

To be true to our faith and our Baptism, we must then cherish towards our Blessed Lady a love that is both filial and doctrinal; we must offer her a worship befitting her eminent dignity. The Church in her official prayer does not overlook a duty such as this. In the Divine Office, she daily repeats Mary's incomparable canticle, whose deep accents ever new and ever living, are as well suited to Good Friday and to the Office of the Dead, as to feasts the most resplendent with supernatural joy. The Canonical Hours are not complete unless the Ave Maria follows the *Pater noster* at the beginning. The last echo of the social prayer is consecrated to the Madonna in a graceful antiphon which varies according to the liturgical seasons.

Again we have our Lady's feasts calling to mind the mysteries of her holy and immaculate life, or the titles conferred upon her by the gratitude of her children for signal benefits received. All Saturdays are dedicated to her, unless in the cycle a feast of higher degree occur, thus depriving her of this filial remembrance; and three times a day the Angelus bell calls upon Christians to salute the Mother of God.

Outside this official portion of the Church's worship of our Lady, innumerable are the practices of filial piety towards the Mother of God which the Church approves and encourages: chief among these we must place the devotion of the most holy Rosary. In this vast field all may choose according to their attraction; for though these practices are praiseworthy and commendable, they are not obligatory. But we must beware of overburdening ourselves with even good practices, lest they should stifle the true spirit of prayer and the true worship of our immaculate Mother, which are fed always by the heart: "When I go into my house, I shall repose myself with her; for

---

[62] Fundamenta ejus in montibus sanctis. . . Gloriosa dicta sunt de te, civitas Dei (Ps., lxxxvi).

her conversation hath no bitterness, nor her company any tediousness, but joy and gladness."[63]

Mary would not be a mother, if she were not condescending; hence she deigns to allow her children to comport themselves with her in various ways. Some love her with an exclusive, sensible and affective love; others, while acknowledging her excellence, her beauty and her dignity, feel their hearts thrilling with only a rational love towards her. One behaves towards her as a little child full of confidence and self-surrender; another takes the attitude of a knight towards his lady and his queen. Some souls from their tenderest infancy are drawn to her, and in consequence of this they have a special characteristic; their ways are more simple, easy and tranquil like those of children who have never left their father's home. Others, on the contrary, not feeling this special attraction, are on that account filled with extreme sorrow, this alone sufficing to prove their real love. At one time it is our Lady that makes known unto souls her Divine Son, and at another it is our Lord that leads souls to His Mother. The love of our Lady is for some the beginning of the spiritual life; while for others this love expands only as the soul grows to perfection.

The gracious Mother of God, as merciful as she is powerful, lends herself to this variety of dispositions and has a smile for all her children, for all belong to her provided that they really belong to her Son, that they listen to his teaching and practise what they have learnt. Then she exerts her maternal, watchful and devoted care to gain them admittance into the heavenly Jerusalem, where, as Queen of Angels and Mother of men, she reigns at the right hand of her Son, in all the splendour of her beauty.

---

[63] Intrans in domum meam conquiescam cum illa: non habet amaritudinem conversatio illius, nec tædium convictus illius, sed lætitiam et gaudium (Sap., viii, 16).

CHAPTER XXII
That the Church at Large is a Sublime Type of the Contemplative Soul

ST. PAUL, in his admirable epistle to the Ephesians, develops the economy of the mystery of our salvation, calling it the mystery of the divine good pleasure, "the mystery of His will according to His good pleasure,"[1] and he brings it before us under the form of nuptials celebrated between the Son of God and mankind. At times indeed the apostle alludes to Christian marriage, the figure of this divine union, wishing that it should worthily represent the sublime reality; at times he treats of the individual union of each soul with God; finally, at times he takes the whole mass of regenerate mankind and brings out the mystery of marriage in its fullest and most complete form, which is the union of the Church with our Lord Jesus Christ, her Head and her Spouse: "And He hath subjected all things under His feet, and hath made Him head over all the Church, which is His Body and the fulness of Him who is filled all in all."[2]

St. Paul considers this divine union as an ineffable mystery, the continuation and completion of the mysteries of the Incarnation and Redemption: "Which in other generations was not known to the sons of men, as it is now revealed to His holy

---

[1] Sacramentum voluntatis suæ secundum beneplacitum ejus (Eph. i, 9).

[2] Omnia subjecit sub pedibus ejus, et ipsum dedit caput supra omnem Ecclesiam, quæ est corpus ipsius, et plenitudo ejus qui omnia in omnibus adimpletur (Eph. i, 22, 23).

apostles and prophets in the Spirit."[3] In the Old Testament this mystery was made known by the inspired writers, in the New Testament it has been proclaimed far and wide by the apostles, one same Spirit working in both and drawing men to one same truth both before and after the coming of Christ. The prophets are the heralds of the bride of Christ; the apostles are more than that, they guard her as the "three score valiant ones who surround the bed of Solomon." The favoured generations are those that have seen the Fountain of life thrown open; that is to say, the side of our Saviour, whence the Church came forth on the sixth day of the week, as heretofore Eve came forth from the side of the first Adam.

The great collective bride of the Son of God is then "a help like unto Himself;"[4] to her the true King of Peace addresses these tender words: "One is my dove, my perfect one is but one, she is the only one of her mother, the chosen of her that bore her."[5] She shows forth with sublime completeness all the features we have described as proper to perfect union; the highest contemplation and the most consummate charity are found in her with a certitude, a stability, a permanence constituting an abiding miracle and stamping her as divine "even to the consummation of the world."[6]

This indivisible union of the Church with God is not a union different from that contracted individually with God by the souls that form the Church. Nevertheless, it will not be without profit to make a study of this consummate union, such as it appears when realized in the Church Militant; in that study

---

[3] Quod aliis generationibus non est agnitum filiis hominum, sicut nunc revelatum est sanctis apostolis ejus, et prophetis in Spiritu (Ibid, iii, 5).

[4] Adiutorium simile sibi (Gen. ii, 18).

[5] Una est columba mea, perfecta mea, una est matris suæ, electa genetrici suæ (Cant, vi, 8).

[6] Usque ad consummationem sæculi (Matth. xxviii, 20).

we shall find an abundance of teaching, so much so that, were any one to seek instruction for his spiritual life in a treatise *de Ecclesia,* he would be very certain of not following a wrong path. The soul that has attained consummate union is an exact miniature of the Church, One, Holy, Catholic and Apostolic. The more she identifies herself with her mother, the more surely does she reach the Heart of Him who has done everything in this world for His collective bride, and who, in the carrying out of His designs, has but one type. Therefore, in studying the Church as the perfect model of the spiritual life we shall complete all that we purpose to say on this subject.

When in the island of Patmos the light of prophecy shone upon St. John, it showed him our Lord's great bride filled with all the sanctity and perfection to which mankind, assisted by the Holy Spirit, can attain. It was said to him: "She is the tabernacle of God with men." In point of fact, her consummate union with her Divine Head makes her one spirit with Him, in so admirable a unity that she will work no works but those which He shall suggest: "But the Paraclete, the Holy Ghost whom the Father will send in My name, He will teach you all things, and bring all things to your mind, whatsoever I shall have said to you."[7] This it is that constitutes the unity and sanctity of the Church; in whatever times or places or circumstances she works, she has never any other than this divine moving principle, so stable and permanent is her union with God.

Although the Church in her militant portion, the only one with which we are now concerned, is still living in time, she already, by her stable union with God and by her Catholicity, possesses somewhat of eternity. In point of fact, as she spreads not only over all times, but also over all places, days in her

---

[7] Paraclitus autem spiritus sanctus, quem mittet Pater in nomine meo, ille vos docebit omnia, et suggeret vobis omnia quæcumque dixero vobis (Joann., xiv, 26).

bosom do not seem to succeed days, and simultaneously she enjoys the benefit of all the divisions of time. Finally she is indeed apostolic; for it was in the person of the apostles that she began, on the day of Pentecost, that life of perfect union with God, that ineffable spiritual marriage which nothing has ever been able to break or to change; and it is by her close intimacy with the Spirit, the Consummator, that she will obtain the final victory and the coming of the heavenly Bridegroom, that the union may no longer be in faith only but in vision. Thus in considering the Church as One, Holy, Catholic and Apostolic, we discover in her in the highest degree the effects of her unitive life.

It would however be very inadequate to study the effects without referring them to their cause. The Father "greatly desires the beauty of that resplendent Virgin, but it is no mere external beauty, the external is but a radiation of the internal splendour: "All the glory of the King's daughter is within."[8] Hence, all the power of the holy Church, all the beauty of her onward march through ages; all the magnificence which she sheds upon her path, even in human things, letters, arts and sciences; all the life that she communicates to whatever comes in touch with her; all, even down to the progress of true civilization, all comes "from within," that is, from her close union with God. From the very beginning its exuberant power appeared in the Church, and unbelievers mistaking its cause cried out: "These men are full of new wine."[9] But Peter, the visible representative of the invisible Head, defended the bride, saying: "These are not drunk, as you suppose, seeing it is but the third hour of the day; but this is that which was spoken of by the Prophet Joel: 'And it shall come to pass, in the last days,

---

[8] Omnis gloria ejus filiæ regis ab intus (Ps., xliv, 14).

[9] Musto pleni sunt isti (Act. ii, 13).

saith the Lord, I will pour out of My Spirit upon all flesh.'"[10]

In this way, the apostle of the Gentiles instructed the newborn children who had just been incorporated into the Church: "In whom you also are built together into an habitation of God in the Spirit."[11] And revealing to them the internal force which is henceforth to take possession of them and to establish them in divine union, he says: "Wherefore become not unwise, but understanding what is the will of God. And be not drunk with wine, wherein is luxury, but be ye filled with the Holy Spirit. Speaking to yourselves in psalms and hymns and spiritual canticles, singing and making melody in your hearts to the Lord, giving thanks always for all things in the name of our Lord Jesus Christ, to God and the Father."[12]

So then, the Church Militant possesses within herself the principle of her life; she draws from her prayer the energies of her supernatural action. Just as the soul animates the body, so does the divine Paraclete animate the Church; and within her, as in the human soul, He produces the "unspeakable groanings" which are always heard by "Him who searcheth the hearts, and knoweth what the Spirit desireth."[13]

No way of prayer is better regulated than that of the holy

---

[10] Non enim, sicut vos æstimatis, hi sunt ebrii, quum sit hora diei tertia; sed hoc est, quod dictum est per prophetam Joel: Et erit in novissimis diebus, elicit Dominus, effundam de Spiritu meo super omnem carnem (Ibid. 15-17).

[11] In quo et vos coædificamini in habitaculum Dei in Spiritu (Eph. ii, 22).

[12] Nolite fieri imprudentes, sed intelligentes quæ sit voluntas Dei. Et nolite inebriari vino, in quo est luxuria; sed implemini Spiritu sancto, loquentes vobismetipsis in psalmis, et hymnis et canticis spiritualibus, cantantes et psallentes in cordibus vestris Domino, gratias agentes semper pro omnibus in nomine Domini nostri Jesu Christ, Deo et Patri (Eph., v, 17-20).

[13] Qui autem scrutatur corda, scit quid desideret Spiritus (Rom., viii, 27).

Church. She leaves nothing to self will; she fixes everything, the attitude of the body as well as that of the soul, even to the slightest movements. Thus she preserves herself in a marvellous manner from the spirit of independence, while she subjects herself in all things to the "Spirit of adoption," whose unceasing aim is to take entire possession of the whole of human nature in order to bring it back to its divine Author.

To suppress all human methods of prayer in order to adopt only the Church's method, is not to throw off all yoke: it is on the contrary to enter the spiritual school wherein it is requisite to make profession of singular self-denial, by renouncing all private judgment and everything that savours of independence. Then the Church imposes her own form, which is the one given to her by the Holy Spirit, and she fashions the soul by a process which in a single day contains all the degrees that the masters have pointed out in the spiritual life. For the Church Militant in her prayer, which is the Divine Office, the "work of God" as St. Benedict says, reveals all the forms of acquired and of infused prayer.

We see her practising meditation in the reading of the Fathers, that is the human and discursive element of her prayer; for it, only the ordinary help of the Holy Spirit is needed, such as we require whenever we wish to apply our minds to divine truths. Contemplation appears in many of the liturgical prayers which express a very simple gazing at divine mysteries rather than a thoughtful analysis of them. Prophetic light shines forth in the inspired writings; while the "Sanctus," the Doxologies, the "*Gloria Patri*," the "Alleluia," the "Amen," and in general all those expressions by which the Church Militant echoes the songs of the Church Triumphant, speak of the inebriation of the soul with the fulness of God. It was fitting moreover that while the Church has to walk in faith, she should be recognized by her perfect and consummate charity, which is none other than the charity of heaven, and this is why she uses the language of heaven, for though at present she is in the state of a wayfarer *(in via)* she belongs to heaven, she "came down from heaven,"[14] as St. John says, and she returns thither, just as the dove returns to the ark carrying the olive branch, a symbol of that perfect peace, flowing from the unction of the Holy Spirit of which she cannot be deprived for one single day, she, the Sulamite of the peaceful King, the Prince of peace.

It is but just that, in the body of her prayer, the Church Militant should follow the teachings of her divine Spouse, contenting herself with developing what, in an abridged form, our Lord has in the *Pater noster* given her. Hence, for the instruction of her children she unceasingly puts upon their lips this divine formula, imitating by this frequent repetition the patience of a tender mother who, when teaching her little one to speak, over and over again takes up the stammered syllable without ever growing weary till it is perfectly articulated. For our mother, the holy Church, in her prayer converses with God, and at the same time she forms us, the children born of her by the Spirit.

But she is principally the mistress and the model of souls who have reached the summit of the spiritual life and have attained that state of sublime ignorance spoken of by St. Denis. The Church prays absolutely as those do who, in the inmost depths of their own souls, adore God unceasingly, and who have but one act, but one most simple operation for their prayer and union with God, because they feel within themselves the constant indwelling of the august Trinity. Observe how in the Office the Church seems to bring everything back to a continual *Gloria Patri*. The intervals between are more or less long, the thoughts suggested in them are more or less abundant; but these Doxologies are always recurring, and are, as it were, the groundwork, the scope, the summary of the whole Office, the centre of the homage paid to God.

We ventured to say that in her prayer the Church Militant

---

[14] Descendentem de cœlo (Apoc. xxi, 2).

gave example even of simple meditation; she returns to it in fact
just as those souls do who, having reached the height of
contemplation, are sometimes brought back by God to favours
and processes of a less elevated nature, in the midst of which,
however, they always preserve something of their sublime
state, which is that of perfect charity. When using simple
meditation the Church always appears as the bride of the divine
Lamb. Resuming the songs of the purgative life she sings them
with such eminent perfection that repentance becomes of a
most exalted kind. The sinner can make her language his own;
but on the lips of the Church every song rises to the
proportions of her admirable holiness, a holiness which is
indeed human, and consequently always within our reach, and
capable of increase, but a holiness so truly consummate that the
purgative life, in its most emphatic expressions, becomes
clothed with the perfection of charity.

In like manner the heavenly splendours of the illuminative
life inundate the Church with an incomparable brilliancy. She
sees clearly, because she puts no obstacle to the light, the force
of which is ever tending to become perfect in divine union. And
yet, in the most pure light of faith, she can stay to contemplate
truth; her eye, strong and steady, can bear the brightness of the
Sun of Justice, and thus she introduces into a higher state those
of her children who are gifted with the light of knowledge, but
who have not yet tasted the sweetness of divine things. No
initiation can be more sure than hers, for having herself the
relish of the mysteries which she contemplates she is a sublime
mistress in the art of communicating light and relish to others.

Above all this the Church appears experienced in the
mysteries of the unitive life; from the lowest to the highest
degrees nothing is hidden from her. Neither is she ignorant of
the nature of passive trials, of which we find a faithful
expression in a great number of the Psalms. But at the same
time she sounds the note of generous self-denial, which in these
painful purifications at once produces the effect intended by the

Holy Spirit.

Moreover, she unceasingly attains consummate union with God by the august sacrifice which is perpetually renewed within her bosom, and which establishes her permanently in her state of ineffable spiritual marriage. For if St. Augustine can say: "Every work which is done that we may cleave to God in holy union is a true sacrifice,"[15] what shall we think of that incomparable sacrifice which is the mysterious reproduction and continuation of the oblation described in these words by St. Paul: "For by one oblation he hath perfected for ever them that are sanctified"?[16] There it is that the Church by the divine Lamb offers to God a sacrifice worthy of Him, and there it is that, participating in the Flesh of that living and immolated Lamb, she is in her turn transformed into Him and offered as the mystic Body of her divine Head, as His fulness and completion. "Already have I communicated of His sacred Body, and His Blood hath graced my cheek,"[17] said the glorious virgin Agnes after having understood the mystery of consummation.

It is in this sacrifice that the Church finds the highest contemplation where God communicates Himself without symbol and without image, because the union is made between substance and substance, and because nothing is more real than that which eludes all visible form. This is the "Mystery of faith—Mysterium fidei"; beyond it there is nothing but the intuitive vision.

The Church is then the type and the model of the contemplative soul. She is Rachel before being Lia; she is Mary before acting as Martha; she gives to the exterior only out of

---

[15] Verum sacrificium est omne opus quod agitur ut sancta societate inhæreamus Deo (S. Aug., *De Civ. Dei*, X, vi).

[16] Una enim oblatione consummavit in sempiternum sanctificatos (Heb., x, 14).

[17] Jam corpus ejus corpori meo sociatum est, et sanguis ejus ornavit genas meas (In Offic. S. Agnetis, V.M.)

her interior fulness, following the counsel of the Apostle: "Let the word of Christ dwell in you abundantly, in all wisdom, teaching and admonishing one another in psalms, hymns and spiritual canticles, singing in grace in your hearts to God."[18]

By her continuous prayer, the Divine Office, the indwelling of our Lord reveals itself; on this point never has she consented to deviate from her customs, and though the imperative duty of preaching the Gospel was incumbent upon the early Christians, it in no way hindered them from following this divine plan: "And continuing daily with one accord in the Temple, and breaking of bread from house to house, they took their meat with gladness and simplicity of heart, praising God."[19] There can be no question here of ordinary bread and food since those who were admitted partook of it with so much joy.

And never, whatever may be the wants of mankind, however much active works may seek to encroach, how great soever may be the miseries of the times, the decay of faith, the importunities of carnal-minded men, the weakness of her organs, the poverty of her resources, never does the Church Militant consent to interrupt her prayer, to change its method or modify its plan. In vain are utilitarian theories held out to her; in vain is the objection brought forward that she must needs take up weapons of defence against unbelievers, and in face of the false, set forth true science, or what touches her maternal heart still more—that she must needs look to the souls that are perishing all around—never will she yield, nor for one single day let anything hinder the exercise of her sublime contemplation. The secret indeed is that she finds in this

---

[18] Verbum Christi habitet in vobis abundanter, in omni sapientia, docentes, et commonentes vosmetipsos psalmis, hymnis, et canticis spiritualibus in gratia cantantes in cordibus vestris Deo (Col., iii, 16).

[19] Quotidie quoque perdurantes unanimiter in templo, et frangentes circa domos panem, sumebant cibum cum exsultatione et simplicitate cordis, collaudantes Deum (Act. ii, 46).

contemplation her link with heaven, and the very motive power which gives efficacy to all her works.

Her enemies so well know what is the power of this prayer that they dread it more than all outward resistance, and therefore they exclaim with such rabid determination: "Let us abolish all the festival days of God from the land."[20] The Holy Spirit, on the other hand, in making the eulogy of king David, enumerates all that the holy king did to enhance the splendour of God's worship: "And he set singers before the altar, and by their voices they made sweet melody. And to the festivals he added beauty, and set in order the solemn times even to the end of his life, that they should praise the holy name of the Lord, and magnify the holiness of God in the morning."[21]

After this there can be no hesitation in admitting that the honour bestowed upon St. Benedict's Order of being so powerful a bulwark of the Church Militant, should be attributed in great measure to that sentence of the Holy Rule: "Let nothing be preferred to the work of God."[22] The Church recognized her own spirit and her own tendencies in this maxim. She seems to be enjoying a foretaste of eternity, when she groups her children on earth in the same way as she contemplates the elect in heaven: "Therefore they are before the throne of God, and they serve Him day and night in His temple; and He that sitteth on the throne shall dwell over them."[23] The state of the blessed

---

[20] Quiescere faciamus omnes dies festos Dei a terra (Ps. lxxiii, 8).

[21] In omni opere dedit confessionem Sancto et Excelso in verbo gloriæ . . . Et stare fecit cantores contra altare, et in sono eorum dulces fecit modos. Et dedit in celebrationibus decus, et ornavit tempora usque ad consummationem vitæ, ut laudarent nomen sanctum Domini, et amplificarent mane Dei sanctitatem (Eccli, xlvii, 9-12).

[22] Nihil operi Dei præponatur (S. Reg., xliii).

[23] Ideo sunt ante thronum Dei, et serviunt ei die ac nocte in templo ejus: et qui sedet in throno, habitabit super illos (Apoc., vii, 15).

in heaven has been represented by St. John as an immense "*Opus Dei*—Divine service," celebrated in a mysterious temple, before the heavenly altar, with harmonious chants and a living incense which is the prayer of the saints, and the smoke of the incense in censers of gold ascends before God from the hands of the angels themselves. The power of the Church consists here below in echoing back these marvellous mysteries of heaven, imitating and reproducing them as far as she can with the means which her Divine Spouse has given her. She knows that one of the severest chastisements of Divine Justice is this: "And the angel took the censer, and filled it with the fire of the altar, and cast it on the earth, and there were thunders."[24] Yes, when the censer, destined to burn the living incense before God, is with its coals of fire, cast upon the earth, then the tempest reveals God's anger, for He no longer beholds in this world the image of the Jerusalem above. The Church Militant then appeases her Lord just as the soul who is still a wayfarer does, by reproducing as far as she is able the prayer of heaven.

But if in one single day the Church Militant provides the most finished model of the soul's onward march to God, even unto perfection, she provides it still more fully in the round of her liturgical cycle.

This teaching is very old, and it was in the third century received by all. We give a proof of this by quoting the following passage from Origen: "To the perfect Christian, who is ever in his thoughts, words and deeds serving his Lord, God the Word, all his days are the Lord's, and he is always keeping the Lord's day. He also who is unceasingly preparing himself for the true life, and abstaining from this life's pleasures which lead so many astray—who is not indulging the lust of the flesh, but 'keeping his body under, and bringing it into subjection'—such a one is always keeping 'preparation day.' Again, he who

---

[24] Et accepit angelus thruibulum et implevit illud de igne altaris; et misit in terram, et facta sunt tonitrua (Apoc., viii, 5).

considers that 'Christ our Passover was sacrificed for us,' and
that it is his duty to keep the feast by eating of the Flesh of the
Word, never ceases to keep the Paschal feast; for the 'Pascha'
means a 'Passover,' and in all his thoughts, words and deeds he
is ever striving to pass over from the things of this life to God,
and is hastening towards the city of God. Finally, he who can
truly say: 'We are risen with Christ,' and 'He hath exalted us,
and made us to sit with Him in heavenly places in Christ,' is
always living in the season of Pentecost; and most of all, when
going to the upper chamber, like the apostles of Jesus, he gives
himself to supplication and prayer, that he may become worthy
of receiving 'the mighty wind rushing from heaven,' which is
powerful to destroy sin and its fruits among men, and worthy
of having some share of the tongue of fire which God sends."
"But the majority of those who are accounted believers are not
of this advanced class; but from being either unable or
unwilling to keep every day in this manner, they require some
sensible memorial to prevent spiritual things from passing
altogether away from their minds. It is to this practice of setting
apart some days distinct from others that St. Paul seems to me
to refer in the expression, 'part of the feast'; and by these words
he indicates that a life in accordance with the Divine Word
consists not 'in a part of the feast,' but in one entire and never-
ceasing festival."[25] For a fuller exposition of this matter we refer
our readers to Dom Gueranger's "Liturgical Year," and
principally to the general preface of the work, in which the
venerable author has in a most clear and elevated style
condensed his whole thought.

[25] Orig., Contra Cels., lib. VIII, cap. xxil, xiii.

CHAPTER XXIII
There is but one Liturgy

OD could not create except for His own glory, and for that very reason the whole duty of intelligent creatures consists in the worship rendered to the Divine Majesty, a worship which is at once both internal and external.

Our Lord Jesus Christ, of whom "it is written in the head of the Book,"[1] Jesus Christ, "the firstborn of every creature,"[2] is the first to render to God this supreme worship decreed from all eternity by the Divine Will: "Behold I come to do Thy will."[3] He came as a creature to pay to His Father a homage the most complete that God could possibly receive, a glory proportionate to God, since it is offered by God Himself, the hypostatic union giving to the human nature of the Incarnate Word a dignity and a splendour unparalleled: "Wherefore when He cometh into the world He saith: Sacrifice and oblation Thou wouldst not, but a body Thou hast fitted to Me."[4] That which our Lord had in view is very evident; the end or purpose of His Incarnation was to enable Him to become priest and victim, that He might thus offer to the Divine Majesty the most perfect and exalted worship that an intelligent creature could offer.

The coming on earth of the Son of God had a further consequence. Whatever else may have been the motive of the

---

[1] In capite libri scriptum est de me (Ps., xxxix, 8).

[2] Primogenitus omnis creaturæ (Col. i, 15).

[3] Ecce venio, ut faciam voluntatem tuam (Heb., x, 9).

[4] Ideo ingrediens mundum dicit: Hostiam et oblationem noluisti, corpus autem aptasti mihi (Heb., x, 5).

Incarnation, it at once brought this result: it associated intelligent creatures with the liturgical act. Raised to the supernatural order, and, by the condescension of the Son of God, favoured to such a degree that for their sake He would become not only a holocaust, but a victim for their sins, these creatures were purified from their faults and errors in such sort, that they themselves were henceforth to concur in our Lord's sacrifice, as members of one and the same body, of which He is the head: "In the which will we are sanctified by the oblation of the Body of Jesus Christ once."[5]

The mission of the Incarnate Word is then the mission of a pontiff, and thus the Apostle St. Paul wished that perfect Christians should understand it: "Wherefore, holy brethren, partakers of the heavenly vocation, consider the apostle and high priest of our confession Jesus, who is faithful to Him that made Him."[6] Now Christ did not in a transitory and momentary way receive this priesthood, but permanently: "But this, for that He continueth for ever, hath an everlasting priesthood, whereby He is able also to save for ever them that come to God by Him, always living to make intercession for us."[7] Thus the sovereign pontificate is eternal, and it is exercised for ever; not only in the adorable person of the Son of God, but in that priestly tribe of which He is the Head, "a chosen generation, a kingly priesthood,"[8] wherein all are priests, although in

---

[5] In qua voluntate sanctificati sumus per oblationem corporis Jesu Christi semel (Heb. x, 10).

[6] Unde, fratres sancti, vocationis cœlestis participes, considerate apostolum et pontificem confessionis nostræ, Jesum; qui fidelis est ei qui fecit ilium (Ibid, iii, i, 2).

[7] Hic autem eo quod maneat in æternum sempiternum habet sacerdotium. Unde et salvare in perpetuum potest accedentes per semetipsum ad Deum, semper vivens ad interpellandum pro nobis (Heb., vii, 24-25).

[8] Genus electum, regale sacerdotium (1 Pet., ii, 9).

different degrees, and all are called to concelebrate with the supreme Pontiff. The sacrifice offered by Him is one, for He could not offer many times a sacrifice which is lasting, and which fulfils by one single permanent oblation all the just claims of the Divine Majesty: "For Jesus is not entered into the holies made with hands, the patterns of the true, but into heaven itself, that He may appear now in the presence of God for us. . . . Christ was offered once to exhaust the sins of many."[9]

It cannot then be wondered at that St. John, contemplating with his eagle eye what takes place in the inaccessible light, should have shown us Jesus, our Pontiff, the Author and Perfecter of our faith, exercising His ministry in the midst of the redeemed creation, of which He is the keystone of the edifice. He celebrates in the midst of the very throne, for He is God; and the annihilation of His Incarnation, the opprobrium brought upon Him by our redemption, far from lessening the honour due to Him, have caused His Father to exalt His name as man above every other name: "And that every tongue should confess that the Lord Jesus Christ is in the glory of God the Father."[10]

It is then in the bosom of the Father's glory, in the centre of the throne that we see the Lamb, standing as a Conqueror and as a Priest, "a Lamb, standing as it were slain, having seven horns."[11] He is slain, for He is the universal victim; He has seven horns, symbols of the sevenfold Spirit that rested upon Him and anointed Him "above His fellows—*præ consortibus*

---

[9] Non enim in manufacta Sancta Jesus introivit, exemplaria verorum; sed in ipsum cœlum, ut appareat nunc vultui Dei pro nobis. Christus semel oblatus est ad multorum exhaurienda peccata (Heb., ix, 24-28).

[10] Et omnis lingua confiteatur quia Dominus Jesus Christus in gloria est Dei Patris (Phil., ii, 11).

[11] Agnum stantem tamquam occisum (Apoc., v, 6).

suis."[12]

He, only, has the power to open the seven seals of the Book, for He is the supreme Hierarch, the Initiator by excellence, and the Interpreter of the most profound mysteries; His victory gained for Him this right. But the moment that He exercises it, the four living creatures and the four and twenty ancients prostrate before Him; their harps proclaim His praise, and their golden vials full of odours, which are the prayers of the saints, send up the smoke of incense, while heaven resounds with the hymn of eternal gratitude from the lips of the redeemed: "Thou art worthy, O Lord, to take the Book and to open the seals thereof; because Thou wast slain, and hast redeemed us to God, in Thy Blood, out of every tribe, and tongue, and people, and nation, and hast made us to our God a kingdom and priests."[13]

Since the Lamb is not only the completion of our human hierarchy, but the pontiff of the universal hierarchy, the angels in their turn proclaim His praise. No sooner had the Father introduced Him into the world, than He commanded them to adore Him; and they with enthusiasm accomplished this order, singing the hymn proper to them: "The Lamb that was slain is worthy to receive power, and divinity, and wisdom, and strength, and honour, and glory, and benediction."[14] To this grand harmony celebrating the victory of the Lamb is joined the praise of Him to whom is offered the sacrifice of the Lamb, and the incomparable hymn sung unceasingly day and night by the heavenly citizens: "Holy, holy, holy, Lord God Almighty,

---

[12] Ps., xliv.

[13] Dignus es, Domine, accipere librum et aperire signacula ejus: quoniam occisus es, et redemisti nos Deo in sanguine tuo, ex omni tribu, et lingua, et populo, et natione; et fecisti nos Deo nostro regnum et sacerdotes (Apoc., v. 9, 10).

[14] Dignus est Agnus, qui occisus est, accipere virtutem, et divinitatem, et sapientiam et fortitudinem, et honorem, et gloriam, et benedictionem (Apoc., v, 12).

who was, and who is, and who is to come."[15] The better to confess that He whom they are adoring is the self-existing Being and the Author of all gifts, they cast their crowns before the throne, thus testifying that their victory comes from Him, and that in crowning their merits He does but crown His own gifts. Then resounds the canticle: "Thou art worthy, O Lord our God, to receive glory, and honour, and power; because Thou hast created all things, and for Thy will they were, and have been created."[16] Now the light which sheds its rays upon this eternal liturgical function, is not an artificial light, a created sun, or any star whatsoever, "for the glory of God hath enlightened it, and the Lamb is the lamp thereof."[17]

Such is the liturgy of the Church Triumphant, a liturgy developed by the inspiration of the Holy Spirit; for it was by Him that the Lamb offered Himself, "who by the Holy Ghost offered Himself unspotted unto God."[18]

But during the days of her pilgrimage our Pontiff would not abandon His bride; and by a wonderful way, and with a wisdom all divine, He found the means of identifying the Sacrifice of earth with that of heaven, since there is but one priesthood, that of Jesus Christ, but one Sacrifice on earth and in heaven, but one Victim, namely, the Lamb conquering yet slain. The shadows and figures of the Old Law drew all their efficacy from the one future oblation of the Incarnate Word, so much so that these rites instituted by God Himself, bore even then some

---

[15] Sanctus, sanctus, sanctus, Dominus Deus omnipotens, qui erat, et qui est, et qui venturus est (Apoc., iv, 8).

[16] Dignus es, Domine Deus noster, accipere gloriam, et honorem et virtutem, quia tu creasti omnia, et propter voluntatem tuam erant, et creata sunt (Ibid., 11).

[17] Nam claritas Dei illuminavit eam, et lucerna ejus est Agnus (Ibid., xxi, 23).

[18] Per Spiritum sanctum semetipsum obtulit immaculatum Deo (Heb., ix, 14).

traces of the true and perpetual Sacrifice which is celebrated in heaven as it is celebrated on earth in virtue of that divine command: "This do for the commemoration of Me."[19] Thus the Church's hierarchy on earth through the wonders produced by the Sacraments, presents to the ravished gaze of the heavenly citizens a faithful reproduction of that which takes place "within the veil, *ad interiora velaminis.*" Our Lord Jesus Christ has then realized this admirable union of the Church Triumphant and the Church Militant; the former enjoys the vision, the latter still walks by faith, and yet the diversity of these two modes in no way lessens the unity of the liturgical work accomplished in both portions of the inheritance of the Lamb. It is the same oblation that is offered on the altar of heaven, and on the altar of earth, with this special glory for our earth, namely, that heaven itself is indebted to it; for the eternal Sacrifice was accomplished first among us; and we afterwards gave it to the angels.

The Holy Spirit, the principle of unity and the link uniting the members with their Head brings about this marvellous association which is the Communion of Saints. He it is that makes the unity of the Priesthood, the unity of the Altar, the unity of the Victim, the unity of the Sacrifice, consummated in heaven and on earth by His devouring fire. He is the fire which our Saviour came to cast upon earth, and which He so ardently desired should be enkindled. Again our Lord says: "I will ask the Father, and He shall give you another Paraclete, that He may abide with you for ever, the Spirit of truth";[20] and as His prayer is always heard by the Father, and always granted, the Spirit abides with us until the second coming, which itself will only be the result of the ceaseless cry of the Spirit and the bride,

---

[19] Hoc facite in meam commemorationem (1 Cor., xi, 24).

[20] Ego rogabo Patrem, et alium Paraclitum dabit vobis, ut maneat vobiscum in æternum, Spiritum veritatis (Joann, xiv, 16).

"And the Spirit and the bride say: Come!"[21] He is the Spirit that contains all things: "For the Spirit of the Lord hath filled the whole world; and that which containeth all things hath knowledge of the voice."[22]

Yes, His continuous working unceasingly provokes an admirable concert, and His zeal seeks to make the "Word of Christ dwell abundantly"[23] in souls, in order that they may accompany the one Sacrifice with spiritual canticles like unto those of heaven, since they can but repeat the praise of the thrice holy God and of the Lamb at once conquering and slain.

The action of the Spirit has not only an external efficacy, it penetrates into souls, it seeks to draw them to the rule and discipline, that is, to the Son;[24] the Spirit does not despair of the sluggish and carnal-minded man, and He closes the sanctuary against him only when he himself refuses to enter. Thus far does the Spirit interest Himself under every form: "Holy, one, manifold, subtle, eloquent, active, undefiled, certain, sweet, loving that which is good, quick, which nothing hindereth, beneficent, gentle, kind, steadfast, assured, secure, having all power, overcoming all things and containing all spirits; intelligible, pure, subtle."[25] These divine and intimate resources are constantly being applied as long as their time of trial lasts, to form, and to adapt men to the sacred ceremonial of the one

---

[21] Et Spiritus cl sponsa dicunt: Veni (Apoc. xxii, 17).

[22] Quoniam Spiritus Domini replevit orbem terrarum, et hoc quod continet omnia scientiam habet vocis (Sap. i, 7).

[23] Verbum Christi habitet in vobis abundanter (Col. iii, 16).

[24] Apprehendite disciplinam (Ps. ii, 12–Vulg.) Osculamini Filium (−Heb.)

[25] Sanctus, unicus, multiplex, subtilis, disertus, mobilis, incoinquinatus, certus, suavis, amans bonum, acutus, quem nihil vetat, benefaciens, humanus, benignus, stabilis, certus, securus, omnem habens virtutem, omnia prospiciens, et qui capiat omnes spiritus, intelligibilis, mundus, subtilis (Sap., vii, 22, 23).

only liturgy.

Yea, even in His unwearied energy, He is not only the fire of the altar, a fire which consummates and consumes the holocaust, but also the live coal[26] which purifies the lips of those destined to sing the divine praises, the live coal taken off the altar of heaven and placed in the human heart as in a censer, that the prayers of the saints may ascend to the throne of God.

That which in perfect unity in heaven and upon earth, the Divine Spirit accomplishes, that in like manner He reproduces in every human soul. In each of us the labours of the whole spiritual life tend only to this end: "For the Spirit Himself giveth testimony to our spirit that we are the sons of God."[27] Man is in very truth a temple wherein there is offered a liturgical oblation after the model of the worship rendered to God by the Church, and this, thanks to the Holy Spirit who takes up His abode within him. "Know you not," says the Apostle to the Corinthians, "that you are the temple of God, and that the Spirit of God dwelleth in you? . . . For the temple of God is holy, which you are."[28] Insisting once more upon this truth, he says: "For you are the temple of the living God, as God saith: I will dwell in them and walk among them."[29]

The idea of the human soul considered as a temple was so familiar to the first Christians that in the Epistle attributed to St. Barnabas we hear the unknown author by a similar teaching consoling the Jews and early Christians for the destruction of the temple of Jerusalem. At the end of his discourse he says to

---

[26] Isa., vi, 6, 7.

[27] Ipse enim Spiritus testimonium reddit spiritui nostro, quod sumus filii Dei (Rom., viii, 16).

[28] Nescitis quia templum Dei estis, et Spiritus Dei habitat in vobis; templum enim Dei sanctum est, quod estis vos (1 Cor., iii, 16, 17).

[29] Vos enim estis templum Dei vivi, sicut dicit Deus: Quoniam inhabitabo in illis, et inambulabo inter eos (2 Cor., vi, 16).

them: "The temple has been destroyed; it exists no more. But let us inquire whether there is not still another temple of God. . . . Before we believed in God the habitation of our heart was corrupt and weak, as being indeed like a temple made with hands. For it was full of idolatry, and was a habitation of demons through our doing such things as were opposed to God. . . . But it shall be built, observe ye, in the name of the Lord, in order that the temple of the Lord may be built in glory. How? Having received the forgiveness of sins and placed our trust in the name of the Lord, we have become new creatures, formed again from the beginning. Therefore, in our habitation God truly dwells by faith, by His calling unto the promise, by the wisdom of His statutes, by the commands of His doctrine; He Himself prophesying in us; He Himself dwelling in us, opening to us who were enslaved in death the doors of the temple that is within; and by giving us repentance introducing us into this incorruptible temple. He then who wishes to be saved looks not to man, but to Him who dwelleth in man, and speaketh in him, concentrating all the powers of his soul in the admiration of a language which he has never heard and which surpasses all his desires. This is the spiritual temple built for the Lord."[30]

Thus in the apostolic times the course of the spiritual life was given in the highest and most complete form. Christianity was never viewed under the common and oftentimes low form that we see nowadays; all at least knew what a Christian is, even when all would not draw the practical consequences of their knowledge.

The baptized Christian then is a temple, a temple not raised by the hand of man. This temple has secret depths into which none can penetrate save only Him who built it and who therein dwells in majesty: "For what man knoweth the things of a man,

---

[30] Epist., Cathol., S. Barnabæ Apost., cap. xvi.

but the spirit of a man who is in him."[31] Behold here indeed a true sanctuary into which nothing profane can be admitted; its entrance is sacred to God alone, the carnal man could not even go down to it; only the man who has been made spiritual by shaking off the tyranny of the senses can enter in. All the masters of the spiritual life acknowledge that there are these secret depths in the human soul, and they admit also the difficulty that most men have in penetrating into the sanctuary of their own soul, there to find the august Majesty who resides within. It is requisite to have been brought in by the working of the Holy Spirit, to which working our own efforts have been joined, not only by putting no obstacle in His way but also by giving to the Holy Spirit a generous and untiring cooperation, which will have made us pass through all the degrees of initiation of which we have spoken in this treatise.

This sanctuary is then like a heaven in which are found all the realities of the other heaven. St. Teresa, speaking of the Seventh Mansion of the Interior Castle, says: "When it pleases our Lord to have compassion upon all that the soul has suffered and that she still suffers in the ardent desire of possessing Him, and when He has already determined to take her for His bride, He introduces her into this Seventh Mansion which is His own before celebrating with her this spiritual marriage. For heaven is not His only dwelling-place: He has one in the soul also, which may be called another heaven."[32]

Hence it need not be a matter of wonder that man, although by Baptism and Confirmation consecrated to God, cannot for all that gain access into his own sanctuary except by the exercises of the spiritual life, for our Lord Himself says: "If any one love me, he will keep My word, and My Father will love him, and

---

[31] Quis enim hominum scit quæ sunt hominis, nisi spiritus hominis, qui in ipso est? (1 Cor., ii, 11).

[32] *The Interior Castle*, chap. i.

We will come to him, and will make Our abode with him."[33]
The express condition then for this intimacy is an observance
of the precepts and an exact fidelity, not a servile fidelity, but
a fidelity of love. The Apostle makes the matter clearer still
when he says: "So the things also which are of God, no man
knoweth, but the Spirit of God."[34] Now, since God resides in the
sanctuary of which we are speaking, only the Holy Spirit can
give the soul experience of what passes therein.

The heaven of the soul possesses then the august Trinity,
and as in the heaven of the blessed so also there we find what
St. John says that he saw in the celestial sanctuary: "And he
showed me a river of water of life, clear as crystal, proceeding
from the throne of God and of the Lamb."[35] This river flows also
in the human soul, of which fact our Lord Himself bears
witness, when He says: "He that believeth in Me, as the
Scripture saith, out of his belly shall flow rivers of living water.
Now this He said of the Spirit, which they should receive who
believed in Him."[36]

The presence of the triumphant Lamb, "standing as it were
slain,"[37] is equally secured for the soul by the adorable
Eucharist, the grace of which Sacrament abides in us, even after
the consecrated species have disappeared, according to these
words of our Lord: "Abideth in me and I in him;"[38] and those of

---

[33] Si quis diligit me, sermonem meum servabit, et Pater meus diliget
eum, et ad eum veniemus, et mansionem apud eum faciemus (Joann.,
xiv, 23).

[34] Ita et quæ Dei sunt, nemo cognovit nisi Spiritus Dei (1 Cor., ii, 11).

[35] Ostendit mihi fluvium aquæ vitæ, splendidum tamquam
crystallum, procedentem de sede Dei et Agni (Apoc., xxii, 1).

[36] Qui credit in me, sicut dicit Scriptura, flumina de ventre ejus
fluent aquæ vivæ. Hoc autem dixit de Spiritu, quem accepturi erant
credentes in eum (Joann., vii, 38, 39).

[37] Agnum stantem tamquam occisum (Apoc., v, 6).

[38] In me manet, et ego in illo (Joann., vi, 57).

the Apostle: "That Christ may dwell by faith in your hearts."[39]

The secret sanctuary of our soul possesses also an altar—it is our heart. On this altar holocausts and sin-offerings are offered and consumed; for there it is that all the acts of the soul are truly consummated, both those that purify and justify her, even to the perfect sacrifice which is consummation in God. It is upon this altar that man offers himself, according to that sentence of St. Paul: "I beseech you therefore, brethren . . . that you present your bodies a living sacrifice, holy, pleasing unto God, your reasonable service";[40] or, according to the Greek text, which expresses our thought still better, "your spiritual adoration." And this victim is all the more acceptable to the Sovereign Majesty, because every true oblation is included in the one sacrifice of the Lamb Himself: "For by one oblation He hath perfected for ever them that are sanctified."[41] Thus everything is brought back to close union with the eternal Sacrifice which, while it gives joy to heaven, is unceasingly renewed upon earth, and is ever bringing about the sanctification of mankind.

The soul accompanies her sacrifice by the incense of prayer, and she can say: "I gave a sweet smell like cinnamon, and aromatical balm; I yielded a sweet odour like the best myrrh."[42] Here again the human soul does not separate her incense from that which the Lord Jesus burns in the presence of His Father: "By Him therefore let us offer the sacrifice of praise always to

---

[39] Christum habitare per fidem in cordibus vestris (Eph., iii, 17).

[40] Ut exhibeatis corpora vestra hostiam viventem, sanctam, Deo placentem, rationabile obsequium vestrum—spiritualem adorationem vestram (Rom. xii, i).

[41] Una enim oblatione consummavit in sempiternum sanctificatos (Heb. x, 14).

[42] Sicut cinnamomum ct balsamum aromatizans odorem dedi, quasi myrrha electa dedi suavitatem odoris (Eccli xxiv, 20).

God, that is to say, the fruit of lips confessing to His name."[43]
And this heavenly perfume of prayer should be so profusely
burnt in the sanctuary as to embalm therewith every approach
to the sacred spot; for it is in this sense that the Bride in the
sacred Canticle says: "My hands dropped with myrrh, and my
fingers were full of the choicest myrrh."[44] Yea, her very
garments are all impregnated with it, so much so that if they
are drawn from the ivory chests wherein they are kept they
shed abroad this perfume which bears no resemblance to the
perfumes of earth: "Myrrh and stacte, and cassia perfume thy
garments from the ivory houses."[45] The bride is so saturated
with this fragrance, that those beholding her cry out: "Who is
she that goeth up by the desert as a pillar of smoke, of
aromatical spices, of myrrh and frankincense, and of all the
powders of the perfumer?"[46] Thus the spirit of prayer
impregnates all the virtues of the soul, and constitutes a most
noble homage, the sweet odour of which is ever rising towards
heaven.

A temple, a sanctuary, an altar, a victim, the very presence
of the living and true God—all these are not sufficient for
liturgical worship, there must moreover be a pontiff. Now man
is truly a priest, truly a pontiff in the august function which is
celebrated in the sanctuary of his own soul: "Thou hast made us
to our God a kingdom and priests."[47] Every baptized Christian

---

[43] Per ipsum ergo offeramus hostiam laudis semper Deo, id est,
fructum labiorum confitentium nomini ejus (Heb. xiii, 15).

[44] Manus meæ distillaverunt myrrham, et digiti mei pleni myrrha
probatissima (Cant, v, 5).

[45] Myrrha et gutta et casia a vestimentis tuis a domibus eburneis (Ps.
xliv, 9).

[46] Quæ est ista quæ ascendil per desertum sicut virgula fumi ex
aromatibus myrrhæ, et thuris et universi pulveris pigmentarii?
(Cant, iii, 6.)

[47] Fecisti nos Deo nostro regnum et sacerdotes (Apoc., v, 10).

is priest and king in the secret temple of his own soul, although he is but a single living stone of the edifice built by the hand of God, of which edifice our Lord Jesus Christ is the cornerstone. Such, in his first epistle, is the teaching of the Prince of the Apostles: "Be you also as living stones built up, a spiritual house, a holy priesthood, to offer up spiritual sacrifices acceptable to God by Jesus Christ."[48]

But to realize all the perfection of this priesthood, man must, freely and voluntarily, offer his sacrifice, after the example of the eternal Pontiff whom we hear insisting on the absolutely free character of His oblation: "No man taketh My life away from Me; but I lay it down of Myself, and I have power to lay it down, and I have power to take it up again."[49] This liberty, which shows Him to be truly a priest, was understood by Isaias, when he said: "He was offered because it was His own will."[50] Thus should it be with man whose will is called upon to cooperate with grace, for God will not receive anything from him by force and constraint. He looks for a voluntary and cheerful offering: "I will freely sacrifice to Thee."[51]

The harps which St. John heard in heaven vibrate also in this new temple; their music is composed of the varied sentiments which are ever bursting forth in the human soul, and which constitute the most beautiful accord, the sweetest harmony, when no breath save that of the Divine Spirit calls them forth. The strings of the harps are in tune and strong

---

[48] Ipsi tamquam lapides vivi superædificamini, domus spiritualis, sacerdotium sanctum, offerre spirituales hostias, acceptabiles Deo per Jesum Christum (1 Pet., ii, 5).

[49] Nemo tollit animam meam a me; sed ego pono eam a meipso, et potestatem habeo ponendi eam, et potestatem habeo iterum sumendi eam (Joann., x, 18).

[50] Oblatus est quia ipse voluit (Isa., liii, 7).

[51] Voluntarie sacrificabo tibi (Ps. liii, 8).

when they are free from all earthly dust, when they are strung up to perfect pitch, and when no counter breath comes to contradict the breath of the Lord. What a living and sublime music is this! What a true echo of the Word!

Exactitude of ceremonial accompanies the music of the harps when all the movements of the soul are well-ordered, and when they obey without resistance the divine moving principle, the Holy Spirit. The formula of this heavenly ceremonial is contained in the very device of the bride: "He set in order charity in me."[52] The external expression of it is called perfect balance and discretion, "the mother of virtues."

Thus the soul renders to God a truly finished worship when she reaches the consummation of charity. Up to that time something is always wanting to the liturgical function celebrated in her temple, whether it is that the soul does not penetrate into the sanctuary, or that the victim is below the mark required, or that the free will of the priest is imperfect, or that the incense seldom burns, or is of low price, or that the harps are badly tuned, or that the ceremonies are performed without precision and without an enlightened appreciation.

We may conclude by saying that it is very profitable for man to be by his state bound to the Divine Office, since God thus constantly places before his eyes the formula of His perfection, such as it is shown in holy Scripture. By means of the Divine Office[53] the monk and the nun receive a deep and continuous teaching, which forms part of their very existence. As long as they are striving to prefer nothing to the Divine Office, and are eager to display in its celebration all the care and refinement which so august a function claims, the science of their own sanctification is communicated to them under the form which they must realize in the depth of their own souls.

[52] Ordinavit in me caritatem (Cant, ii, 4).

[53] S. Reg., lxvi.

And if it came to pass that in some liturgical function the souls called to take part in it were all very near the perfection of their own private liturgical worship, that is to say, the highest reach of the spiritual life, the angels would, in the midst of such an assembly, well nigh think themselves in heaven. God's satisfaction would for certain be unbounded, and the radiation from such a centre would be the wonder of the whole world.

As a matter of fact, whenever a man realizes within himself the ideal of the worship which we have described, God at once bestows choice graces, which are a sure sign of the presence of the creating and sanctifying Spirit. But on the other hand, how sad would be the spectacle presented of souls bound to the prayer of the Church, but without zeal for their own spiritual progress, leaving their interior temple without adornment, their sanctuary without beauty, their altar without victims or perfumes, their harps out of tune and without harmony. What would be said again if the genuflections, prostrations and other ceremonies were so disorderly as to make them almost a mockery, if the pontiff of this secret sanctuary, having become negligent, slothful, regardless of the Divine Guest who dwells therein, were to think that he had done enough because he had not allowed it to be utterly profaned? Yet such is the picture of souls who neglect the care of their own perfection. God has every right to reproach them with their inconsistency in wishing to have in the Church that which they no longer wish to have within themselves; such an inconsistency is severely punished, for the very reason that the soul has received special grace for the celebration of the sacred liturgy.

But if we conclude that those charged with the prayer of the Church ought above all others to have a burning zeal to reproduce within themselves the realities they are unceasingly celebrating, what shall we say of those who have furthermore been raised to any rank in the sacred hierarchy, and who are associated with the eternal priesthood of our Lord Jesus, "the

Pontiff for ever according to the order of Melchisedech."[54] Holy Church thoroughly penetrated with the sense of their nobility, and full of admiration for their greatness, says to them: "Understand what you do, imitate that which you handle, so that, while you celebrate the mystery of the death of the Lord, you may study to die, in your members, to all vice and concupiscence."[55] This is the teaching already given by the Apostle St. Peter: "For unto this are you called; because Christ also suffered for us, leaving you an example that you should follow His steps."[56]

In fact, all who have been divinely elected to participate in the functions of the sacred ministry find in those very functions a principle of personal sanctification, provided that they accomplish them with a real understanding of what they are doing. Then their ministry magnificently falls back upon themselves; they purify and are purified, they sanctify and they are sanctified. Only, they purify, illuminate and sanctify by reason of their sacred character, whereas by their own personal ministry they cannot be purified, illuminated and sanctified, except in the measure in which their will, in virtue of a kind of voluntary initiation, assimilates what in the sacred rites is applicable to them. This assimilation is the *Imitamini quod tradatis.*

How unutterable the consolation of one responsible for the sanctification of others, and for the exercise of an awful

---

[54] Sacerdos in æternum secundum ordinem Melchisedech (Ps., cix, 4).

[55] Agnoscite quod agitis; imitamini quod tractatis; quatenus mortis Dominicæ mysterium celebrantes, mortificare membra vestra a vitiis et concupiscentiis procuretis (Pontificale Rom., De Ordinatione Presbyteri).

[56] In hoc enim vocati estis: quia et Christus passus est pro nobis, vobis relinquens exemplum, ut sequamini vestigia ejus. (1 Pet., ii, 21).

ministry, to know that in devoting himself with intelligence and faith to this ministry he advances the work of his own sanctification. He has in his hands the formula, the method of his own personal perfection, and by penetrating himself with the rites, the ceremonies, the words, the substance and the form of the Liturgy, he gathers most practical instruction on the true spiritual life and holiness.

From the earliest times St. Denis, the prince of mystics, treated of the divers degrees of the sacred hierarchy and of the relations of each of them with a definite portion of the Christian people. His words are as follows: "The class of those undergoing purification is composed of those who cannot as yet be admitted to see or to participate in any of the Sacraments; the class of the illuminated is that of the holy among the people; the class of the perfect is that of holy monks."[57] The first class he considers to be intrusted to deacons; and in fact, in former times the catechumens and penitents left the Church after the reading of the Gospel, which is the deacon's ministry, and they had no participation in the Sacrifice. The second class, the illuminated, has a close relation with priests; whilst those who have embraced the perfect life seem to have a bond of filiation with the episcopate.

These divers degrees are determined in proportion to the soul's proximity to that sanctuary in the centre of which God resides. Those who are leading the purgative life are in the porch of this temple. They must lay aside the life of the senses, and perseveringly practise virtue, that having put on the nuptial garment of the new man, they may be admitted to contemplate some of the mysteries, that is to say, to enter upon the illuminative life, wherein man, being no longer either so much weighed down by the senses, or distracted by the tyranny of his passions, can at last enjoy the light of divine things, and

---

[57] De Eccl. Hier., cap. Vi, n. 5.

catch from afar, as it were by flashes, a glimpse of the sanctuary into which he may not yet enter.

Finally, the unitive life, is an entrance into the Holy of Holies, that is, into that close intimacy with God which is in truth, the end for which man was created. Here he can and ought to offer to the Lord the true sacrifice, being no longer obliged in a certain sense, to offer victims for his own sins, since there is now no obstacle between himself and God.

It is but too true that nowadays these distinctions no longer exteriorly exist, any more than do the relation which in the beginning existed between the divers portions of the faithful people and the corresponding degrees of the hierarchy. But as regards their advancement, souls are none the less before God in one or in another of the three degrees of the spiritual life of which we have spoken.

To these relations of the soul with God corresponds exactly the measure of her action upon men. If our eyes could contemplate invisible things, they would see that souls have an influence over others in exact proportion to their own advancement. The higher they rise, the more widespread is their influence; their power is in effect, in proportion to their nearness to God. Their nature, it is true does not change, but just as an object grows warm the nearer it approaches a furnace, and itself radiates in a larger sphere, so is it with the soul by reason of her proximity to the divine furnace. In this sense we read in Psalm XVIII: "And his circuit even to the end thereof: and there is no one that can hide himself from His heat."[58]

The soul exercises a ministry corresponding to her state, and radiates diversely all round about her upon souls belonging to the purgative, the illuminative and the unitive life. Experience shows that souls more easily and with fewer

[58] Et occursus ejus usque ad summum ejus; nec est qui se abscondat a calore ejus (Ps. xviii, 7).

dangers and trials pass through these degrees of the spiritual life when they are assisted by another soul who is in a higher state than they themselves are. The history of sanctity studied from this point of view is very instructive; and we can thus explain how it is that saints seldom stand alone. True pontiffs, they attract souls to themselves in order to unite them with God; they sanctify while stooping to those who belong to a lower state.

Happy the souls that know how to work the treasure contained in the sacred liturgy, and this not for the sake of loving it with a sterile and purely external love, but that they may draw into themselves and reproduce the symbols and the forms which contain realities so full of life. Under the Old Law God loved nothing so much as the temple; but by the mouth of the Prophet Jeremias He severely blamed those who thought that they might take every liberty because the temple was theirs: "Make your ways and your doings good; and I will dwell with you in this place. Trust not in lying words, saying: The temple of the Lord, the temple of the Lord, it is the temple of the Lord."[59] Otherwise, continues the prophet, if you do not cease from your presumption, thinking that the temple can stand in place of obedience to My precepts, behold what shall be your chastisement: "I will do to this house, in which My name is called upon, and in which you trust, and to the place which I have given you and your fathers, as I did to Silo."[60] Undoubtedly the nation that possessed the temple was a privileged nation, but the temple could not dispense with fidelity; and before being honoured in the temple, God requires

---

[59] Bonas facite vias vestras, et studia vestra: et habitabo vobiscum in loco isto. Nolite confidere in verbis mendacii, dicentes: Templum Domini, templum Domini, templum Domini est (Jerem., vii, 3, 4).

[60] Faciam domui huic, in qua invocatum est nomen meum, et in qua vos habetis fiduciam et loco quem dedi vobis et patribus vestris sicut feci Silo (Jerem. vii, 14).

us to adore and serve Him in the invisible sanctuary which He has within us built for Himself.

We must then, with King Solomon repeat: "Thou hast commanded me to build a temple on Thy holy mount, and an altar in the city of Thy dwelling-place, a resemblance of Thy holy tabernacle, which Thou hast prepared from the beginning."[61] This is our task here upon earth; that tabernacle already on the mount had been shown to Moses: "Look and make according to the pattern, that was shown thee in the mount."[62] St. Stephen, in the great discourse which won for him the palm of martyrdom, reminded the Jews of it. Let us then build up this tabernacle according to the Exemplar and the Model, our Lord Jesus Christ; let all enter into this liturgical unity which receives from the Holy Spirit its life, its beauty, its consummation, and enables every creature in heaven and on earth and even in the depths of the ocean to cry out: "To Him that sitteth on the throne, and to the Lamb, benediction and honour and glory and power for ever and for ever. Amen."[63]

Finis

---

[61] Dixisti me ædificare templum in monte sancto tuo, et in civitate habitationis tuæ altare, similitudinem tabernaculi sancti tui, quod præparasti ab initio (Sap., ix, 8).

[62] Inspice, et fac secundum exemplar quod tibi in monte monstratum est (Exod. xxv, 40).

[63] Sedenti in throno, et Agno, benedictio, et honor, et gloria, et potestas in sæcula sæculorum. Amen (Apoc. v, 13).

Made in the USA
Monee, IL
05 August 2022